Toward Globalization
with a Human Face

Edgar Krau

University Press of America,® Inc.
Lanham · Boulder · New York · Toronto · Plymouth, UK

Copyright © 2009 by
University Press of America,® Inc.
4501 Forbes Boulevard
Suite 200
Lanham, Maryland 20706
UPA Acquisitions Department (301) 459-3366

Estover Road
Plymouth PL6 7PY
United Kingdom

Library of Congress Control Number: 2009922304
ISBN-13: 978-0-7618-4560-7 (paperback : alk. paper)
ISBN-10: 0-7618-4560-7 (paperback : alk. paper)
eISBN-13: 978-0-7618-4561-4
eISBN-10: 0-7618-4561-5

Contents

Preface

There is an old dispute as to which factor is playing the main role in the permanent changes which modify the face of society, determining its content and direction. The Marxists upheld the primacy of the forces of production, technology and the instruments of work, which would bind on society certain production relationships. The latter, so they say, find their expression in the juridical and ideological suprastructure of society. Marx (1859/1953) pointed out that the material mode of production was conditioning society's social, political and spiritual processes in general. Many people have rightly voiced opposition to the peremptoriness of this statement. One cannot object to the assertion that the transition from feudalism to capitalism was brought about by the changes in the modes of production based on the "new" tools in the weaving and the metal industry, by the steam engine, the loom, etc. But it would be mistaken to overlook the forceful influence produced on the economy by the ideological factor, by the science, the technology and the arts of the Renaissance and Enlightenment in the previous centuries. Was not slavery abolished in the United States, although it was entrenched economically and cost-effective? However, it was morally intolerable and as such, it did not fit into the new culture and spiritual ideals. Instead of speaking of a simplist economic determination of social and cultural processes in society, one should think of a dialectical interaction of the two. In a final account, both must be congruent. The domain which is lagging behind, realigns itself with the one that has taken a forward leap. Steadiness only belongs to movement and change themselves, as had already been told at the dawn of history by Heraclitus. "One cannot step twice into the same river", he has said.

The factor, which spurs the movement lay in people's needs, and they incite to ideas and action plans. It was precisely Marx, who has drawn attention to the fact, that human beings are planning their acts. The difference between the bravest bee and the poorest craftsman, so Marx says, is that the latter has a plan before doing his work, a mental image of it, before he starts his work bahaviors. This is true of an invention, of shaping a metal piece in the lathe or of brokering a deal at the stock exchange. What we must add, is that it is not a single idea that pops up in the person's head, as a certain activity is intended. The idea on a future activity is part of an entire mental system linked to the person's overall idea-treasure and aspirations, acquired through education and life in society.

Revolutionary modifications in the economic style or in a particular production technology occur at the meeting point of ideas heralding a change in society's *values* with the representations of technology or of the economic setting. As such, society's *culture*, comprising the values, ideas, customs that exist in society, is at the cradle of every nascent socioeconomic system and of its modifications. It follows that the analysis of a social system and of its upcoming or more distant development is best done through its culture. This is the approach of our book, borne out by the history of this society, the boom followed by the global finacial crisis and economic downturn. The book will help achieving a better understanding of these phenomena, which are not accidental economic occurrences, but represent the failure of a social system. At fault is not only business and the behavior of the market, but the contemporary culture driving toward wrong economic behaviors.

In our society the technology to which economic growth is mostly endebted is communication through the *Internet*. Its economic counterpart is *globalization*, and both are promotng a new culture, we shall call it the *Internet Culture*.

This book is a critical essay on contemporary culture, the way it manifests itself in the various domains of social life. The culture of our days is so very different from what has hitherto been the image of a modern society, that it deserves a special name, and which name could be more appropriate than the technological invention around which it has crystallized, the Internet. The latter has become a fetish of modern society. Its influence does not lie in technological characteristics and advantages only, but in the values, the aspirations, the behavior and the lifestyle of people who are embracing it.

The apparent unlimited liberty from every moral code and obligation, which is the gist of this culture, meant unhoped opportunities for inidividuals who wanted to break with tradition, and for corporations, who enthusiastically adhered to it. In this business-promoted form the Internet Culture was adopted first by the intelligentsia, by artists and people of the Academe, and then by public opinion. Therefore, in our analysis we shall very much lean on the testimony of the mass media reflecting public opinion, the newspapers, weeklies, journals. The peculiarity of the Internet Culture lies in the fact that all new postulates and principles first appear as practical behaviors reported by the media, and only later a theorization is spun around them. This makes the analysis a difficult task. The analyst has two options. He may chime in the choir of eulogy and apology of all what happens, even be it in sharp contradiction to hitherto accepted ethical principles. Alternatively, he may try to discern between the good and the bad, expressing disapproval for things that may lead to a social and moral collapse. The economic collapse follows very soon. We apologize, if
in this approach of ours the negative aspects of modern culture seem more emphatically presented. The intention is to hold a mirror in society's face and show

what is wrong. Don't blame the mirror, when the face you are seeing is not nice, says an old proverb.

Today the offspring of a revolutionary, developed communication system is the *globalization* of economic and social processes. It shares all the advantages and the drawbacks of its breeding factor, the Internet Culture, but adds its own flaws. They do an enormous damage to people's livelyhood, aspirations, to their physical, social and psychological security, to their family. Therefore a process of initiating changes in this society has already begun. Its aim is to restore humanistic values and a culture built on them. The new upcoming culture will proclaim the priority of the human person's wellbeing and happiness over the exclusive accumulation of shareholder wealth, disguised as abstract numbers of "economic growth". All this amounts to putting a human face on what is currently understood by globalization.

The solution of the heavy problems raised in this book does not entail the renouncement of the achievements in technology and in the global economy, which this society undoubtedly has, but a shift in its value emphasis and priorities. It should and will hopefully turn into a *globalization with a human face*. It will be sustained not by the greediness for ever bigger profits of a few, but by the solid foundation of morality, leading to the wellbeing of the large masses of people, by the respect for their national and cultural traditions.

Chapter One

After Postmodernism: the Internet Culture of the Contemporary World

It would not be mistaken to say that today the word mostly used in public is *Internet*. This reflects an astonishing career if considering the limited origins of the Internet's destination in the '1960s as a computer program allowing for a direct linkage between government agencies in case of a feared communication breakdown in the aftermath of a nuclear attack on the US. The Internet technology also developed out of intrinsic necessities of communication. After World War II, at the cradle of computer science, a link between computers had to be established through intermediary means like perfocards or magnetic tapes, which had to be physically transported to the location of the distant computer. In the '1960s scientists started to seek ways to create direct linkages between distant computers in order to optimize the transmission of information regarding decisions on millitary operations, business transactions, scientific research and training methods.

At that time the scientific world mainly used the concept of Cyberspace. Scientists and the media explained that in the information age the fundamental particle of the material world was not the atom but the informational bit, and that the basic belief of people ought to be in the reality feeling of the screen images, i.e. that behind the computer screen there was an actual space. Then came the Internet, and it was declared that the Internet was Cyberspace (Welcome to Cyberspace, 1995). The signing of the Transmission Control Protocol (TCP/IP) in 1983 may be considered as the official birthday of the Internet. The new communication instrument fulfilled many of the hopes vested in it. In world affairs it enabled a free flow of information defying censorship, especially in totalitarian countries, like the former U.S.S.R. Thus it made an important contribution to the implosion of the Soviet empire. The success of the Indian Chapas revolt in Mexico is also much endebted to the spread of information on the events which took place before the revolt broke out and on the government's attempt to crush it. Many people are considering that the great liberating democratization of the world is happening because of the Internet (*Fortune*, May 27, 2002).

In business, thanks to the communication via the Internet, distribution costs shrank, buyers and sellers could now meet without costly marketing campaigns. In this sense everyday life was made easier, there were less irritating ordering letters, banking correspondence, marketing as such has been made much easier. The internet screen has also created the characteristics of a virtual office, and thereby has reduced the office space an organization needed, sometimes instead of nine floors four would suffice.

In education digital landscapes have become a powerful tool for learning history and geography, and also for knowing the important creations of art throughout the world. People are drawn closer now, there is the possibility to chat with people from all over the world and to make acquaintances with persons having similar interests or to whom one is feeling attracted. If sex is the interest, the Internet is again a facilitating tool for meeting or exchanging all kind of virtual phantasies. Of course there is no guarantee that the underlying intentions and the content of such fanatasies abide by social consensual norms. In January 2004 a man named Meiwes was tried before a German court because he had murdered and cannibalized another man, who advertized on the Internet his desire to be dealt with in this way (Are you a cannibal? was the ad's title). The court sentenced Meiwes to $8^{1/2}$ years in prison, after it had reduced the charge to manslaughter, proving that even murderers get a lenient sentence when they were hired through the Internet. As to cannnibalism, it does not figure in the German criminal code. In the same vein, another socially dangerous use of the Internet was the organizing of group suicides in Japan, plotting together young people who fancied to kill themselves, but had not the courage to do it, and neither had they received psychological help. Recently, on the 12th of Oktober 2004, such a group of nine prsons were discovered in a wood near Tokyo. In the last years the Japanese suicide web.- site has created the mobilizing link among 34,000 suiciders.

To strike a merrier note, in the Internet era a key modification of lifestyle has also occurred in entertainment, although it did not necessarily mean an increase in socialization. Kids and adults are sitting for long hours in front of their computer screens, passionately attracted to all kind of computer games, a majority of them unloaded from the Internet. They do so with the participation of game partners who may remain anonymous. It happens that because of such virtual games, social activities, families or jobs are being neglected. There is, however, also the content problem of these computer games, which may be quite opposed to anything what is traditionally called public morality, but about this we shall speak later.

In the domain of public life it has been generally thought that the new communication technology would spur mass political participation. The challenge was to re-empower voters, to strengthen the link between them and the legislative and executive branches of state power. In the meantime the Internet has indeed had a strong informative political influence on the public, but not always in the direction of strengthening democracy. Alongside with the increasing importance of the existing media, there has been a growing presence of more extremist and violent opinions in both the rightwing and the leftist spectrum. If it had been thought that the Internet would strengthen the public power of the media, it rather appeared that the Internet has turned into a power *per se* with which the other powers must reckon.

In the ordinary meaning of the word, the Internet does not belong to anyone. The so-called "hosts" are companies merely offering search and link services. Even the US National Science Foundation, which has created a number of centers with supercomputers, is only aiding the process, but not controlling and regulating it. As a matter of fact, control would hardly be possible technically, because today more than 150 million hosts are connected to the Internet and their number is still growing. This situation has had tremendous consequences. In a sense they have changed the face of the world.

Firstly, the information highway can be used by everybody who enters a subscription contract with a provider of linkage services, and this server company cannot know in advance who their new clients are, and what they intend to communicate. Presently it seems that the Chinese Communist Party alone has been capable of exercising a certain control over her Internet browsers by the aid of "government hackers", but even this control has proved not to be a hermetic one (*Fortune*, December 24, 2001). In the West only very recently there are attempts to prevent the continous presentation of materials inciting to crime or spreading hatred vis-à-vis religious or ethnic groups, or political organizations, but all this only *post factum* .So, whatever limitations governments or parliaments would seek to impose, after a democratic vote or a referendum on the public presentation of materials contrary to the ethics and the beliefs of the nation's citizens, the Internet makes their striving worthless. It imposes a new meaning on the concept of democracy, which ceases to be the control and power of the people expressed through the will of its majority.

A second noneconomic consequence of the Internet concerns the entire rhythm of social life. The continuously improving technology of the speed of transmission and presentation accentuates the speed of all processes in social activities to the point where there is no time for lengthy deliberation. Decisions have to be made fast and the decision takers are under continuous pressure, whether they are considering the buying of commodities, the offer of a business transaction or of a job. Click here, click there, click now, the image on the screen will instantaneously disappear and with it the opportunity. By its intimate technical constraints and the structure of its advertising style, the Internet promotes a lifestyle in which thorough weighing and deliberation are downplayed and impulsive immediate action is emphasized instead. This feature brings to the foreground two other possibilities with heavy consequences: a) the transmitted message may be manipulative and not necessarily true, and the decision taker has no time to carefully consider it under all its aspects, b) preference is given to the dazzling and shrill presentation over content matters. It is easy to see how such features are passing from commercial publicity to the domain of public life, and the havoc they are wrecking there.

With this third charateristic links up a fourth, paradoxical one: the Internet promotes the transmission of an unheard wealth of information. All libraries, all research laboratories open their doors before the eyes of the stunned re-searcher.Never in history have there been such large possibilities of learning what is done by other scientists throughout the world. This is a very positive development. The point is, however, that the richness of information prevents its selection and careful consideration, and preference is again given to the shrill and glaring, while the scientists are under pressure to come up with some dis-covery of their own. They will present it in the Internet where there is no need to be previously verified and replicated, whereby sometimes the "discovery" only amounts to glamorous wishful thinking.

The Internet linkage embraces the whole of the globe. In a daring forecast McLuhan (1962) saw how the speed of information spreading would transform the world into a "global village". The Internet has made his prophecy come true. Scientists, business people, politicians and private persons from all around the world are participating in instantaneous real time decision making and they are capable of instant reactions to each other's ideas and actions. The consequences are again much beyond the limited domain of communications, producing the phenomenon that has been called *globalization,* a global outlook and strategical planning in politics, business, scientific research and in the private sphere of life. Globalization is not necessarily good or necessarily bad, the question is what you do with it and what content it does assume in your planning strategy. All this is to say that globalization, as also the change in the economy, in the rhythm of life, the change in the meaning and the structure of authority and power, are indicating the modification of the whole texture of society, of moral principles and of the possibility to apply them. All these are consequences of the new communication technologies used by the Internet, and they amout to what might be called *a new Internet Culture of human society.* In this book our task is to describe this phenomenon, to trace the benefits of its positive sides for human-ity, but also to warn of its fallacies and to discuss the ways by which the latter might be avoided.

Culture is a multilateral phenomenon, which in Kluckhohn's (1962) view comprises explicit and implicit patterns of behavior acquired through social in-teraction and transmitted to other generations through symbols. Culture includes ideas and especially their attached values, which are common for a group of people. Kluckhohn stresses the adaptive value of culture. Behaviors which are conform to it are rewarded with satisfaction, they keep people alive, healthy and reproductive. Because of people's specific needs, culture may create problems for the individual, but it also solves problems, or some of them at least.

Linton (1945) defined culture as a configuration of learned behaviors and of their results. This definition underscores two facts: first, culture is not a loose package of elements, customs, but an integrated configuration based on society's values, and second, culture is learned (Kluckhohn also equalled it with socialization). Instinctive behaviors, nor the basic drives, which are behavior's ultimate motivators, have ever been regarded as parts of culture, although they influence it. Although culture is learned, it becomes a part of the person's identity, her social self. In André Bazin's (1968) words, the individual transcends society, but society is also and above all *within* him. Even speaking the same language, the English and the Irish have different identities. Anderson (1997) points out that we live our lives as the selves we believe ourselves to be, and that every civilization creates its own concept of the self. Therefore one could speak of a "social heredity" (Linton). Culture becomes society's way of life by which each of its members is likely to give a predictable answer to certain situations.It however used to happen that people persist in giving a culturally elaborated answer, even if it is incongruent with the facts they are refusing to perceive and to verify. Sperber (1996) points out that the facts of culture become *representations* that are interpreted by attributing beliefs, desires and intentions to individual or collective actors, in a manner that makes behaviors appear rational. He thinks that culture is foremost made up of contagious ideas, a true epidemic, and of the artifacts of tools, writings, artworks, the presence of which permits the propagation of ideas.

The use of a taxonomy linking culture to physiological processes of disease is, of course, inappropriate, because even if the author explains that there is no morbidity in culture, the well-accustomed connotation of the words remains. For our discussion the approach nevertheless presents interest, because it sheds light on the author's conceptions, which are reflecting the modern Internet Culture. Culture, a fact of social sciences should, so Sperber says, fit into nature by reducing the mental to the neurological (mistaken again, the mental is *based* on the neurologic, but cannot be reduced to it), by naturalizing the mental, by reconceptualizing the whole domain, and by eliminating all concepts that do not refer to natural entities (it cripples culture which is a social-anthropological and not a biological fact), and finally by granting naturalness more liberty. If taking into account the direction of the idiosyncratic use of the concept by the author, the way is paved for the triumphant entry of pornography and of all possible, even monstruous phantasies, which no social institution could stop from now on. We are told that the resisting institutions must be "reconceptualized" and should disappear. In the book there is, for instance, a lengthy attempt to prove that marriage cannnot be defined, whence it cannot have legitimacy. The physiological foundation of cultural representations links them to people's self, because cultural representations have to meke sense for the subject followiing from the benfit which the adherence to a concept can bring (*Ibid*. 34, 47).

If Sperber related culture to the self, conversely, Anderson (1997) links it to culture, saying that every civilization creates its own concept of the self, which people construe through the use of language and with the aid of the social environment. The modern self is presently being replaced by a postmodern concept, which characterizes it as decentered, multidimensional and changeable. Such changes are not only produced by convincing life experiences, but also by stories told of the person and which empower the subject (Anderson, 1997).It is here that the Internet Culture enters with its full impact, because stories are essentially virtual constructions, creations or "adapted" versions of real events.Any way, Anderson points out that different areas of the brain register different versions of any event. Therapists help people to deconstruct nd then resconstruct their stories, i.e. their selves. Therefore Anderson speaks of virtual personalities (*Ibid,*. 237). It follows that for the brave adherent to the Internet Culture the self is a story having very little in common with the real lilfe occurrences. If this is so, how can people give at a court session or in a newspaper report an accurate version of an event in which they or their friends, or party have been involved, when their own image is based on a self-enhancing phantasy? The Internet Culture glorifies the virtual. There is no truth in how people present themselves, or in the events told by them, be they personal or in which society as a whole is involved, e.g. weapons of mass destruction ready for use in Iraq.

Indeed, the self-concept undergoes modifications, as a function of the objective changes in the individual's or the group's social and economic situation, but also, and this is the point, according to what they believe on themselves. By 1956 75% of adult Americans, including lower-class, blue-collar workers, and even those with their income barely above the poverty level, began to think themselves as middle class, because they took on what they thought are the middle-class values (conservative ones), and were persuaded by skillful politicians and aggressive advertising that they are middle class.

It ensues that in a certain sense the cultural interpretation pre-exists observation. Picasso has said, *"First I find and then I seek"*. This method is much favored in the kybernetic conception, where we start with finding an image, and only then we are looking for its relationship with reality (Moles, 1967). Perception as such appears as the projection of a sensorial message on the interpreting screen (*écran de repérage)* of human culture. This means that people sees the world through the spectacles of their culture, which at a closer inspection is the subculture of the social group to which they belong.

Belton (1996) points out that we live in and belong to a mass culture. It leads to a mass identity, but we used to deny it. Anyway there is an erosion of the older distinction between high culture and mass or popular culture, philistinism and kitsch. In this sense Crary (2001) remarks that the crowd, the obvious bearer of the mass culture, is shifting to a lower cerebral functioning, resembling infantilism or savagery. He adds that *homo democraticus* is a man without qualities, without an identity, a lifeless cog, a kind of automaton, put into motion by external forces. We may ad that this "modern man" remains ferociously individualistic, his integration into society is realized by the mass cultre, which addresses the lowest common biological drives.

The two most important problems which the study of culture must address are: a) culture indepth pervasiveness, understood as its ability to influence and change people's personality, and b) its capability to resolve the great contemporary problems of the world. Within the first domain the argument had in the beginning concerned the semantic problem, as according to D'Andrade (1965), propositions about language are confused with propositions about the world, and as such, no real culturally imposed personality differences are being measured. Still, Tupes and Christal (1961) have found culture as being one of the basic personality factors, and Linton (1945) had emphatically upheld the concept of a basic different personality type apparent in each culture. Such a configuration of traits supplies common perceptions and values, and it makes possible a unified emotional response of the members of a certain society in which those values are implied.

In a multimethod crosscultural study Paunonen, Jackson, Trzebinski and Fosterling (1992) came to the conclusion that, although personality factors proved to be highly congruent across linguistic and cultural groups in speakers of European languages, researchers needed to broaden their perspectives. They consider the many cultures for which values, socialization practices and lifestyles are substantially different. This attests to the heavy impact of culture on the behavioral personality type.

As indicated, the pervasiveness of a culture pretending at universality has also to be evaluated as to its impact on the treatment and the solution of the great problems of the world. These are the problems which no country can solve on her own (Gielen, 1990): the rapidly spreading degradation of the environment, overpopulation, the increasing economic disparities between haves and havenots. There is also the debt crisis, the spread of chemical and biological weapons, the growing number of refugees, the containment of ideologies of hatred and - we might add - of terrorism. If the Internet Culture deserves its name as a culture of the contemporary world, we shall have to see what traits it bestows on its basic personality type, and how successfully it tries to tackle the great problems of our time.

Nations diffuse their values, and the culture based on them, into areas where their power reaches (Kluckhohn, 1962). This explains the influence of the former Soviet culture in the countries of the former Eastern Bloc, and the present-day influence of American culture in a situation in which the US remained the sole superpower in the world. The more powerful will the trend for globalization be, because of its backing by mighty economic groups in the US, the more enforcement will develop for the culture dominant in the U.S.A.

The Marxists have always contended that societies' culture is decisively influenced by what they called the "mode of production" based on the technology dominant at a certain time, and which determines the relationships among people engaged in the production process (Marx, 1953). It is hard not to see the rational kernel of this theory, but the German, English and French cultures in the XIXth century were very different, although they all were based on the capitalist production mode. Even if in general lines this was true, the difference between French *libertinage*, English Victorian prudishness and American tolerance and practical outlook was very large and not at all neglectable. On the other hand, there had been all the time common characteristics between the "capitalist" cultures and the one of the victorious proletariat in the "great socialist Soviet Union", which, so we were told, had new socialist relations of production: there was a positive attitude towards the family, the education of children, a negative attitude towards theft and murder. These differences make the Marxist paradigm unreliable as a universal theory of culture and of its links with society.

The Internet Culture presents a radically different picture as compared to all the other cultures we were used to in the past. First, it is not linked to a new production mode, let alone to a new type of relations of production. The Internet is an enhancing accessory to existing production modes, whether in China or in the US, it does not change the relationship among people as far as the ownership of the instruments of production is concerned. The socioeconomic framework remains a free market economy (even with vestiges of socialism in some countries), although it may take on some special characteristics in comparison to the pre-Internet economy. What sticks out, mainly refers to the so-called suprastructural building of society. In the Internet Culture the hitherto customary cultural universals and the basic institutions based on them, like the family, the fatherland, the institution of criminal justice, are all coming under attack, and the widely propagated tendency is to weaken and to finally cancel them. That makes a radical difference between the Internet Culture and all the other cultures existing beforehand.

The differences between the so-called capitalist culture and the "socialistic" one lay much in the interpretational content of certain value-concepts, like democracy, authority, loyalty, freedom for political dissent. The Internet Culture rejects the formerly acknowledged values and proclaims new ones: there is no public morality, anything goes, the more it is shocking, the better it is. Surprisingly, there is no acknowledged legitimacy of dissent from the dominant leftist "political correctness", and not only are rightist-conservative opinions vehemently reprimanded, but their authors are reduced to silence by the best methods known from the arsenal of daddy Brezhnev. Had it not been for the Septembr 11 attack on the Twin Towers, the tendency had been to acclaim terrorists as freedom fighters instead of tracking them down and prosecuting them. If the liberal protest movement in the '1960s was one of resisting authority and power, today their former activists enlist power (Post, 1998), marginalize those whose opinions are different, up to the point where no real freedom of expression is possible (Gavison, 1998). At the same time they deplore the changing of the names of streets and towns which glorified former bolchevik heroes guilty of mass murders. They deplore the tearing down of statues of Stalin or of Dzerzhinski, his former secret police chief, in the aftermath of the implosion of the Eastern Bloc in 1989 (Levinson, 1998).

The Internet Culture is not bothered by such contradictions, because it is the offspring of the post-modern culture in the '1980s, contradictory in its very nature (Kellner, 1989), devoid of meaning and nihilistic, where the moral seriousness of modernism had been replaced by irony, cynism, commercialism. It has been a game with the vestiges of what had been destroyed (Kellner, 1989). Like the new Internet Culture, post-modernism ranged from philosophy to the arts, economic practices and everyday experiences. The common element in post-modern currents was the heightening of advesarial tendencies of modernism, while instinct and pleasure were regimented to carry the logic of modernism to its furthest reach (Bell, 1980). Social life was swallowed up by computer technology, while real things and phenomena were substituted by models and simulations (Baudrillard, 1983). The social scene was dominated by class polarization, labor over-supply, capital over-accumulation and over-consumerism. The loss of employment security led to the bizarre situation of poor people living in a hyper-rich world. (Cooke, 1988).

The Internet Culture has its roots in post-modernism, but it goes beyond it and is qualitatively different. First of all, post-modernism repudiated global models of social analysis and global solutions, and has replaced them with a focus on local group differences and the ways in which the individuals adapted and helped reshape their local environments (Herman, 1999). The Internet Culture is intimately linked to a global outlook and strategy. Globalism is its primary *raison d'être*, and localism is forced to integrate into the global strategies of the information emitters.

Sharp differences between the Internet Culture and postmodernism also appear in regard to other characteristics. The playfulness of post-modernism did not take tradition seriously, it spurned all hitherto venerated traditional concepts in religion, in the arts, and in social life: the fatherland, the family, the institutions of king or president, friendship and love. The Internet Culture goes one step forward and its aim is to disband them, to get rid of them. Jameson (1996) sees the roots of this phenomenon in the fundamental incapacity of the new culture (he calls it postmodernist) to deal with time and history. There is the feeling, especially among artists, that all has already been said, and that all the artist can do is give a *pastiche* of past events, an aimless and humorless parody of the past, seen through our pop images and stereotypes. As a result, we live in a continuous ever-changing present, which obliterates the past and its traditions.

The preoccupation of Jameson was to describe what happens in the seventh art, the movies. He did it very pertinently, and analyzed what corresponded to the artistic manifestations on a philosophical level. However, there is the need to evince the causal process which developed in the reality of society and produced the occurrences on both levels; after all, "art is the mirror of nature". What happens in the arts, the modifications in contents and styles, is much caused by developments on the socio-cultural level (which, of course, has its own causes and conditionings). Nevertheless, the arts and mainly the movies, may strongly further some tendencies and withhold others. In the case we are dealing with, I should see the cause of peoples's incapacity and the lack of desire to deal with the past correctly in three characteristics of the Internet Culture: a) the pressure for urgency, followed by b) superficiality of general cultural and historical knowledge, both entailing c) the fetishism of the present.These features are the consequences of the Internet communication technology turned into a   mass phenomenon. The Internet-imposed urgency, which became a stereotype, has caused people's interests to be narrowed down, and is preventing the allocation of time and energy to general cultural or historical knowledge, which is regarded as superfluous. The present considered as the embodiment of the wonderful invention called the Internet, and is fetichized, past forms of culture look ridiculous as they are seen through the " lenses" of the present world perception. However, in the present people are unable to find any fulfillment of happiness. Therefore artists turn towards the past, although for lack of knowledge and interest they are incapable to describe it accurately. From our persent world perception only remains what is inducing an emotional shock and cries for momentary attention, the squalor, the sick mind and dirty sex without love, all what is negating the image of customary and the traditional conception of what is beautiful in life. The predecessor of such an attitude was *La charogne (The Carcass)* of Baudelaire and other works of his, but at that time such an art was marginal, now images like these are dominant. Today society's ideals comprise the rudest forms of material and immediate satisfactions only. If people fail to reach them, the virtual world produced by drugs will help them overcome.

With this basic attitudes the Internet Culture purposefully destroys the lasting character of human attachment, be it the loyalty between business partners, owner or management and worker, citizen and homeland, husband and wife or between friends. Some human links are declared as nonexistent, such as the loyalty between organization and workers, others, like friendship and marriage are only temporarily admitted, as long as they are profitable. Love is reduced to the sexual act, the psychological link within the family is destroyed, there are ever more cases of parents killing their children, or conversely, of children killing their fathers and mothers, or their peers or innocent bystanders. It happened in the U.S.A., in Germany, in Italy. If these juvenile perpetrators are caught and tried (official statistics show that 85% of the cases are never caught), the strongest contrition they express, is that they made a mistake (Garbarino, 1999). Then come scores of writers publishing heaps of books, in which they argue that such kids must be pardonned and receive psychological treatment. The damage in life and in property had already been done, so we are told, there is no justice to be made. There is only a system, whose aim is not to render justice, but to play by the rules. In this play the victim is forgotten, and in the forefront appear the rights of the defendant, from whom society reluctantly agrees to separate "donec corrigetur" (until he will be corrected), as sounded the medieval censor's verdict on Aristotle. Killers are not Aristotles. But then, neither he was ever corrected. All what happened was that the Church accepted him in her bosom as he was - and so does modern society wih the killers, no matter how ferocious they have been, and will actually be when again turned loose on the public.

It would be a mistake to think that the legal acrobatism to achieve leniency for violent and convicted criminals is an American phenomenon only. The Internet Culture is universal, and its manifestations are appearing everywhere. There are reports from Germany, from Israel, where in July 2002, amidst public uproar, a gang rapist of a 13-year old girl got a sentence of 1 1/2 years in jail, or from Spain where every two of three perpetrators of domestic violence are acquitted. In pure despair the Spaniards created a special government commission,

Observatorio sobre la Violencia Doméstica, for a follow-up of the trials of these cases and of what happens after sentencing (*ABC*, June 16, 2002).

Even if they are in their innermost bewildered by such a position, which is actually favoring crimes against life and property, number of people accept it nonetheless, because it seemingly conveys the pretence of tolerance. The postmodern culture was indeed tolerant, although not respectful. They tolerated all kinds of religious beliefs and ceremonies, mysticism, they did not oppose the way of life of gay people. The Internet Culture is onesided, it cannot be straightforwardly characterized as tolerant. New authorities replaced the old and only the form of domination changed. In the name of freedom from tradition women were trapped in new forms of sexual objectification and bound to a consumerized and sexualized household (Ewen, 1980). The Internet Culture is tolerant vis-à-vis all kind of deviants, like homicide criminals or sexual deviants, but intolerant towards all possible ideological dissent or towards people who wish to pursue a more conservative world outlook, would it only be in their private life.The Internet Culture gives relief to some phenomena, e.g. an exaggerated preoccupation with gays and lesbian, with Hindu mystics, especially when it can be linked to sex (see Anand, 1995), with Satanism, while it is fighting and delegitimizing the official doctrines of Christianism and Judaism.The demand voiced by groups of scientists to have an open mind vis-à-vis religious theories has been repudiated by some "modern" authors as an attack on reason , whereby they declared that an open mind must not be confounded with an open sink (Gross, Levitt and Lewis, 1998). It is true that Christmas appears in every Hollywood production, but not as a conveyor of the Christmas message of tolerance and love to humankind. It simply features as a shopping time, its hero is Santa Klaus in the part of the sales-promotion man.

Post-modernism had been characterized by its playfulness. The computerbased Internet Culture creates and lives in a virtual world of images, symbols and words. In the words of Anderson (1997) in the past, the language has described the world, today it creates it. He should have added only that this created world is a virtual one, merely existing in the mind of the speaking creator and of his friends. This explains why in the Internet era the great world problems are not solved, there is only much talking going on about them, pictures are taken, learned arguments are emitted, but nothing is done. In June 2002, the world press was full of images and articles about the victims of hunger in underdeveloped countries. However, at the United Nations FAO conference in Rome, of the 29 invited industrialized nations only two sent their chiefs of government, namely Italy the host country and Spain, who was at that time presiding the European Union. The majority of the delegates wanted a declaration in which there should have been an explicit mention of peoples' basic right to food, but the rich countries, including the US, opposed this formulation. After much hackling a compromise was adopted asking governments to reinforce striving in this direction (*Corriere della Sera*, June 10, 2002). This, of course, will not solve the problem, even a formal declaration can be withdrawn, as did the US onesidedly with the Kyoto protocol on environment protection. But here the leading country of the new culture opposed even a declaration, in order to shun just the idea of welfare states. Then why hold such conferences at all? Conferences are good because there is the possibility to talk and photographs are being taken. "Ours is a time of diarrhetic speech", declares Brown (1998), very much alluding to the Internet. Even when waging a war, the talking and the snapshots are more important than the results on the ground. The war in Afghanistan is a good example. For every logic mind it could have been clear from the beginning that an air war could not capture Bin Laden and neither solve the terror problem driven by homeless, multinational perpetrators without an urban infrastructure. Important, however, is the smoke seen on the TV screen. What a picture! Besides, in the Internet era it is difficult to send ground troups against the enemy. It can only be done when the government is sure that the own casualties will remain at a low level (as they hoped it would be in Iraq), because the government cannot ask its soldiers to give their lives for the fatherland. Everybody lives for himself; the individual is important, society is not.

This statement asks for an explanation. As a matter of fact the Internet Culture has some ideological-political roots. It is not completely apolitical and only the consequence of using a new communication technology. By its very nature the computer technology was introduced into mass usage and spread by students of the most important industrial nation, which was (and is also today) the U.S.A. The generation, which started using the computer technology and invented the Internet, was the one which shook America in the '1960s with its radicalism. The movement was against the contemporary institutions, for finding a meaning in life that is personally authentic (Brinkley, 1998). They had slogans but not a coherent ideology, as did the Old Left. In the end they seemed driven almost entirely by cynism, nihilism, hatred and rage. Disaffection and rebellion led them to the drug culture, the sexual revolution, the cult of eastern religions (Brinkley, 1998). Some of them mitigated their conceptions and integrated into the civil society, however the basics of their outlook remained. Being young, brilliant intellectuals, they achieved leading positions in their careers and their conceptions had a strong influence on the whole of the culture in the American society. We shall say more on this issue when dealing with the values of the Internet society.

It ensues that culture is a complex phenomenon based on values. They are not exclusively determined by production modes linked to technology and the relations developed on this basis. Values constitute the cultural expression of needs. While needs are individual, value preferences have a double anchor: They stem from individual needs, but at the same time they are adhered to by social groups. It becomes clear that it is not a technological innovation alone that creates a new culture, be this technology important as it may, but its impact on people's needs and on the mode of their satisfaction. The same may be said of production relations depending on the ownership of the tools of production. In Western countries there has been no change in ownership characteristics for at least a century, when family enterprises went public, but the culture has changed, and is again changing today with the introduction of the Internet.

Seen in the context of society, the Internet Culture is a signifying denomination, as one would speak of the Rococo or the Middle Ages, its meaning and content originating in society's new values which engender new behaviors and attitudes. The new Internet era started when extremist post-modernist values joined the new computer and communication technologies. Stock maneuvers, global organizational strategies, enterprise mergers, lay-offs, deceit as a business practice were known from the beginning of the market economy, but they were not key phenomena.Now they characterize *the* economic behavior altogether, preventing and replacing any other mode of thinking and acting.

It has always been said that "publicity sells dreams", but in the '1960s and the '1970s it was known and agreed that publicity presentations had some substance and were not simply lies told in order to enhance the selling of commodities, as were the ads in the XIXth century. Today many advertisements have no substance at all, like the letters distributed in millions of copies, "Congratulations, you have won . . . . Imagine what you could do with this money", and then follows a proposition to pay a certain sum for the transfer of that money, or to order something worthless, but described with colorful superlatives. Of course, in reality nobody has won anything, and what remains is only the illusion and the dream. Only 30-40 years earlier, in the middle of the XXth century, reflecting the progress in which all believed after World War II, organizations tried to raise the "dream substance", for it to enhance the truth of the advertising message. It was stated that the future of advertising belonged to loyal and honest publicity, a helper and educator of the consumer (Krau, 1967). When I wrote these words, I drew on the business culture and practice, and on the literature of that time, but today I humbly and contritely recognize that I did not and could not foresee the economy based on the Internet Culture, which was to come upon us 30 years later. I thought, mistakenly, that an established positive trend in the economy and in public affairs would continue to develop along the same lines and not be negated altogether, like in a ridiculous class exercise in Marxist dialectic. In the next chapters we shall seek to find out why this happened, but one theoretical conclusion seems clear already: progress is not a linear phenomenon in domains involving sociocultural aspects, and this includes the economy. The economy is not only tightly linked to technology-based production relations, as the Marxists had thought, but to the sociocultural lifestyle of society, and both these aspects have an equal impact. It is not true that changes in technology first influence the economy, the relations of production, and then the latter engenders changes in the social suprastructure. The modifications produced by the new computer and communication technologies were not economic first, and only then followed by modifications in thinking and behavior. Perhaps rather the converse is true. The economic consequences followed from a new mode of thinking, of conceiving reality, triggered by the new technologies. Also in Keynes' (1936) views ideas, intelligence or even "animal spirits", emotions decidedly influence behavior, but the intelligence and the emotions he referred to were arbitrary individual creations. I have argued (Krau, 1998) that every society follows a culture-bound model of socio-economic management, and that this is the framework in which the various strategies of investment, management, employment, saving and consumption are designed and applied. Who is referring to an individual only seen as an investing, working and consuming person, is referring to an abstraction. The individual exists as a member of a social group adherent to a certain culture. He or she is using various technologies under the encouragement, the limitations and within the models put forward by society's culture.

Culture conditions the link between the individual and society and the link between society and its activities (biologic, economic, political, scientific, educational, religious, artistic) within the various frameworks (cosmic, environmental, technologic, cultural). In the Internet era the computer screen raised to the level of a fetiche has led people into a virtual world, while the Internet economy anchored in credit-card shopping has given enforcement to the virtuality. The cash flow so important up to now for business proceedings does not count any more. There are assets to substitute the cash, and their nominal value has risen continuously. The rising stock prices made people feel rich, and so did credit cards, people borrowed to feel even better (*Fortune*, April 2, 2002). Reality is being ignored for the profit of virtuality. In this lies the main characteristic of the Internet era and of its culture. It reinforces wishful thinking and plays down rationality, precaution, self-discipline. In the economy savings are disreputed in favor of obsessional spending, in social life impulsive drives are extolled, while religious or moral restraints are disregarded and scorned.

The Internet Culture is egoistic, the needs of the other or of the public are disregarded, there is no place for them in the virtual world of the computer game, where the hero has always his way. He shoots down every opponent and uses all the others to satisfy his wishes and fantasies. Paradoxically, there is also a tendency for unification, for nullifying all the cultural differences, which existed among peoples and countries. Today nothing has remained of the pluralism upheld after World War II. It is important to understand the essential mechanism of this unification trend in the Internet Culture. The latter is not imposed by a political authority, although there is a participating political factor. Herman (1999) points out that although strategic interventions occur, they are of distinctly secondary importance. What happens is the result of the forces of the free market, whereby the powerful have similar economic interests everywhere, and they protect their interests naturally and without an overt conspiracy. Herman does not use the concept of Internet Culture, but his analysis of the "propaganda model" in communication (Herman and Chomsky, 1988) describes as a matter of fact a manifestation of the contemporary Internet Culture. It is known, however, that every materialistic business motive is always presented in an ideological gown, which in this case is the globalization of communication. As already indicated, this means the spread of the culture of the most powerful nation, at present the U.S.A. The rival tendency is a unified European culture, meaning first of all the vanishing of boundaries and of cultural differences among member nations. It should be looked at with the same wariness. In the '1930s the Germans had coined the term of *Gleichschaltung* (cultural and administrative equallization in an approximative English translation) for their own political purposes, and the term has a very negative connotation ever since.

The unifying tendency of the Internet Culture has two manifestations. One reflects the underlying motivation to facilitate the achievement of a global market in which commodities need not be adapted to the specifics of local culture, a need which had very much complicated the selling of American cars and of other commodities in Japan and in Europe (and vice-versa). The second manifeststion of the unifying tendency in the Internet Culture is the mass culture it produced. People, as a rule, deny it, defining themselves as unique individuals in relationship with a specific gender, class, race, etc. This denial does not obscure the fact that today the concept of individual opinions and tastes is obsolete, and we live in and belong to a mass culture (Belton, 1996) promoted by the mass-media and mainly by the Internet. All what we consume are mass products produced with a mass technology, which alone can justify the heavy investments put into it. Mass products create a mass culture. The Internet society is not the first in history to advocate a mass culture. Communist societies did the same, trying to erode the distinction between a high-culture elite and the masses. However, between these two cultures there is a sharp difference. The Communists tried (whether they succeeded is quite another story) to raise the masses up to a high-level classical and scientific treasure of knowledge, the Internet toils hard to give the process a downward direction in spiritual, aesthetic and general cultural knowledge and interests. The process tends towards the least common denominator, so that the advertized commodities and the advertising style itself should fit everybody without the obligation to "educate the masses" which would require huge investments. Besides, as already discussed, the Internet Culture shuns all what is close to tradition and to classical culture. Therefore, what remains is the lowest level of "basic instincts" in social behavior and entertainment, the plumpest "casual wear" regardless to the occasion one participates in, or the most offending lack of clothes. Remains a kind of modernization in art annihilating authenticity.pIn the modernized version, the action of Romeo and Juliet is developing between two contemporary mafia families, as also Carmen of Bizet is taking place in an American boot camp.

The declared aim of such artifices is to bring culture and the arts "closer to the people". However, the damage done by these manipulations is colossal. It marks the loss of general knowledge, skill and beauty in life. To this we should add that there is no real contradiction between the unifying tendency concerning the commonness of the level of general culture and aspirational style and the egoism of the Internet Culture. Students in American campuses have repeatedly declared in the last years, half in joke and half seriously, that after all, Shakespeare was a dead white male, and there was no point in studying him. Implicitly they stated that the difference between them and Shakespeare is that the latter is dead, while they are alive - what a blessing for mankind! Had the talker been black or female, there had been two additional differences. In this statement there is not only a hitherto inconceivable ignorance but a value judgement too, crazy in its disdain of the past and in its self-aggrandizement. Said Jean de

Salisbury, "We are like dwarfs standing on the shoulders of giants. We see more and farther than the masters of the past, not because the sharpness of our look or because we are so tall, but because we are held up and raised by them" (*Metalogicus*, III,4). The representative man (or woman) of the Renaissance era was a spiritual giant with the greatest possible universal knowledge. Who or what is the representative man (or woman) of the Internet Culture? I entrust the readers themselves to make the judgement. Mine would not be politically correct. Right now our problem is to analyze in detail the manifestations of the Internet Culture in the various domains of society's life. We shall start with the economy.

Chapter Two

The Globalized Economy: from the Bull Market to System Failure

In recent years, in the corporate world much is spoken of four simultaneous economic revolutions, namely: 1) globalization, 2) computerization, 3) changes in management structure and style, and 4) information. According to the already mentioned trend of economists to isolate phenomena and narrow down them to their own specialty, these revolutions are considered economic in their causal texture and society's role should be to embrace them and learn to adjust (Stewart, 1993). On the top of all came the Internet and intricated the processes which already tended to structure and stabilize.

Globalization expresses the linkage of business occurrences in one country to what happens elsewhere. The great companies are international, and the strength of international commercial links constrains organizations in one country, e.g. the U.S.A. or Britain, to find answers to decisions made by competitors in Japan, Singapore or in France.

The computerization of the economy in recent decades has even more revolutionary characteristics, because the entire field is relatively new and its development has had unforeseen effects on production technologies, company administration, marketing and distribution. In the latter domain the interlinking of computers may give customers more insight into the way commodities are produced, and what their real qualities and deficiencies are. It also gives the same insight to competitors and industrial spies, since the more computers of the business world are interconnected via the Internet and private networks, the more exposed they are to break-ins (*Fortune*, February 3, 1997).

Another change computerization produces is a shift in the power balance within the organization in favor of top management. Computerization allows for the reduction of employee headcount, including the retrenchment of lower-level managers .Their work activity is taken over by the computer, and supervision is made much easier. If the "first economic revolution" posed a problem of power struggle among organizations in different countries, the "second economic revolution" entails power shifts between organizations and their customers, and within the organization in favor of top management. The real meaning of these revolutions seems to be in the shift of the external and the internal power balance of the organization and of management.

The third revolution in the economy is taking place in management, and it revolves around the dismantling of middle management, the drastical flattening of organizational hierarchy and the installment of an organizational structure capable of being modified frequently. The newly created term is *reconfigurable*, and one of the CEOs interviewed by Stewart (1993) wanted an organization reconfigurable on an annual, monthly, weekly, daily, and even hourly basis. This idea had been aired less presumptively by Warren Bennis back in the '1960s, (Bennis, 1966) as he spoke of the possibility of temporary authority systems, temporary groups, temporary leadership, temporary assignments and democratic access to the goals of the firm. With scientific sincerity he had added that in the minds of many people these ideas brought confusion, disorganization and stress. They do so also today.

There is an additional less publicized aspect of organizational reconfigurability. The CEO-champion of a perpetually reconfigurable organization tacitly assumes that around him all will crumble and change, while only he himself will remain firm, hard and immovable like a rock in his managerial chair. The more he swirls around the others, the solider his powers are to become.Therefore he will stick to reconfigurability, and so will his colleagues in other companies, regardless of the damages they inflict. Here again the economic revolution plainly translates into a shift in the internal power balance of the organization, and again in favor of top management.

It is stated that as for now the highest capital asset is knowledge. It can be captured, deployed, and it creates an edge over competitors. There is a double consequence, so we are told, first a widening gap between the pay of college-educated employees and those with less education, and second, there is a boom of the knowledge-entrepreneurial business, consulting firms, for instance.

The importance of knowledge and more education in the economy of today is certainly a positive feature, and so is the gap between the pay given to people with more and with less education.But this is not the whole truth.College education is worth more, indeed, but only *if and when* people succeed in getting a job where such education is required.Actually, 25% - 30% of American college-educated youths are overqualified for their jobs, and paid in accordance with their lower function, and not with their higher education. Neither minority groups, nor women have been able to translate their educational achievements into financial status (Fitzgerald, 1986; Hartmann, Kraut and Tilly, 1986).

Also the second characteristic of the knowledge revolution in the economy, the spread of consulting firms, ceases to be a blissful development, if we are envisaging that the greater majority of those people had been employed, and had lost their jobs without gaining the security of their existence by self-employment. The failure rate of these small entrprises is very large, 40 per cent of them disappear in the first 6 years (Labich, 1993). In his time Francis Bacon of Verulam could peremptorily state that *Scientia est potentia,* Science Is Power, today the fourth economic revolution makes this adage less sure on the micro-level.

Each culture creates its own model of strategic management, sanctioned by the dominant societal profile of value preferences, which will also characterize the management model of organizations as such. The XXth century produced the socioeconomic management models of collectivist authoritarian societies, of liberal-individualistic societies and of collectivist societies with participation in decision making. In recent years we were witnessing the crystallization of a European management model in the EEC countries, which may be called a bureaucratic welfare model (Krau, 1998). The advent of the Internet introduced a factor of change into this pattern. The Internet started its develoment in the liberal-individualistic society of the U.S.A., and is essentially endebted to is values. The greater the dissimilarity between the liberal-individualistic and the other management models created by national cultures, the greater will also be the opposition to the new economic model of the Internet economy. The latter superimposes itself on the existing management models, bending each of them according to its own characteristics. This fact adds to the complexity and the contradictions of the economy today.

The economy triggered by the new communication technology of the Internet is in itself a contradictory one. The advanced achievements are sticking out in glamor, but there are also negative sides, which stay hidden for a lengthy time. What is sure, is that technological progress in the key industry of communcation has changed the face of society, starting with its economy. Business is relying on communication, and today the PC business is the computer industry for all practical purposes, with a despotical concentration of technological influences and profits.The sibling of computer-communication is the networking industry, which e.g. has already transformed cars from a transportation instrument into a multimedia data receiving and processing center. Presently the PC and the Internet are linking up with the cellular phone. Every day the inclusion of a new gadget is proposed. Today medical control and security gadgets are preferentially advertised. Of course, every coin has a reverse, and the public gets medical and security systems "that are crying wolf all the time", spreading fear and uncertainty.Then there is also the problem that every public campaign leaves behind institutions that don't go away, and according to Parkinson's (1959) law deploy a febrillous activity in order to prove how much they are needed.

There is also a caveat concerning the exclusive feetishism of technology, neglecting the share of human talents and activities. The best example is the American intelligence dossier that led to the war on Iraq, and was exclusively based on all kind of technological gadget information. The authorities have spent on spy satellites and secret listening devices more than the gross domestic product of many countries, but the information was wrong, because it had not been corroborated with plain old-fashioned human intelligence on the spot (*Newsweek*, February 9, 2004). Perhaps it should be added that there had been the human intelligence of the UN inspectors, but the US leadership did not believe what they reported and preferred the fantasy extrapolation of data furnished by technological gadgets. We have here two important elements of the Internet Culture, the fetishism of technology and the faith in an image, which is knowingly manipulated and presented as the truth.

At any rate, be you enthusiatic or wary, the Internet, as Castells (2000) points out, is not simply a technology, but the central technological medium of the Information Age. It is the heart of the system, as the network becomes the social structure of society, and it functions in every aspect of life, from business to social organization. Nonetheless, Castells adds a caveat. Surprisingly, the Information Age is aggravating social inequality, because increasing the wealth of a society in which education and cultural capital are unequally distributed, also increases inequality. One cannot agree with this remark which puts the blame for the growing inequality on culture and faulty education. It is an oversimplification, which for one, doesn't see or neglects the noneducational factors of economic clout, and then doesn't inquire into the causes of the lack of education or into the sustaining elements of a culture that doesn't foster schooling. For the same reasons one cannot agree with the enthusiastic statement of Seligman, former president of the American Psychological Association, that today there is more money and more happiness *(APA Monitor, 1998, 20,* 10). The question is always, who has more money and who is happier, and how much does this happiness last? And finally, is the Internet linked to this happiness and in which way?

Analysts agree that the Internet is a commercial reality with great potential. Powell (2000) points out that the developed world will soon be on-line all the time, in our cars, home and offices. He also claims that the Internet will make the demographic time bomb go away, but this again is the expression of an uncritical elation: we already know that the gap between haves and have-nots is increasing in the Internet society.

Economists emphasize that the concept of being always on-line, always connected, is a very powerful one. On the business side it means access to anything needed at any moment, and on the consumer side it has a strong impact on people's interaction with companies. In the year 2000 there have been approximately 200 million consumers who used the net. The rise of the Internet seems the biggest business story for the years to come (*Fortune*, October 9, 2000).

Opinions are, however, divided regarding the meaning of this "business story", and as to how it should be obtained. In the past years the jingle was *growth* through mergers, the takeover of other companies or the development of one's own organization. Mergers are still continuing, especially in the communication industry: Bertelsmann, the editorial and music giant has acquired RTL, Vivendi, leader in pay television (Tele+) has bought Universal, a major Hollywood enterprise, Granada has fusioned with United, etc. The success of mergers depends on the common willingness to build a common new organizational culture, on being honest about all aspects of the deal, and on taking care of people's careers in the acquired organization. Hostile takeovers do not respond to these requirements, and the acquired entity sticks like a bone in the throat of the raider. Therefore, generally, the raiders' aim is not to build a big viable organization, but to quickly sell their prey. Such action brings money "at the end of the day", but does not improve social production. We are here witnessing one of the main features of the Internet economy. In many cases the *value added reflects stock maneuvers and is therefore not real, but virtual, without reality coverage, and only creates a bubble which finally will go off.* In a previous book (Krau, 1998) I have emphasized that economic progress depends on real added value. This means an innovation, an improvement in technology, so that the public would be able to receive more products they need, with an improved quality (a real improvement, not a merely advertized one) and in better conditions (quicker, at a more affordable price, in improved supplying conditions). The globalized economy promised to satisfy these conditions, but did only patially so. One should also be wary of jingles like a referral to an allegedly existing steady production growth. Such growth, if it is obtained, causes stock prices to rise, but then the market may bring in a "useless" verdict. You can't sell products of which the market is saturated, or the price is not affordable. In the last years we had some good examples for such production rises in the car industry and in hotel building. They finished in huge losses. The Summer of 2002 saw the crush of the communication giants of Enron, WorldCom, Xerox. In 2003-2004, in the name of globalization, the Italian Parmalat and the German Mannesmann followed their dubious example, the first with an embezzlement of more than 500 million euros, the second with the suspicion of an illegal bonus of 56 million. The Italians complain that 2/3 of the wrongdoing was due to foreign frauds (in the Cayman Islands for example) and only 1/3 of it was "truly Italian". This does not change what has happened , but gives an illustration of what globalization really includes. In all these companies there were unlawful accountant temperings involved, but the latter only delayed and aggravated an existing business situation of severe loss. In a classical economy things like this could never have happened on such a scale. There have been frauds and bankruptcies in the past, but not as a mass phenomenon. Obviously, the Internet economy is not what analyst-poets have claimed. Its entire system is faulty, starting with the basic assumptions, the principles of business conduct, the relationship with internal and external factors, the operational gamut. Let us discuss all this in detail.

The classical organization had a relatively stable strategy of conduct, like the preservation of an already conquered market or innovation and the expansion to new markets, and contingent plans to reach the planned objectives. It did so amidst the adamant resolve to strengthen the internal unity of the organization, without which the objectives could not be realized.For the Internet enterprise the jingle is "more money at the end of the day", and it does not matter how.This means the exploitation of people's credibility (customers, suppliers, credit institutions), the use of not entirely legal means of operating and accounting, and a planning up to "the end of the day" only, without caring for later events.Such a conception brought the catastrophic boom and fall of the dot-coms, the organization raiders, the continual slashing of the payroll, and last but not least, the deceitful advertisements and accountings.

The public reacted by blaming outstanding representatives of the world of business, if not business as a whole for lack of morality, and some extended the reproach to political leaders. Unwilling to accept the blame, the defenders of the Internet Culture tried to demonstrate that the human nature does include violence, the deceit and the hunt after lust we are witnessing. In this context a scientist was brought to the fore, the American Napoleon Chagnon, described as "the most famous anthropologist in the world, living or dead" (*Scientific American*, March, 2001). After a controversial research conducted on an Indian tribe in the Venezuelan jungle, he reported that 40 p.c. of adult males in the 12 villages he had sampled, had participated in killing people. The men who had killed, were more successful in obtaining wives and had more children than those who had not killed. They were admired in their culture.

It would not be nice to make a direct linkage between Chagnan's adulated warrior killer, wealthy and reproductive, and the Internet business hero. Still, astonishingly, there has been much admiration voiced vis-a-vis professional corporate "job killers" like "Chainsaw" Al Dunlap, walking from one organization to another with the declared task of "slashing and slashing again" the payroll and throwing people out on the strets, breaking up their careers and in many cases their families, with the sole aim of making possible additional short-term profits, as the company saved their salaries. Of course, in the long run no company can thrive wih a slashed, despirited , hostile work force, but the Internet Culture is not built to create lasting things. Click here, click now, and cash now!, these are the commands. After people like "Chainsaw" Al Dunlap (there are others too, it could be the Swedish Barnevik in Europe), completed their mission of destruction, they used to be hired by other organizations to do the same exploits there. The company they just left faces another business hero, the Raider.The heyday of these people were the '1980s when they took and disembowled companies for sport and profit .Carl Icahn or Ron Perelman employed buy-and-break strategies, they threw out management and used the company itself as a collateral to finance their swashbuckling.

While the "corporate killer", the first hero of the globalized economy accepts the framework of the organization which hired him, and slashes, "kills" the staff only (?!), the raiders slaughter the organization itself. What happens to the staff is a consequence, although their fate is not much different from what had happened to them with a "corporate killer". .In the gallery of economic heroes of the globalized society, i.e. of people who basically influence the economy, and are therefore much appreciated, "successful and reproductive", there is also a third hero figure. He does not wage a war against the staff of his organization, like the "corporate killer", neither does he slay his or other organizations like the raider, he kills financially with a smile all those who trust him, be they customers, shareholders or banks, playing the gullibility card of the public. Some of the afflicted victims plainly call these people swindlers.

Garry Winnick, despite his lack of experience founded Global Crossing in 1997. One year after going public its stock was valued at $38 billion. How did he do it? His business plans changed all the time, luring costumers and investors by overstating the capabilities of the company's network. He was hailed as an industry giant, and indeed billions of dollars flowed out of this company into the pockets of insiders. A little over two years later all was finished, the company was plight. Global Crossing had raised more capital than it needed, it had built a network with more capacity than the world demanded, and its leaders had greedily confounded a public company with their own pockets. Winnick got rich quickly, but the shareholders lost their money (Cresswell and Prius, 2002).

A big organization has to focus on production and marketing, the stock market should reflect the organzation's real production and marketing potential, nothing more. The woe of the contemporary economy is that management's focus is th stock influenced by maneuvering, rumors and fantasies. In the old days the focus was on the service to the public by producing a much needed product, but now it is on money alone, and money is linked to the stock. Much more money and much easier can be made through stock manipulations. Forgotten is the truth that the stock and its monetary expression must be backed by the material value of the commodity produced by work. Not only is the sole focus of the Internet Culture the stock, but if it doesn't evolve as the finance people would like, they falsify the financial data. Nobody really seeks to improve the underlying process of production and distribution of material goods through the investment in human skilled work. This means that the contemporary organization, like the classical one, ought to deal in the first place wiht the process of managing production and marketing, and this includes a correct policy of employment and financing under the conditions of new technologies and contemporary culture. The latter must be improved, but it cannot be ignored. First of all, the technological progress has to be accepted and it is a factor of change. However, its pace must be controlled, and also its usefulness for society. The Internet Culture is promoting perpetual changes for the sake of change and without justifying their necessity. This situation is leading to organizational bankruptcy, because the market accepts only changes that are necessary and satisfy the needs of at least a sizable group of the public.

Second, the influence of the psychological factor in the economy has to be accepted. The Internet economy is resting on it. It is true that such a process is not devoid of danger, because the world and the economy are real and not virtual, they are subject to real laws and not governed by whimsical dreams of wealth. Nevertheless, the psychological factor is largely active, it cannot be decreed inexistent, and the only thing that can and should be done, is to bring it under control, to use it in the interest of society and the public.

It is generally agreed today, that one of the causes which exacerbated the Great Depression of 1929-1932 was the psychologically induced "doomsday" propaganda in the mass media. The government also decided to make budget cuts, when the economy badly needed spending injections, in order to be put on its feeet again. This lesson has been learned in the present recession, and it is a positive development to maintain public trust in the economy, but exaggerations may turn into a costly mistake. Investors are conjured not to give up, to spend more, to go to pricy restaurants, to resume firing infotech workers (Colvin, 2001). The market is irrational, we are told, there is no way to understand it, so let us go and spend, all will be fine, there is no reason why the bull market should not continue, it is such a wonderful thing (*Fortune*, March 19, 2001 and June 14, 2002). "Ignore the prophets of doom", we read in the Endnote of the *Special Issue of Newsweek* in February 2008, the month in which the present deep recession started."Despite terrorism and the many errors the Administration has made, the world is better off than ever".The wrriter of this article, Rose, a managing editor of Foreign Affairs, continues saying that more than a third of the world's population now lives in countries with an economy growing 10 percent annually, and an interconncted global economy is open to all new comers. Who benefits from this growth? Has the managing editor not heard of the horrid poverty in India, in Latin America or even in Harlem? The public should surely have faith in the economy, but not blind faith. Psychology, faith and confidence cannot and must not come in lieu of economic analysis, a sound management policy and the weighing of the social consequences of leadership decisions. Specifically, a new economic boom needs capital accumulation which should also lean on the populace's savings. Some analysts triumphantly declare that the "negative wealth effect" of a plummeting stock which drained the wallets has had no significant impact on spending, bacause interest rates and inflation are low in the US, the prices of houses are rising and they have been causing renewed purchases of homes and mortgage refinancing. Credit is easy for consumers, it is harder for business. *Fortune* (September 30, 2002) concludes, "Pundits have waited two years for consumer spending to falter. It hasn't. And it won't". The media are enthusiastic. Hammering the necessity of spending into the public brings momentary relief, but then the public's empty reserves prevent the investment in log-lasting commodities, whereby also the reinvigoration of the economy in the long run.

The industrialists of today do not consider this side of the process, they want money *now*, and believe that that if they succeed in overcoming their present cash predicaments, their overseas investments will take care of the capital flow needed to-morrow. They forget that the Internet economy is global. More often than not, when the Dow Jones goes down, so does the Nikkei in Tokyo and the Hanseng in Hong-Kong. During long years of Western propaganda efforts the ordinary citizens in the Far East have been coaxed to waive their traditional saving attitudes and to spend. Nowhere are there any reserves left.

The media have repeatedly reported that American banks are very generous in granting big loans without the due investigations of collaterals, but they are very careful in giving small loans. This is another mistake which has worsened the impact of the Enron and WorldCom frauds. Still, bankers are not worried because of the insurances. It seems their solution lies in also bringing down the insurance industry. They simply are incapable of renouncing the stereotypes of the Internet Culture - what counts is the moment, click here, click now! The world is a virtual place, therefore one has to use virtual methods to cope with its predicaments. The application of this rule bred new accounting practices which presented losses as gains. AOL Time Warner reported a "one-time, noncash charge", in plain English, a noncash loss of $54 billion (*Fortune*, May 27, 2002). It didn't affect current operations. But the stock could have been sold for a then existing high price and put in the bank with a high interest. Instead, the company mistakenly and only for the sake of gambling, bought another stock, the price of which went down. The operation was presented as a one-moment giant loss, but after a quarter of a year the balance sheet looked better, no "goodwill" amortizations for acquisitions that last for 40 years and eats away at profits - the Internet society lives in the present.

By this method a faulty management decision was made because of the "bubble" and the "principle of growth", but no legal cheating has been done. The latter occurs when research data are being falsified, and losses are accounted as gains. Merryl Lynch has been accused of just that (*Fortune*, May 27, 2002). The list goes on from phony book keeping to allegations of insider trading. Between 1992 and 2001, 609 cases of fraud were referred to US attorneys by the Securities and Exchange Commission, 525 of them were closed and 187 cases prosecuted, 142 of them found guilty, but only 87 persons went to jail (Leaf, 2002).

The problem is that you cannot trust any more the information published by the companies themselves, you cannot trust any more the published reasearch data, because lots of data are phony and tampered, and finally, and most horrendly, you can neither trust the accountants' statements. Andersen, who tried to cover up the Enron fraud, is not the only accountant office, which destroyed public trust in the profession.

It appears that accounting self-regulation is not working as had been expected, and the most glaring example is acountants' unwillingness to deal with conflict of interests. The auditing firm cannot work both for the public (as an auditing institution) and for management (as a consulting institution) (*Fortune*, January 7, 2002). Generally, acountants seem embarrassed by their watchdog role and have treated their public responsibility as though it were a burden, the more so because they do not get big earnings from this activity. This happened especially to Internet insiders like Mary-Meeker, a much admired analyst, who came to see herself not as an analyst, but as a player. After the disasters she causesd, she defended herself by saying that she felt protective toward the phenomenon she helped launch. It was the Internet bubble. Says Elkind (2001), "The story of Wall Street over the past two decades has been in many ways the story of eroding ethical values, of greed taking precedence over client loyalty, and degradation of standards". The situation worsened when the uncorrect accounting linked up with executive greed, a destructive characteristic, which turned against other companies, but also against the own shareholders and employees. At Enron it was not the CEO alone who by his greedy mismanagement brought the disaster upon the company: it was also the indifferent, gullible board itself. First of all, there are too many insiders on American boards (from 7 to 9).

There are directors aged over 90 and others regularly missing from board meetings. What can be expected from the decisions taken by such boards?

There was a bizarre spread of corporate and public trust in those who presented themselves as experts. This gullibility was supported by the Internet Culture which furthered the tendency of people to believe in virtual stories and fairy lands, whereby corporate leaders posed with arrogance as the new supermen. There was arrogance in Enron, and greed, deceit and financial chicanery. Their financial statements were by intention obfuscate, indicating the origin of their earnings as being in "wholesale energy operations". Their compensation plans seemed oriented towards enriching executives rather than generating profits for shareholders, whereby employees were kept in the grip of continous fear, because of a forced rating system by which the bottom 20% had to leave the company. Thus employees were busy with atttempting to crush each other, and cover up for their own mistakes (*Fortune*, December 24, 2001).

In general, although statistically the situation on the labor market is not desperate in the industrialized countries, the attitude towards employees has worsened even in Europe. In France the jingle of *délocalisation de l'emploi* (synonymous with the American "outsourcing") has become widely spread. In the US the trade-unions are weak, there were almost no strikes, and the Internet Culture has caused a change of attitude for the worse towards the work force. Gimein (2000) gives the example of Wal-Mart, a trade giant, the employer of one million people. They are constantly asking of its employees to do more with less people, but branch and department managers since long do not know their employees, and after all the talk on democratization and the right to leisure, a mandatory six-day working week has been introduced. Once the workers were important in the eyes of management and made a difference, but now only customers do. No wonder that nobody does believe in management's promises any more.

Analysts admire the steady increase of production in the U.S.A.There is, however, no reason for stunned admiration. The spiral is turning downward. If the productivity miracle was for real, the profits plummeted, however, some say by 21% from mid-2000 to September 2002. One cause was the formerly strong dollar (this at least has changed in 2006, and today the weak dollar is accused), also a result of the psychological-cultural war for supremacy conducted by any means in order to achieve an everlasting bull market in an American supereconomy. Some blame the former Federal Reserve chairman Alan Greenspan for not stopping the Internet bubble by raising the interest rate in 1998 already. However, others think the Fed chairman behaved normally, since he was a fervent supporter of the free market and had strong faith in the new economy, a faith forcefully sustained by the media and by corporate interests. Where does this leave us? At the recognition, that the culprit is the entire global Internet Culture itself, which by its intrinsic faulty characteristics has led to a *system failure*, first in the economy, but also in other domains of society's life. It has produced what analysts call a "go-nowhere economy" bearing the spectre of a double-dip recession (Bernasek, 2002).The stock market rout has accelerated a sharp decline of household wealth, there is a credit squeeze because of accounting scandals and weak profitability, and finally, consumer, business and investor confidence has been badly shaken. The tight credit market and the downgrading of consumers' debts increases the cost of capital, it becomes more expensive and harder to invest, while consumer spending remains at a standstill, although people may not cut back on spending drastically. Housing prices have remained strong, and mortgages could unttil 2005 be refinanced at low rates. Just, promotions and salary raises will be hard to get. In 2008 there already are signs of a deepening recession. Consumers are cautious and will be saving more. In one word, it is not a débàcle, but a stagnant economy going nowhere. Any additional crisis can produce a double-dip recession .

Daily newspapers and some TV interviewees would not agree with this analysis, because, so they say, the Western economy has lastly shown unmistakable signs of recovery. In 2003 the Dow Jones has stepped over the 10,000 point barrier and in the Fall of 2006 the 11000 points and then 14000 points, but later it fell back to 12000. In these results the digital revolution, linked to the Internet, the latest in a series of technological revolutions has definitely had its share. All new technologies have deeply transformed the economy, producing decades of prosperity. So it has earlier been with the railroads in Britain and in the US. They helped putting afoot the inputs that industry needed. The same is happening with the information revolution. Systems, machines business processes are all getting connected, the digital technology is making business smarter, tiny processors can see, listen and pass on the information and even provide a collective intelligent action.

However, the analysis discovers several dubious points in the economic recovery which present the whole image in a very dubious light. First, the more cautious European analysts agree that the whole process of economic recovery is very fragile, and even in the US there are experts warning that corporate America looks more an athlete pumped on steroids than a naturally fit competitor (*Fortune*, 15 Sept. 2003). They refer to the fact that there has been an incredible swift return to what looks like speculation with shaky small companies performing spectacularly. The term coined for the phenomenon is "echo bubble" or BWave and reference is made to what happened after the crashes of 1929 and 1968. These secondary bubbles rapidly splat, and wiped out all bubble gains before a new bull market started (*Fortune*, 23 February 2003). Secondarily, the digital technological informational revolution has produced a structural change in the American economy. The manufacturing sector is about to collapse, "Made in America" is fading away (*Fortune*, 24 November 2003). Already some years ago Belton (1996) warned that the U.S.A. could not any more be considered a producing industrial economy, it is today a service economy. In this sense also Craik (1994) concluded that in our days leisure is the big business.

The third drawback of what is called the economic recovery, is that it is a jobless one. True, in the recovery year 2003 nearly 300,000 jobs have been added, but this leaves a net loss of one million jobs, (*Fortune*, 24 November 2004). Although forecasters believe in a 3.5%-4% economic growth for 2004, it is far from bringing relief to to the job market. The characteristic feature of this recovery is performance growth with ever fewer people. If there is need for additional work force, only temporary workers are hired (*Fortune*, 29 September 2003). Then, there is the problem of wage level. Today in the US hospitals and restaurants hire, but they are paying substantially less than before. The explanation of this situation is that the chief motor of the economy, the manufacturing sector, has been maimed by a wrong economic policy. Manufacturers are stuck with too many factories and must cut prices to compete globally and satisfy shareholders' appetite for ever bigger earnings. This means laying off workers and try to even produce more with fewer of them or else outsource the whole production process. If until now the retrenchments only concerned shop workers, the big innovation is that a country has been found where office and computer jobs can be transferred: it is India. It holds a vast market of English-speaking educated workers, happy to take jobs in software, accounting, consulting for 10%-20% of what would be paid to an American worker. (*Fortune*, ibid.). D. Kirkpatrick, Fortune's senior editor for Internet and technology is very enthusiastic about offshoring, and this reinforces our contention that what happens is a reflection of the Internet Culture. He writes that we should not even try to stop offshoring, because for each outsourced dollar the US gains $1.12, and 30% of Indian offshoring is performed by US coompanies which *own* the Indian ones. Job turnover is a sign of a healthy economy (but he forgets that here there is no job change, people become jobless!). Kirkpatrick's solution is to demand better education and training (it is an empty slogan if structurally there are no jobs), and then he asks for social programs to cushion the blow (*Fortune*, February 23, 2004, p. 29). The haughty absurdity of such a solution is obvious. Apart from the horrific social costs, welfare recipients are supported by the taxpayer. It would benefit society much more socially and economically if those people could work.

So what will Americans do for a living? Work for the industries of the future, answer the companies-paid analysts, but the problem is, as one interviewee says, "we create new products and when they become mature, much of the production moves overseas, and we move on to the next big thing". Till when? What a paradisiac outlook. Will America become a nation of leisurites, a kind of Video-game Planet? But there are two problems. The first one is that capital accumulation goes on also in the countries where the American jobs have been outsourced. After a number of years, they will by themselves design, produce and market the products outsourced to them, sell them cheaper and conquer the markets which provided the money for American leisure. In 2006 this process was well under way.It is more of an American problem, because the European Union is maiinly outsourcing their manufacturing activity within the EU to the economically less developed members, and thus "all remains in the family", and the unequality of wages can be set at the conference table. For psychological reasons this method is unlikely to be used by the Americans soaked with a superpower or a hyperpower conception, which is pushing them to a price war or even a "gun-boat policy" as had been used in the XIXth century. US detractors say that the war in Iraq is an expression of this policy, but sure is it neither would work with the European Union, nor would it with China or Japan (it did work in the '1800s).

At this point the first depicted problem of the future Internet-leisurite American society meets the second. It is the problem of poverty and a decreasing living standard of the lower social-economic strata. It is bound to lead to political and social trouble and violence. Again, the US is more endangered than other developed countries. Precisely, because of the outsourcing of American work, the economic situation of those countries is rapidly improving and the people there can see the future with confident hope, while in the US the situation is endemically deteriorating and no hope is in sight. Beth Schulman (*Fortune*, 29 Sept. 2003, p.27) considers that 25% of the doomestic work force of the US don't earn enough to stay out of poverty. These low-paid workers are far from being also low in skill. In fact, she says, they are very skilled, a majority has high school education and they are vital for child care, nursing homes and other essential jobs of the new service economy. Nonetheless, they can reach no upward mobility, and after 25 years in the work force their wage is still unsatisfactory. As a matter of fact, the financial situation is improving at the very top only. The earnings of the others are pressed down. In a leading pharmaceutical company, we are told, managers asked employees to take pay cuts to help pay for the launch of an expensive new drug. They were not promised job stability in return, the sole purpose of this intervention infringing existing contracts was to enable the company to meet the targets promised to shareholders. Such cases happen because managers are promoted not for espousing high-minded values, but for making the numbers (*Fortune, ibid.* p.54-55). This means that we are speaking not of some managers who have lost their way, but of a generalized organizational culture imposed by society, mainly the American society, as we have seen. The situation may be looked upon as a systemic process, which will inexorably go its way if not recognized as such and willfully stopped.

What has been said should not induce the thought that only the American economy struggles with setbacks and problems. The European DWS Investment report on the 50 enterprises which participated in the stock index Eurostoxx50 maintains at the top only the Finnish Nokia, while two giants, the German Telekom and the French Télécom plummeted, the first to the 38th position, the second to the 50th position. The Italian Eni, however, rised to a fifth position. Following this disclosure, the DWS report asked for improving corporate governance, transparency, respect for minority shareholders (one share, one vote, one dividend), attention to the composition of the social organs of the organization and the presence of independent directors (Co*rriere della Sera*, September 21, 2002).

These measures proposed by experts in stock exchange are certainly aiming at curbing the mishappenings that lately plagued especially corporate America.They have one major flow: they see the stock exchange isolated from the economy and the latter isolated from society's culture. It is not a system failure they are addressing, but negative occurrences in one sector of the economy.

From all we know now, this is the wrong approach. Just as the Internet Culture is not just regulating the behavior of Internet browsers during *gophering* activities, the investing, stock buying and selling behavior of executives is not an isolated domain of acticvity, but embedded in a culture-bound strategic conception on society, the company and on themselves. There is a continuous thread linking together society's values, personal values and behaviors in the different domains of societal life and the activities of organizations in all these domains. In my previous book (Krau, 1998) I have described the *culture-bound models of strategic socioeconomic management* existing in the various parts of the globe. In the meantime the new advanced Internet technology has achieved dominance in the liberal-individualistic model of the world's strongest economy, and is tending to achieve a global character, leaving behind pockets of more collectivist or pluralistic attitudes in Japan, China or in Europe. The bankrupt Japanese banker who, after closing his institution and laying off his personnel in the recent Asian bank crisis, went to the TV studio, and with tears in his eyes begged entrepreneurs to hire his former workers, who lost their jobs, is the hero of a conduct model which went underground, and is therefore obsolete.

Japanese stock has not substantially risen since the recession of the '1990 and nothing they did has changed the situation, but they abide by their traditional values and business style, and they do not feel misery-stricken, even if accused that the Japanese system isn't really capitalism. So many businesses which should die out are given loans by the banks and are staying alive (Powell, 2000). Fujio Mitarai, the new boss of Canon pledges a non lay-off policy with life-time employment. He maintains a large production base in Japan, even though costs are lower overseas and 70% of his sales are outside Japan. This policy works, and Canon steadily reduces the market share of the American Xerox (Holstein, 2002). American markets continue to function because they are ruthless, Powell (see *supra*) points out, but as the Canon paradigm shows, the much criticized Japanese system has inner resources allowing it to be very competitive, even if stocks are not fabulous and their *zombies* are alive.

The new chief manager in the Internet society lays off workers with a self-confident smile, a feeling of power and satisfaction. Retrenchments reduce production costs and the "retrenched" company should be worth more on the stock market, bringing him additional "performance-bound" earnings. It is a wrong, momentary judgement, because in the long run, a high quality production cannot be upheld with a reduced, exhausted by multiplied tasks, and despirited work force. In this situation the great advice of occupational experts to employees was, "be your own boss, become independent". The advice was ill-conceived, as the débácle of the dot-coms proved. There were several reasons for this event. Firstly, not all the ideas of the new start-ups were needed on the market, secondly, not all the new entrepreneurs had the necesary organizational and marketing aptitudes. Finally, after a short initial free flow of credits, the banks refused to give them to small undertakings, and approved crediting for big companies only, where they thought they would have no problems with the repayments of debts. In that way the banks have choked the new small initiatives, and succeeded in losing billions of dollars instead of only thousands, now that the big corporations are frauding them and go bankrupt. Again a wrong decision, but these are the new rules of the game.

What is being said is intended to underline that the faults are not in isolated sectors of the economy: *The Internet Culture caused a system failure of the economy which manifests itself in all its domains*: 1. The stock market 2. Credit and finance policy 3. Technology's place in society 4. The relationship between the organization and its clients, consumers, and other organizations 5. Internal organizational management, the relationship between management and employees 6. Management and society's social setting 7. Globalization.

Of course, there are new markets in the developing world for the existing products, but the populace has no money to pay for them. Once there was a joke told on a successful salesman who sold refrigerators to Eskimoes. Woe is the company, General Electric or any other one, which would stake its present or future on such practices! Developing countries must be helped to acquire a decent standard of living, which first includes commmodities of primary necessity. In the industrialized world there is no real desire to help them reach this stage, the latest proof is in the watery, sterile document of the conference on "Sustainable Development" held in August 2002 in Johannesburg. With such an attitude the developing countries of the Internet world are shooting in their own leg, but investing in underdeveloped countries brings dividends in the long run only, whereas the purpose of the new culture is immediate profit.

Some analysts are indeed complaining of a systemic failure of the conomy, but it so seems, they coined the term to exonerate the wrongdoing by individual organizations like Enron, WorldCom, Global Crossing, etc. Others theorize the issue. The point is that the Internet Culture produced the licence for individual wrongdoings, gullibly embraced by banks and individual investors. In a letter to *Fortune's* editorial board, Th. Rieger writes (*Fortune*, July 22, 2002) that if a company pays its executives obscene amounts of money, it also gives unsecured loans to its officers, while making expensive and unwise acquisitions, nobody should invest in such a company. We are adding that this is valid not only for the US, but also for the EU, as the Ackermann case teaches with his illegal merger bonus of 56 million. Nevertheless, these features reflect the intimate features of the Internet Culture, therefore investing in such organizations seems normal and is (or had been at least) generally done. *This* is the manifestation of the system failure.

Other manifestations of it appear in the "new" relationship between the company and its costumers or with other organizations. Until now management lore held that the company aspires at winning and holding ever more customers, thus enlarging its share on the market. Not any more, say Selden and Colvin (2002), if the company's aim (its sole aim - *E.K.*) is to enrich its shareholders. Modern managing of an enterprise is managing a portfolio of customers and not a collection of products and services (the people working there are not even mantioned). Analyses with the newest computer programmes show that not all customers are equally profitable, some buy only "sales" items, but then call service rep too frequently. Today, due to advanced computer technology, such custoemrs can be identified the moment they call, and then put to the lowest-cost channels: automated phone lines, longer queues, the website, so the most profitable customers, who buy for greater amounts of money, could be served more quickly. For the unprofitable cutomers the treatmenet described above would be a disincentive to call. The company should also cease to send them announcements of big upcoming sale actions.

In other words a company should only serve customers of big money. The others should be treated as second-class people and driven away. Very cautiously Selden and Colvin (2002) only gave the examples of two Canadian firms who were living by these rules: the Toronto-based Royal Bank of Canada and Fidelity Investments, which obviously had no rep service. This was a very necessary cautionary measure, because such "progressive and modern" measures may dangerously backfire. I remember a TV interview of an Israeli hotel owner, who, in a time when tourism crumbeled in this country, and he had asked for government help, he was asked why did he not lower his very high hotel prices, so as to accomodate internal mass tourism. The man proudly answered that his enterprise is organized for rich tourists. Two months later, with the same pride he went bankrupt.

For our discussion it is important that the new management methods à la Big Brother were prompted by the Internet Culture establishing the duty for reaching a maximal profit and made possible by the existence of the internet web sites and by the new computer programmes. They were used to gather more data on customers and then make unwelcome selections with the aim of discriminating against parts of these customers, humiliating them, so they would leave and would not "soil" the company with their presence.

The role of the new technology is a very curious one even in its economic aspects. Its declared role is to make activities more easy and comfortable, to bring to the users the possibility of new connections and activities they could not have dreamed of. However, in the Internet Culture technological development is driven by the desire to heighten profits and not by society's needs. Computer processing power doubles every two years, said Moore 40 years ago, but an unstated corollary to this law holds that at any given time all the machines considered state-of-the-art are on the verge of obsolescence simultaneously. This is so, because they are designed to run for a few years oonly, and then they overtax and befuddle the computer. Microsoft's recent Vista spells doom for aging machines, which otherwise would be still able to function. Therefore the new economy's problem becomes the high-tech trash (*National Geographic*, January 1, 2008) in two senses. With all the due politeness, but an expensive gadget designed to break down after a short time, and spoil the host machine too, is trash. Secondly, there is the problem of depositing this trash somewhere on the globe. It is preferentially done in developing African countries, which the globalized economy turns into trash repositories. It should be added that in many instances the new products are not better, not easier to manage, but they are more expensive, and the advertisement plays with the slogan "new vs obsolete" so very familiar in our times. One could give the very recent example of genetically modified crops forced upon the market with the presentation of dubious research results. Presently, there is no known certain advantage of the Gmcrops. While traditional produces are well in supply, the former enlarge the gap between rich and developing nations, and they also introduce new and insufficiently studied biological dangers. Here is the crux of the matter: The basic medical principle of *Nolli nocere!* (Don't cause any harm!) proclaimed in the oath of Hippocrates should also apply to all the technological inventions and discoveries.

One will also have to reject as untrue the new slogan ventured by corporations that in the new world technologic development is driven by customers as an expression of the "tectonic shift" from customer-centered to customer-driven (*Fortune*, July 22, 2002). The driving force behind animal cloning and bioengineered crops are not the conservative American farmers, neither the European peasants, fearful of the negative effects of the new produces, and who are also afraid of risky investments and unnecessary changes in their working settlements, nor the public who reject these products.The driving forces are the money-greedy companies, which accept the risk of biologcal catastrophies for the sake of a new profit avenue.

The point is, the attitude of the organization vis-á-vis its customers has ceased to be client-centered, but neither is it client-driven. It is simply an attempt to dominate the client through the new Internet-created methods of advertisement. Things are even more complicated when looking at the company's link with other organizations. Emery and Trist (1973) had demonstrated that the *environmental texture* in which the companies exist (the concept had made the object of an analysis back in 1935 by Tolman and Brunswick) acts as a *causal* texture imposing certain templates and modifications of organizational behavior. An environment with many organizations of the same kind which want to take over each other's part of the market may cause "turbulent fields" to appear, bringing the whole economy into an earthquake like motion. I have added (Krau, 1998) that in the contemporary world one ought to speak of *global turbulent fields*, also involving the social-political structure. In this situation organizations must come to some sort of understanding, even short-living ones. They cannot exist as a chain with its link members independent from each other. They have to cluster into complex ecosystems requiring alliances with partners, collaboration even with competitors, while maintainig the contact with customers. The problem is that the Internet society has written permanent change on its banner. All understandings and alliances are short-lived, on the agenda are forced mergers and hostile take-overs. The link of common (ethical) values intended as a solution to this problem (Church and and Emery, 1966) has not materialized. The common value of the Internet society is immediate material profit, and this includes the steady planning and striving for taking over or liquidating competitors, surpassing them by ever new technologies.

The new era marks the end of user-friendly products, appliances, packaging, user's instructions. If the latter exist, they are written in a technical, unintelligible language, on the package they appear with tiny letters, so as to make their reading impossible under time pressure, and without spectacles for people beyond forty. The company phones promoted to a key communication medium have become an instrument to lay off workers. Everywhere there are too few telephone switchboard operators left to ensure a personal communication with the customer, who must stumble around on his way in a maze of preset tape answers. This after an unrealistic period of waiting spiced by tapes containing music chosen by the company or by political comments from the radio, again selected according to the executive's preferences. Political brainwashing while you are waiting is a new invention of the Internet Culture for a more efficient use of time.

At any rate, the practices that have been mentioned, cause two obnoxious consequences: first the end to transparency in organizations, and second, the end to ergonomics. The Internet organization is, despite all lofty declarations, neither designed to bring a sense of comfort to the customers, nor to make work comfortable for the human operator. The sole principle is to make more money quickly, and therefore factory occurrences described in the times of Dickens and Zola are restored to their former glamour. In an era when "modern" architecture advocates the abolition of separating office walls, and the concentration of white-collar employees in big open halls, computer software is ubiquitously designed to produce unnecessary beepings and other noise pollution. It is designed to write single-spaced texts that are difficult to read and that destroy the eye, while there is no preoccupation to sufficiently protect the computer operator from screen radiation.

The end of organization transparency strikingly appears in the relationship between the company and the public. Letters are not answered. If nevertheless, a company letter is sent, it has no date, no address of sender, often even not a phone number, it used to bear no lisible signature, and frequently only mentions a website without an e-mail. When a phone number is given, it is impossible to reach a personal representative of the company for lack of sufficient phone operators.If the company sends a phone message, it appears under "private number" or "unknown number" on the costumer's answering machine (or, if the addressee answers the call, the employee will describe himself as Johnny from. . . without giving his full name). The organization wants to stay anonymous in order to reduce its responsibilities in possible law suits. The products and the services are as they are, the exacting of responsibility is made impossible by all means of "advanced" technical tricks.

While the communication in which an organization is involved, is enhanced by modern advanced technology, it is outmoved to impersonal tracks of online-internet. As a byproduct of this process, the buyers are de facto denied their right to a fully infomed choice.If it is an internet online transaction, the buyers only receive the information preset in the ad, they cannot ask questions, and they are under psychological pessure of a backgroud with sparkling colors and noises to speed up their decision.

In the "old days" many books described the process of buying with its stages of 1) catching the potential buyers' attention, 2) convincing them while involving them emotionally by presenting the commodity, 3) describing its positive features and 4) answering all the buyer's queries and doubts 5) provoking a positive buying decision 6) followed by action and 7) ensuring costumer satisfaction (Kitson, 1927). True, even now organizations promise consumer satisfaction, but an unsatisfied internet buyer cannot even contact the company, which he feels has sold him trash. He is better advised to save his health, his time and his money on futile telephone conversations with a tape, and simply give up.

As a consequence of the advent of hi-tech, not only bilateral commmunications become impersonal, but also bilateral actions which should essentially be personal, like health care. Medical science has become pure technology in recent years. Checks and controls are performed by computer-controlled equipment. This information could and should be very helpful indeed for the physician to reach an infomed decison concerninng the symptoms of an illness and for the appropriate treatment, but it is misused in several directions. First, the patients are nilly-willy submitted to endless check procedures. Ever new and renewed checks are required from them. I could tell dozens of such cases beginning with a phoetus in which an ultrasound check discovered a little enlargement of the kidney basis, and from that moment on there was no end to external and intrusional checks, medicines and proposals for operations immediately after birth. Needless to say that the parents have decided not to operate the child, and that despite their decision the child developed absolutely normally and no problems have arisen with the kidneys since. I saw patients who after a heart attack from which they had recovered, were transformed into psychological invalides by permanently submitting them to all kind of effort tests, checks and analyses. The poor patient who got very satisfactory results in this week's check, awaited with anxious scare the checks of the following week. The doctors in the Internet society do not rely on computerized analysis data for help to reach *their* decision, but the act of diagnosis is handed over to the computer, and the doctor only proclaims it vocally. Where are the physicians as knowledgeable dispensers of medical care? They are swallowed up by the new technology, which relieves them of the responsibility they should bear for the diagnosis and the treatment of their patients, *and* it allows them to substantially enlarge their and the medicare institution's income by shackling the patient to permanent checking ups. Where is the physician's scientific knowledge? The routinized computerized work erased it from their memory, or they think it is wiser not to use it, the computer will do the job for them, and if things turn out badly, the responsibility is not theirs.The global Internet society is one of "legal violence", and scores of money-hungry lawyers are watching for every medical mishappening to start a lawsuit for alleged malpractice. To blame the fetichized computer is the doctors' best defence.

In the economic system failure of the Internet society an important part plays the internal management of the organization, which includes the relationship between the organization and its employees. Of course, bad management is not only the misjudgement of a company's human assets. It mainly rests on a success-oriented culture with unrealistic perfomance goals and wishful thinking, until the violation of rules becomes the standard, unfavorable facts are explained away instead of facing them, and management is looking for a quick fix at any (moral) cost (Charan and Useem, 2002). In other words the causes of economic failure in organizations are much rooted in society's culture and in psychology, in the simple denial of unpleasant facts, of data which are incongruent with management's wishful thinking. We have here a key evidence of the Internet Culture which first sets managers into a virtual world they take for real, and then destroys the communication with them, so that subordinates are affraid to thell them the truth. We were mentioning here the common mistakes, but each failing company was brought down by its own particular sins. Together they reach an impressive record attesting to the system failure of the economy. In the USA 257 public companies with $258 billion assets were bankrupt in 2001 compared to 176 companies with $95 billion in the year 2000 and already 67 companies in the fiirst quater of 2002.

The organization of the Internet economy bets on technology and not on human assets in the production and the communication processes. Management thinks that the use of advanced information technology and the outsourcing of labor-intensive production activities will do the job.An analysis of nation-wide data for the last 20 years done at MIT has found that for every 1% of investment increase in information technology, the average firm employment has dropped by 0.13% within one or two years. On the other hand, the outsourcements have largely favored the plague of counterfaits in the foreign countries, causing the US losses in worth of $200 billion over the last decade.

The organization of the Internet economy is slimmed down until it reaches extreme limits, it is delayered, meaning the lay-off of mid-level managers, the responsibilities are devolved to lower levels, carefully supervised by top management (Peters and Waterman, 1982). One might say, "Not so bad, a smaller well motivated army with less supervisors can give better results". .Such an outcome is opposed by the basic principle of the Internet organization to deny employees every chance of stability, because their "job at risk" (Hartley, Jacobson et el., 1991) is a permanent status.Research has confirmed (see ibid.) that these employees have higher levels of anger, anxiety and related forms of stress.

It has to be added that the organization of the Internet economy in principle avoids to give its employees contracts for longer terms or tenure. Whenever it is possible stable employees are substituted by temporary ones or by part-time workers hired from man-power companies. Research has shown (Krau and Kimelman, 1991) that in fact we are dealing with a new basic policy aiming at hiring cheap labor, while avoiding institutionalized employment relations with the new job holders. To every logical mind it must be clear that an organization which applies such principles is heading for disaster. An employee whose job is continually at risk, who is denied the rights to promotion, pension, etc., and who frequently has not even a legal relationship with the enterprise or the institution for which he/she works, is not and cannot be passionately motivated to add value to the wealth of his bosses. The "delayering" takes away the professional supervision, because top management has other problems to care for and lacks the deeper and subtler knowledge of the work process, even if working with a special computer software.

This is true practically and also for the new organizational theories put forward. Kanter (1989) speaks of a post-entrepreneurial organization, flexible and highly responsive to environmental changes, slimmed down by contracting out in-company activities, and authority loosely devolved to lower levels, but tightly kept to management aims through a universal sharing of organizational mission. Whose common mission? Kanter answers with the concept of stakeholders in which she surprisingly includes the partnership with competitors in market exploitation, together with the own workers, awaiting to be "slimmed down" .Obviously she understands neither human psychology, nor the mechanism of competition on the market.And then, we got a new theory at the World Economic Forum held in Davos in 2001, more known for the antiglobalization protests on the streets. Speaker after speaker talked about how emerging *business webs* or value networks are connecting *modular* or *molecular* corporations (*Fortune*, March 5, 2001). There would be no more companies, which design their own products, and then build and package them. Because of the Internet, companies now have the ability to strip down their business to its essence, to focus on where the greatest value creation and profit lies. The rest may be eliminated through partnerships and outsourcing. And what happens to the employees? There is another question too: If the organizations become "molecular", then why the unsatiable appetite for mergers and take-overs? They say of Bernard Ebbers, the founder of WorldCom, that his appetite to eat other companies knew no limits, although he didn't bother to digest them, and the result was chaos. Others, like General Electric, knew better how to integrate their acquisitions, but our point is, that such market behavior belies the much vaunted partnerships, business webs based on value networks and all similar rhetorics in contradiction with the real Internet Culture. The dominant model of strategic socioeconomic management in the Internet society is an extremist liberal-individualistic one. In this model power belongs to everyone capable of seizing and using it, while state organs maximally refrain from interfering. A power balance is though exercized by public opinion, but only in matters concerning liberal-political values like environmental awareness, the prevention of racial and sexual discrimination. Since the individual organization is sovereign vis-à-vis the general society, social consequences of management actions are nonvalues and not taken into consideration, even if they were to damage the entire society in the long run (Krau, 1998). To clothe such a model in collectivist values of partnership is a contradiction in terms. We shall speak more about values in the next chapter.

To the aid of the Internet organization come two basic principles of the new culture: a) the world is virtual, if it doesn't yield to your wishes and does not look like you would like it to, simply change the data, present the virtual gains existing in your imagination instead of the real ones, and b) if a hero in a computer game is in trouble, in order to assert his power, he guns down all what moves around him.It is just a game, isn't it, and society has a violent character.

Norton (2000) says ironically, "First impugn the motives of your opponent; second, assume the very thing you ought be proving; and finally, don't bother with any data or analysis to support your position". McLean (2001) adds, "Start with arrogance. Add greed, deceit and financial chicanery. What do you get? You will get Enron". The Enron, Worldcom, etc., cases expose not only dishonest accounting methods, but also deeper processes of faulty communication and repartition of influence within the organization. The mismanagement of the big companies is caused by a systemic failure of the present-day economy, it manifests itself as such and exacerbates it with its consequences.

True, it is impossible to monitor the actions of every employee and external consultant or accountant, but precisely here the organizational culture has to step in providing internalized guidelines and shields against wrongdoing for employees and for executives. The Internet Cuture does just the opposite. There is no collectivity to reckon with, in the executive's eyes he/she is the lonely hero of a virtual world in which only the benefits and the enjoyments are real. Charan and Useem (2002) point out that Enron's culture encouraged profit taking without disclosure, Andersen's culture engendered conflicts of interests without safeguards.

In its very essence, organizational management is a form of power behavior having its hallmarks set by the dominant culture of society. On the market organizations are in competition, and competition is also a power struggle, and so is even the attempt to influence the public to buy the commodities and services offered by an organization. The gist of power lies in dealing with resistances. Weber (1947) defined power as the probability that a person could carry out her own will despite resistance. The content of power behaviors in organizations does not merely characterize a one-time event.Power is a strategic behavior, its meaning lies in the strategies of which it is a part and the latter reflect the goal aspirations they are intended to serve. As a strategic behavior power has *dimensions*, which constitute a formal attribute, because they belong to every behavior in which power is acted out. One must deal with the following dimensions of strategic power behaviors in organizations: 1. External vs internal directedness (towards competitors, suppliers, costumers, authorities, mass media, trade unions - or towards internal interest groups, owners, lower ranks in the hierarchy), 2. Attraction vs fight 3. Offensive vs defensive directedness 4. Acceptance vs despising moral and legal limitations (Krau, 1998).

In the economy of today the *external directedness of power struggle* is a necessary and ever-present feature of macro-organizational behavior. Its efficiency and success may be predicted from the predominance of the external locus of power over the internal direction, when more energy is invested in internal intrigues and skirmishes, and less remains for the struggle with external factors. However, in dealings with people having less power, power exercises may give the manager a feeling of ego-aggrandizement. The less balances are in society, the greater will be the emphasis on power behavior, and the greater the temptation to seek personal power satisfaction in economically unjustified layoffs, "corporate killings".

The Internet hero loves power for its own sake and for the money it brings him. He uses power in both directions, against his co-workers, "because they are there", as said Sir Edmund Hillary when asked why he climbed on Mount Everest, and against all possible other companies, because of the illusion that every growth of the company adds value to its stock and clout to its executives. In the '1970s and '1980s there was a definite category of enterprises who did not seek to enlarge their share of the market and introduce new products, they only sought to defend the place they held by all means (Miles, 1980). Today the pressure from external competitors, and the internal pressure from shareholders and fellow executives to enlarge their profits, is so strong that this category of organizations has ceased to exist. They changed or died.

In this context we ought to speak of globalization, as one of the outstanding events brought about by the Internet economy on the international level of the market. Take for example L'Oréal, formerly the image of Paris sophistication. Under its new chairman Owen-Jones, the company developed the strategy to buy local cosmetics brands, give them a face lift, and export them around the world. The new public is carefully sought out, and the product's name, package and brand is adapted to it. Thus, Maybelline, a dowdy US makeup house, acquired by L'Oréal in 1996 became a hit in Japan and in Middle America. While in the past 75% of the comapny's sales was in Europe, now it is only 49% from its $13.7 billion annual revenues (Tomlinson, 2002). Obviously the managing of such a diverse gamut of products could not be done without the modern online communication techniques and the marketing it made possible.

Nevertheless, globalization is a much more complicated phenomenon as presented usually, because we are only shown its positive fanade of easier communication throughout the planet, of an enhancement of distributing and production facilities, as also the better circulation of capital, with an interdependence of stock markets all over the world. The periodical meeting of representatives from the seven great industrial nations (sometimes eight with the inclusion of Russia) tries to control and to coordinate the events, lest they become the kind of turbulent fields of which all are afraid. The analyst who tries to study this phenomenon is struck first by the violent resistance globalization meets by social activists. These are not the usual strikes with agitating speeches made by trade-union leaders or univerity teachers, but the international gathering of reinless, violent crowds, chanting, looting and destroying, sometimes as an accompaniment of a discussion forum where the pertinent ideological questions are being debated. In November 1999, in order to protest against the meeting of the World Trade Organization, held in Seattle, tens of thousands of demonstrants invaded the city. Their violence constrained the authorities to declare a curfew and the summit failed. In the next year, in January 2000, the meeting of the WTO was held in Davos (Switzerland), as thousands of violent demonstrants again made their entry. There were violent clashes with the police, a number of stores belonging to McDonald (the symbol of a global company) were looted. At the G8 meeting in Genova, in July 2001, 150 thousand "no global" protesters appeared, the damage caused by them was estimated at 40 billion Lirettes, one demonstrator was shot dead by the police, tens of other manifestants ended up in hospital.

It was a turning point, the crisis was near. The governments finally got it that the social problems raised by the "No Globals" had to be taken seriously, because the dimensions and the violence of the demonstrations could no more be considered to be merely a police matter. Unfortunately, the main intention is until this day to hold nice speeches, and not to invest larger sums of money, because "there is no fortune at the bottom of the pyramid", and underdeveloped countries are hung up on existing rules and procedures (*Fortune*, October 28, 2002). On the other hand, the "No Globals" understood that some form of structure had to be created in order to control the movement, otherwise it could degenerate in mob and/or antisemitic violence, as it happened in Rome at the international FAO meeting (*Corriere della Sera*, 10 June 2002). The leaders want to maintain the disobedience, but in some nonviolent form. It may be late for this, because the movement is infiltrated by violent guerillas who suddenly apear at any demonstration. Also, some groups want the repeated use of the squares: from Catholics to social centers, from trade-union organizators to ecologists. In Germany increases the preoccupation to find a structure, but people say it should not resemble a party. There should be voting, but decisions should be taken by consensus, or at least with a 90% majorty (*Die Zeit*, 29 May, 2002).

At the beginning of the '1990s Magnet (1993) hailed the new computerized technology, because it required less and less labor and raw material. The technological revolution, he pointed out, makes possible to manufacture a product anywhere and to sell it anywhere. The liberalization in Latin America, in China, the collapse of the Soviet Union has made available a store house of cheap labor to capital-rich countries. However, in this way the job growth in the rich countries is halted. At the same time the situation of the developing countries does not essentially change for the better, because wages remain miserable, and the native culture, which lent social acceptance to a lower living standard of life is supplanted by a foreign culture with its slogans of high economic aspirations, infulfillable for the natives. What is even worse, the new culture reflects mainly one foreign country, the U.S.A., whereas in historic tendency there is the affinity to the former colonial powers, France, Spain, Portugal, etc.Globalization is the enemy of local cultures, as they impose the American model - I have called it the liberal-individualstic model of socioeconomic management with competition on the loose (Krau, 1998).The world is invaded by CocaCola and McDonald, therefore the protest of demonstrators target these companies.Yet, the big companies are convinced that their strength is in the international and not in the national markets.

It so appears that the great companies are seeing their own immediated interests only. They do not fathom that this short-sighted policy jeopardizes their own existence in the long run. This conclusion is also corroborated by the curious finding that the terrorist attack on September 11, and the following war against terrorism did not influence the global economy substantially. People are contracting international businesses, they travel, and if there was a reduction in economic growth, it happened before September 11 (*The Marker*, February,

2002) - we shall add, as a result of the burst of the Internet bubble.

Globalization may be a quite useful business tool, on a higher level of political thinking it is neither good nor it is bad. It depends upon the possibility to limit the phenomoenon so as to allow national cultures to flourish, and not to impose a single model of socioeconomic management, whether it is a blessing or a curse. Said Vincente Flox, the president of Mexico, "there has to be more globalization, but within a dialog with Porto Alegre, there must be interchange *and* aid, so that the poorer populations would benefit" (*Corriere della Sera*, 4 February 2002). Even so globalization continues to be a concealed form of the use of power, but it should be a wisely used power.

This brings us to the last power dimension, which has special importance in our days, *acceptance of vs despising moral and legal limitations* in the exercise of power. Balances are imposed on power behavior by law, culture and by social and moral responsibility. It had been stated (Carr, 1968) that business has its own norms and rules, different from the rest of society, and therefore a number of things we normally reprove, are permissible in business. However, Shaw and Barry (1989) point out that by divorcing business from morality, Carr misrepresents both. He treats morality as something we give lip service on Sundays, but which otherwise has no influence on our lives. As to the special "business code of conduct", one might ask, where in this conception is the boundary between business and mafia, which also has some codes of behavior between rival families? As time goes by and the Internet Culture takes over more and more, these questions are ever harder to answer. There are links among some individual business executives and mafia bosses, and regarding the morality lip service on Sundays, in the Internet society even the latter does hardly exist any more. The only hurdle for this kind of "advancement" is the law. But, as Shaw and Barry (1989) say, law cannot cover the variety of individual and social conduct, and it also cannot be taken as an adequate standard of moral conduct. There are various conducts not (or not yet) explicitly forbidden by law, but highly unethical and unprofessional, like the selling of stock by top officials, a phenomenon which lastly happened *en masse*. As investors were losing 70%-80% or even all their holdings, top officials of those companies were getting immensely wealthy by taking advantage of their inside information and of the bubble to cash in millions of stock handed to them via risk-free options (Gimein, 2002). We are again reminded that the Internet society does not recognize loyalty towards one's organization, shareholders, friends or colleagues, only towards oneself. The situation may be remedied and such events prevented only if intervening at a more general level, by changing the culture. Morality is the basis of law, and the latter functions as a kind of least common denominator of morality in society. Both morality and the law are depending on society's culture, whereas both, but especially the law, has a strong component of society's self-presentation, because it is openly heralded, and not only understood by covert consensus. Therefore a deed may be unlawful but condoned by the more advanced (?!) public opinion.

Let us take an example: The aforementioned authors opened their book with Ivan Boesky, Wall Street biggest speculator's pleading guilty to a felony charge of stock manipulation in 1987. He could have been indicted for a wider range of criminal activities, but in exchange for his cooperation, the prosecution reduced the charges. He was sentenced to a four-years term of imprisonment and a fine of a hundred million dollars. The authors exclaimed in 1989, "A brilliant career has nose-dived and crashed".Not in the Internet society of today! After two years in jail Boesky went free, and because he had cared to put a greater part of his fortune on his wife's name, he got after her divorce 20 million dollars, a house worth 2 millions and an annuity of $200,000. A similar fate had the junk-bonds hero Michael Milken, denounced by Boesky. He paid a fine of 1 billion dollars and did $1^{1/2}$ year time in prison. Today his fortune is estimated at 800 million dollars and he is hailed by public opinion, he has founded a research institute and an institute for investment into private schools. He has written two books on diets. Hollywood treats him like a star. As to the heroes of today, Jeff Skilling, delegate administrator of Enron, kills his time skiing in the Andes, Dennis Koplowsky, former president of Tyco International is in this Summer on a cruise in the Atlantic.Both are under investigation for white-collar crimes, but the authorities did not even retain their passports. Their careers are definitely not broken, only the careers of their victims are. Some of the latter suffered financial losses beyond any repair.

Every time things like this happen, analysts used to ask "Why?", but they are concentrating on the perpetrators' deeds only. This is not entirely appropriate. In forensic psychology it had much been spoken of the "criminal couple" (Mendel-sohn, 1956) comprising the delinquent and his/her victim, which in the stade preceding the crime felt attracted towards the criminal and towards the situation of risk. In the case we are debating here, the clients, inclusive the banks and the financial authorities trusted the criminals, their gullibility made possible the fraudulent behavior. True, swindlers have always been, but again, now the phe-nomenon has a mass character, and society's defense is weak. The swindler's punishment is a lip service only. "Who is saying that crime doesn't pay, write *The Times* (London), the *Corriere della Sera* (Italy) and other leading newspa-pers, doesn't know what happens with the summits of American finance". The fault lies with society's culture, the Internet Culture which requires the public to trust business ("go to pricey restaurants!, etc"), but does not require from busi-ness to stand by its word.

In the past, as also today, the building of consumer confidence has been a basic condition for business to succeed. However, in those days success was reached through the truth of the publicity message and of the content of adver-tisements, through the image of the corporation as a model of a positive attitude towards the public and the company's employees, inclusively in the case of con-sumer complaints (Krau, 1967).

Also today, business organizations consider public relations and their image in a pivotal role within the new integrated marketing communications (Harris, 1998). It should be an outside-in process that begins with the understanding of the individual consumer, and the latter does the integration of the informations received. (Yes, but the question is what kind of information do the consumers receive and how).The publicitary aim is not to reach publics, but individual people pointed by data bases (How about the invasion of privacy, and the exposure of these innocent citizens to a daily flood of junk mail, mostly with a deceptive content?) Also today, every institution or corporation has two assets on which success and survival depends, its Brand, the image and the reputation of the company, including its financial assets, its performance and people, and its brands, as the products or services it sells (Harris, 1998). One wonders, what is the meaning of company performance and reputation, only the millions encashed by shareholders and chief executives or the service to customers and the creation of a place of work bringing satisfaction to employees and happiness to their families and the community in which the company works? It does not mean that an organization should oversize its work force. Nevertheless, when a conclusion is reached as to the number of necessary workers, then the game of "cut and cut again", although it may create an increase in stock values, is creating by the same token hatred within the work force and in the community. Hence it will also spill over to consumers.

The new integrated marketing communication sees a priority in establishing links with the community, for them to exercize a positive influence on individual costumers. The organization uses various methods like sponsorship of events, VIP fan clubs, endorsement by a third party, the support of causes that benefit society as a whole. Again, such methods are not new, but as they are done today, they are raising serious doubts and questions, if one goes into the details.Let us start with the organization of events. The marketing in the Internet society usually comprises of sweepstakes and the allocation of prizes. The 50th aniversary of the "Tide" detergent was celebrated in 1996 with a prize-winning contest for the ten best photographs of the *Dirtiest Kid in America*, which then figured in the local magazine, and the company donated for every entry fifty cents (?!) to a nonprofit organization. Harris (1998) resumes the benefits of such actions: People trust nonprofits, and will see the company as one who cares about people, as well as about profits. Such contests are fun and offer winners the chances to win a prize and fame for one day (for what, for being the "dirtiest kid in America"? - very educational for them, and for the entire society!) We are given another educational example when Ben & Jerry, the producers of ice cream with innovative flavors, unveiled a poster proclaiming, "We want you to be our CEO", and invited applicants to send a 100-word essay demonstrating thir qualification. More than 22,000 applications were received, but then the new CEO was recruited by professional headhunters. Those who are working in the field of vocational counseling know that the term "headhunter" designates firms which are "hunting" for qualified people without or before the latter would even think of making an application. This means that from the start on the company did not intend to use the applications it asked for from the public to select its new CEO. In the Internet Culture such a procedure may be the normal way to elicit confidence and to link up with people, in the past it would have been regarded as a deceit incompatible with business ethics.

De George (1982) has pointed out that if a corporation made a statement, which it knew or believed it was false, to another company or individual, who one had reason to think he(it) would believe it was true, such statement is a lie. A statement or any ad is misleading if it makes claims in such ways that, when ordinary people read it quickly, without great attention, they will make a false inference or draw a false conclusion. Needless to say that lying or enouncing misleading statements, has always been considered unethical.We shall discuss the value problem in the Internet Culture in the next chapter, for the moment let us accumulate more facts about it, and take a close look on the donations of 50 cents or more to nonprofit organizations. Who are they? Marconi (1996) tells the story of a Body Shop whose chief executive gains substantial attention by the media, because she purports to sell only "all-natural products", while passionately fighting against testing cosmetics on animals. This way she was able to reach a larger public through wide editorial channels, in print and electronincs. In other words, in a part of those nonprofit organizations, as in the case under discussion, we are speaking about plain politics. In numerous cases the corporations use political methods in promoting their case, like lobbying in Congress or forming coalitions to bring their case before the public and the courts. A good example is the Dairy Coalition, which energetically fights for the admission of genetically engineered food. It is an issue raising the spectre of an enormous potential danger for humankind. Therefore its solution should be found by patient, impartial research, and definitely not by a partisan presentation of uncertain facts gained from not rigorously controlled experiments which also use political pressure in asserting the results.

Chapter Three

Values and Ethics in the Internet Culture

In the previous chapters we have discussed cuturally determined behaviors of individuals and groups in which the values of the Internet society find an eloquent expression. Our intention is now to deepen the analysis in order to expose their philosophical-ideological and psychological roots, which make them ubiquitous manifestations in all domains of contemporary life. What we have described in Chapter II as a system failure of the economy is in fact a system failure of the gobalized Internet society caused by values which are leading to the destruction of human solidarity based on morality, common tradition and common spiritual values. Joas (2000) points out that the loss of values may be perceived as the symptom of crisis of a society, with the decay of families, the neglect or the vandalizing of public spaces, drug addiction, unmotivated acts of violence. All these are phenomena, which appear in the Internet Culture of our days. The latter can therefore be characterized as a society with a deep value crisis.

Values constitute the cornerstone of substantive or content theories of motivation, which seek to explain what specific entities motivate people, energizing and sustaining their behavior (Campbell, Dunnette, Lawler and Weick, 1974). Values have been found to designate an important psychological phenomenon, which mediates, in Zytowski's (1970) definition, between the person's affective orientation and classes of objects offering similar satisfactions. It follows from this definition that: a) a peson's profile of value preferences reflects his/her need profile, and b) a person's profile of value preferences expresses attitudes vis-à-vis situations, behaviors and events. A strong positive attitude will be attached to situations related to values with a high preference position, while situations linked to a low value preference will elicit indifference or negative attitudes. The impact values will have on behaviors depends upon the relative salience of the role behavior in the repertoire of the idividual's roles in the various stages of life. In their classic study on the quality of American life Cambell,

Converse and Rogers (1976) emphsized the role of need-based aspirations, although they attested to the existence of a process of adjusting them to changed life situations. The question of emerging need-based aspirations expressed in value objectives was addressed by Krau (1987, 1989) in two studies.

The research sample consisted of 913 high-school students, boys and girls in equal proportions, half of them in the last grade, and the other half in the IXth grade. The research was conducted in Israel, the sample included Jewish and Arab public schools and Catholic monastic schools located in urban and rural areas. The latter were divided into neighborhoods of a high and a low economic status The research instrument was the Values Scale of the Work Importance Study elaborated by an international team in which I participated. The international character of the reasearch gave the possibility to compare the Israeli findings with other countries (Krau, 1995; Super and Sverko, 1995).

School was indeed found to inculcate the principle content of values and the main elements of society's culture. There are, however, two qualifications: school's influence gradually declines, and in late adolescence the common societal value profile remains confined to the rejction of unacceptable values (non-values like Authority, Risk Taking and Prestige). This phenomenon also appeared in Portugal, Australia, Italy and Yugoslavia. In the US Physical Prowess was added to the rejections and also Cultural Identity. In Israel and in Portugal Physical Activity was also rejected as a value (Krau, 1995; Super and Sverko, 1995). In Krau's studies (1987, 1989) it appeared that the profile of value rejections was characterized by a remarkable stability acros all samples and age groups as all agents of socialization were contributing to this situation.

The data suggested that the source of value determination appeared more so in the subculture of a socioeconomic environment, also integrating national and religious features. Socioeconomic level appeared as a factor of *longitudinial stability* in individual value profiles. As people are passing through the periods of their life course, a majority of them cling to the valus of their original socioeconomc level. Krau (1989) used the method of value profile determination in retracing the path of social ascent in the careers of opeople. Age-related social experience is leading to a *horizontal stability* of values in people of the same age. Then the combined influence of the two factors is presiding over the transition in values between high school students and adult workers.At any moment a common rank profile of values in people indicates a common developmental stage and/or a common developmental path of social mobility.

The importance of value preferences must be considered in the light of life domain saliences. In American, Canadian, Italian and Yugoslavian high scools (we are talking of a research conducted prior to the division of Yugoslavia) leisure seemed to be the domain of utmost salience, but work rises to the first place when value expectations in adults were concerned (Krau, 1995; Super and Sverko, 1995).In Israel this happened only in white-collar employees, while for blue-collar employees Home was more important. In all countries the values of Ability Utilization, Advancement and Achievement showed the highest correlation with the salience of work (in Australia it also correlates with Creativity, in

Portugal with Autonomy). However, all this is only a part of the truth, because the study also evincecd significant correlations of work saliences with Risk Taking (US), Physical Activity (US, Israel), Altruism (Australia, US), Prestige (Australia), Authority (Portugal), and one will remember that these are the least preferred, the rejected values. It therefore appears that the salience of work in human life is not an entirely positive experience. Work salience covers the whole meaning of work, which for many people is an instrument of self-realization, but it partly appears as an imposed activity with aspects that are preferred least of all, but are accepted in order to earn a living and achieve personal development.

What if public opinion of a society reaches the conviction that the path for personal development is not linked to work? Would work still be people's salient life domain? Obviously not. Here the hidden, inferred negative valuation of work in the 1987-1989 research presaged in fact the coming of the moral-spiritual profile of the Internet Culture a decade later.This does not mean that the globalized Internet society rejects work and does not recognize it.On the contrary, work is considered very important for society, but for others, not for the person him/herself. However, neither society as a collectivity is valued, nor are *the others*. Hard work is requested (otherwise you starve), but society dos not value it, and does not educate for it. Handicrafts and handiwork are straightly disregarded, only intellectual work is given some consideration. This new culture was not imposed on society, it organically grew out from hidden thoughts and problems for which the *old* society did not or could not seriously try to find the answers.

What did then and does today make work to be so unpopular? Work is a purposive, generally collective activity in which individuals are interdependent and obeying to certain rules, whereby the purpose of the activity and the rules themselves are represented, stated and enforced by other persons who are nominated or elected by still others to play the role of a leader. Even if a person is a free lancer, he/she must accept the rules imposed by the market, the public or the organization, which buys his/her production. Empirically and anecdotally the reluctant attitude towards work of today's generation is well known, but the phenomenon is of a much more fundamental nature. Work, formerly a basic value of human society, nowadays clashes with the chief values of the Internet Culture: freedom, equality, leisure and permanent enjoyment and pleasure. To speak today of the Protestant Work Ethic described by Weber (1947), ensuring employee satisfaction by the simple exercise of their occupation, resembles to excavating archaeological findings from the times of dinosaurs. This is not to say, that today the work career is not an instrument for achieving self-realization (Krau, 1997), but society imposes on many people an interrupted career and a self-realization image not linked to a definite vocational activity. The transformations in technology bring about frequent changes in the occupational activities as such, and the Internet Culture imposed maximization of corporate profits used to cause lay-offs and the frequent change of the employing organization, and/or also of the occupation as such.

There is a corresponding shift in the aims of self-realization. My reseach on self-realization in the "old" society (Krau, 1997) showed that about 30% of people saw a certain vocation as the path to reach their end-state of self-realization, and about 50% had seen their self-realization in making money and achieving power. This purpose can only be achieved if the person deploys a work activity, even if it is not tied to any specific occupation, as the self-realization of the first group.Finally, about 20% did not link their self-realization to work. They aspired at spiritual experiences, marriage, wandering in exotic regions, etc. Such are the life purposes today strongly emphasized by the Internet Culture (except marriage perhaps), and to which bow all modern heroes of movies and TV talk shows. A minority of people seek spiritual experiences, the majority may simply be characterized as the *Leisurite* type of Super. Since work remains an economic necessity, the beginning of an orderly career is postponed in order to make a several-year-long trip to India, Thailand, the Saharian desert, Peru, etc. There they experience the sublime freedom and happiness of dangerous sites, kidnapping, drugs (and for many an Indian jail or a Malayisian gallows for drug trafficking). Then, if they are still alive, they come home and look for a job in which they continue to only seek excitement and not the passion of a life-time activity.

The intrinsic work ethic as such is disappearing even in Germany. In 1993 *Times International* (May 24) linked the decline of Germany's economy to the decline of its work values. The country which taught the world important qualities of reliablity and service, sees how today others make better products and cheaper, because in Germany the working week is 36 hours (today it is 35 only in the Western parts). She has one of the highest pay rates, there is a general lethargy, and they have the highest rate of sick leaves (including a high percentage of unjustified cases). The journal concludes saying, that it is not the workers who are sick, but the work ethic. Here is how characterizes his work Stanley Big, described by the redaction of *Fortune* (*148*,7,88) as a *real executive*, "In between the coffee and meals, and planning for the coffee, I work. The nature of my work is unimportant. It is not odious; it's probably a lot like yours. . . I have to be there".

Nonetheless, to say that people in the Internet Society do not want to work would not be true. What I have described as the categories of end-state images of self-realization (Krau, 1997) taps general human behavior, and so work-addict people do exist in the Internet Society, only their activities have changed and so has their place in the social ladder. Perhaps the rapid changes in socio-economic life have brought to the fore a miscellaneous type, seeking realization in certain occupations *and* leisure activities, or leisure *and* money. At a more thorough biographical analysis one of the classical types will prevail. Sir Richard Branson praised on *Fortune's* (*148*,7,2003) cover page as "the man who has everything" gets up every morning at 5 o'clock, so he can have two hours to think of his business when all the world is quiet. He works all the day, but then mixes all with adventure in business, in hot-air balloon races, in meeting beautiful women. His job provides the education he was never able to get in a classroom. The journal purports to present him as the prototype of the new society, but here it is wrong. His success does not come from his anticonventional, unsettled activities, from his failure to finish school, but from his extraordinary busines capacities *and* work addiction. How many such people do we know? And then, this is a very narrow vein in which such behavior leads to success. Try it in research, in building and in hundreds of other careers and you will fail. Branson replaced the school knowledge necessary for his business with sources offered by real life, but in other careers they are irreplaceable. Therefore the picture presented by *Fortune,* although it is a good journalistic spin, is a false presentation, educationally at least. To call Branson a business genius would not be entirely wrong, but to compare him with the giants of mankind, Michelangelo, Dante, Goethe or Thomas Edison, who created art works or technological works admired for centuries, is out of place. What does he leave to mankind except his own feeling of good?

What is guiding the men and women in the globalized Internet Society? First are the qualities required by the Internet technology, as they are translated into values and aspirational goals of the personality: a) the exclusively valued hitech *and* the contempt for all what is not hi-tech, b) this is leading to an exclusively valued present, *and* to the contempt for all what is past and tradition. The shortness of memory is astounding. It has been reported that some Americans doubt whether American astronauts have really set foot on the moon (*Scientific American*, February 2003). A corollary of this fallacious memory trait concerning the past, is the emphasis on a perpetual restlessness, a constant change, a thirst for the new for the sake of the new, and for more for the sake of more (see Giroux, 2001).Joas (2000) joins the choir asking that we liberate ourselves from the pressure for constancy. The marvellous and exciting things, like a good wife and a good health become customary and are discarded, points out the Italian *Corriere della Sera* (18 December, 2003).

We shall only be troubled by what disturbs the exercise of our self-indulgence, like viruses, poisons, accidents and terrorism. Towards all other things the attitude is one of apathy, and this latter will be the suicide of Western civilization. Giroux (2001) remarks that in the US people are more interested to know who will be voted off from the Island of Survivors than who will be the next president of the United States. c) In accordance with what has been said, society's central preoccupation becomes the computers, the Internet, *and* the depreciation of all traditional means of information retrieval, e.g. books or older scientific journals d) In connection with this behavioral style a new value is joining, the fetishism of science, as an enhancer of the individual's functioning.Its expression is the craving after the *smart pill* which makes people superior to their colleagues (i.e. their rivals). A new kind of *moral Darwinism* appears, which, with the cult of the winner also establishes the struggle of all against all and cynism as the norm of all practices (Bourdier, 1998). In day-to-day life this aspiration manifests itself in healthy people buying medication designed for the sick with schizophrenia, the bipolar disease, Alzheimer and other diseases with which, however, the medication designed for them has very modest results only.

Against all scientific evidence an intense promotional propaganda convinced masses of healthy people and some of their doctors that those pills help improve people's memory, intelligence and attention concentration. Hall (2003) points out that scientists are cautioning against the use of such medication for two reasons: first they have no better effect than e.g. caffeine (simply coffee in its traditional name), and second, there is the problem of side effects in the artificially concocted chemicals. But of course, the poor pill-swallowing guy pays his/her tribut to science, to progress, he/she feels good, and so do the pharmaceutical factories which earn lots of money, as do the physicians who hand out the prescription. All are happy, except the really sick, because they continue to suffer from cancer, Alzheimer and from all the other diseases for which the medications had been designed. To them they are giving little help, because they have been hastily approved without the sufficient and hitherto legally obligatory research guarantees (Hall, 2003, 40).

Other values follow the technical interaction with the computer and the Internet browsing: e) urgency and speed as the most desired behavior characteristic; it entails the speediness of analyses which causes cursory actions and biased decisions, f) the valuation of virtuality vs the reality of events; it entails the gulllibility of customers, the lack of responsibility, the tendency to deceive, success aspirations neglecting the reality of goals (it's only a game!), g) the desire to communicate with others, but maintaing one's anonimity vs the opposed tendency to discover the personal data of the other, use and abuse them in business and in private life, and finally h) ascribing to technology a higher value than to people, mainly in business.

These values straightly built on the technological means of activity and the mode of handling them grew into traits of personality like egocentricity. The computer operators are sitting alone in front of their computers screen, and if while browsing the Internet they decide to chat or to collaborate, this is just a gesture of convenience, they have no obligations to their partners, and their sole aim is to make themselves feel good. Hence follows the disregard for others, but this tendency slashes back, because, if you have no regard for others, these others have the same scornful contempt for you. So you cannot escape a growing feeling of alienation, which strengthens every time you are overlooked, cheated, treated with indifference. Another trait that naturally appears is the rejection of loyalty to friends, lovers and business partners. The given word, even in contracts has no more value, and the slogan of "I changed my mind" used with a very high frequency destroys all credibility betweeen partners and friends. Then there is the disregard for any rules, social, religious which might prevent the person from feeling good, and finally the disregard for the truth.

The Oxford Dictionary (Honderich, 1995) characterizes *alienation* as a harmful separation which sunders things that belong together. The Marxists who introduced this term into the current speach, referred to the worker's alienation from the instruments of production and from the product itself designed and/or manufactured by him, because they all were owned by others. People may, however, be also alienated from the social process they cannot influence, or even understand, or from a society with which they cannot identify any more.

While all these characteristics also remain valid in modern times, they receive an additional impulse in the globalized Internet society by the fact that the individual is sitting alone in front of the computer screen, chatting with people he/she does not know and cannot trust. This situation is inevitably leading to feeling estranged from the others and from all what is going on around. The essence of the human person is in her links with the others. Therefore the enslavement of the individual to playing with the Internet leads to his/her depersonalization, the renouncement to be an individual subject with personal opinions, having an individual lifestyle and values corresponding to his/her personality and personal history. The forceful loneliness of their situation is leading to the acceptance of an *alien* mold of behavioral style dictated by others and which the individual feels is not his own. It is perhaps this alienation from humanity which makes understandable (but not acceptable) the growing fetishism of animal predators in this society. They too are lonely hunters chasing their own satiety and pleasure only. In a fully developed stage of this process the alienated individuals do not feel that they belong to a collectivity, and therefore they do not obey to the rules of moral, civilized coexistence, not even to the rules suggested by human mercy, love or friendship. In this sense the computer has transformed people into robots.

It may sound curious, but in the kind of culture we have described shunning principles and authority, there are broad discussions on ethical theory going on and voluminous books on this subject are being published. When you read them, it however appears that their aim is to obfuscate the problem of moral principles and to search for the fundament of morality in the individual's changing feelings linked to pleasure and comfort. The philosophers of old times thought they needed an anchor of morality, which in their view would prescribe what are the good and acceptable ("virtuous") behaviors which should be accomplished, and which are the bad ("vicious") ones which should be avoided. Plato anchored morality in the divine, Socrates in the knowledge of the truth. He taught that people are neglecting virtue only because they do not know it, "otherwise virtue is so bright that our will is necessarily inclined to follow it". The Sophist had considered morality linked to the situation of the individual, "It is not good to steal, but you may steal from the enemy". Socrates rises above this situational conditioning to the height of principles: "In no situation and towards nobody is it allowed to perform injustice", he says, and he refuses the aid offered by Kriton to evade from prison, so he might escape from the death penalty. For Aristoteles the exercise of virtue brings happiness, which in his view is not hedonistic (sensual enjoyment), but eudaemonia, spiritual enjoyment, the development of the soul in order to perform all the feasible good one can do and the practicing of virtue. The latter is temperance between the extremes in Aristoteles' view, leading to a perfect, complete life, which is not a contemplative state of pleasure, but essentially an activity for the benefit of one's family, friends and fellow citizens (*Nicomachean Ethics*).

We presented these quotations, because they do not appear in the broad phi-

losophical discussions of today, and there is a need to restore the truth on philosophical thinking. Modern writings quote the *names* of the fathers of philosophy, but then use truncated and selected quotations in order to create the impression that all the history prepared the advent of the Internet Culture. This is not
true: Socrates and Plato stressed the lasting character and the general validity of
moral laws and principles, and Aristotles the necessity of action for the benefit
of others.

Modern thought tries to demolish the objective source of moral laws, religious or otherwise, external to the individual. Curzer (1999) declares that since
God asks to perform immoral acts (e.g that Abraham kill his son), morality cannot be based on religion, and neither should we assume tat it takes precedence
over other values. The priority of morality, he continues, stands in need for justification. Currently we cannot achieve certainty about the moral rules, and if
there is no *right way*, peoples and cultures cannot be blamed or commanded
because they act in a certain manner. In the qutations put forward by Joas (2000)
it appears that in our culture the good is not considered more beneficial than the
evil, and what counts is that people should admit freely all their desires regardless to the moral point of view. Diminishing the concern for otherrs, morality in
this society is a self-legislation to the benefit for oneself. In order to obfuscate
the matter completely, while maintaining an appearance of learnedness, Curzer
(1999) and his colleagues (Mackie, Nussbaum *see ibid.*) use the semantic and
semiotic confusion as a preferred method of "scientific" argumentation in the
Internet Culture. The substance is redued to the discussion of weird concepts,
the judgement of facts is substituted by the judgements on terminology. In ethics
the argumentation on principles is replaced by a discussion on concepts, like
Normal Absolutism, different actions in different situations.or the same action in the same situation, (is the concept of absolutism justified in this context?). There is also mention of Extreme Absolutism, in every situation people
have to do the same thing, Descriptive Relativism, in the same situation different
cultures act differently, Normative Relativism, different people should do different things when they are in the same situation. With the last category are we still
speaking of morality and moral principles? For the pilosopher of the Internet
Culture all assertions have the same value, there are no general principles, and
there cannot be. Morality roots in the individual: everyone has his own morality,
which means doing what makes him/her feel good. The Internet Culture proclaims John Stuart Mill (1863/1944) as the morality guru when he says that morality is about (seeking) pleasure and avoiding pain. He is highly praised because of his egalitarianism, when he says that each bit of pleasure and pain
equally counts, whether it is experienced by a saint, a sinner or a dog. We should
not be confounded by the romantic glamour of the term *equality*. It has also been
used by the Marquis de Sade, who in his book *La nouvelle Justine* (1797) has
described what in his mind stood for a moral conception, in which the equality
of all beings by birth gives everyone the right not to sacrifice himself for the
others, whose destruction is necessary for his pleasure and happiness - sounds
familiar? Lawmakers have always considered that the well-being of a drug

dealer or a killer should enter consideration only after the well-being of morally behaving people has been ensured. The Internet Culture has quite another angle of view. Time and again our cities are the scenes of violent demonstrations against killing animals or against conducting medical experiments on animals. We are vocally and violently reminded to put a hold on the extinction of species, as there are also vocal and violent demonstrations against the death penalty. Has anyone seen similar demonstrations against letting hard working honest people become destitute and homeless? Human populations approaching extinction in the Americas and in Australia are photographed by archaeologists and progressive journalists, paraded in front of their lens (to make us feel good in our comfortable homes), but nobody insists on any measure to help them. Then there is this curious campaign to preserve the white sharks, the terrible killers of the sea, and the curious cult of dinosaurs, the fierce ugly predators of past times. Clearly, there has to be a link to the present-day culture otherwise such an inclination would be weird, to say the least. On a symbolic side these creatures are an integral part of the new culture: the violent power of the predator is the salient value of the Internet Culture, therefore people addicted to to it feel some kind of identification with those animal predators. Joas (2000) has set the origins of morality in the natural selection of species stating by this that animals heve also values and explaining our *moral rapprochement* with predators. The *predator* of the Internet society sees himself as a lonely shark going along with any ideology, without any obligation to prevent poverty and pursuing his interests and pleasure only. Such an image is sustained by society's mass-media.Here are some recent titles of the cover page of *Fortune*, one of the greatest economic journals of to-day: August 11, 2003: *The Power Issue: The 25 Most Powerful People in American Business*, September 29, 2003: *Vivendi, Vidi, Vici* (How Bob Wright Walked Off with the Spoils of Messier's Empire), October 6, 2003: *The Man Who Has Everything - The Money, the Family, the Island.* In the preface the redaction says that it is a special issue about getting the most out of life as a business person. It is full (the redaction says) of stories on health, great ways to reward yourself, etc. I didn't see health stories there, if not the proposal to hold business meetings naked in Finnish saunas - a question of semantics; October 13, 2003: *The World's Most Powerful Women in Business* (*The Power 50*). Is all this about managing, trends in business, stock? No, it is about the models of the new society, about people who destroyed other organizations, walked away with it while having fun. To have fun despite of all and everybody is the life motto of this society.

This discussion raises the question of what relationship there is between the society's *morality* and naked egoism as a sanctioned "moral" guide of behavior. This latter is what economists expect normatively to happen with the new *Homo oeconomicus* (Sigmund, Fehr and Nowak, 2002), and they are very disappointed that the results of their "ultimate game" experiment showed the intevention of emotional considerations into people's decisions.

The much vaunted slogan of liberty is a problem in itself in this society, and it had a similar evolution to that of democracy. Liberty is not the absolute freedom of the individual, because there are others too around him/her. Therefore, it has to be submittd to Pareto's (1919) *utility*, it may be used and stretched only until it clashes with the liberty of others. Insisting on the individual's liberty beyond this point leads to terror and violence towards others. The process starts with the rejection of tolerance and of the liberty of others to voice their opinions.The desire for liberty is selectively applied only to those whose opinions are the same as yours. Against the others there is a merciless fight in which all means are allowed. We used to hear that terrorists are freedom fighters, politicians speak of *good terrorists* and *bad terrorists*. This is of course nonsense. There are no "good" and "bad" terrorists, terror is terror, and it is perpetrated not only with pistols, bombs and knives, but also through threats, false denunciations to the organs of law and order, through the destruction of the assumed rivals' careers.

Real liberty is not absolute, but means voluntary obedience to the moral values and the laws accepted by the majority. As also democracy, liberty means the submisson to the majority without a relentless and violent fight against the values and the laws upheld by the majority. Changes should be brought only through lengthy convincing, and not by mob violence, riots and willful misuse and misinterpretations of the concepts of liberty and democracy, in order to achieve shortcuts and give violence a semblance of morality and legality.

The Internet Culture has a special semantic, like the Soviets, who also presented their régime as the most democratic on earth. .Such slogans, initially forced upon the public may later be absorbed by its culture.Some 30 years ago I participated in the international team of the late Prof. Osgood in his endeavor to elaborate an international Psycholinguistic Atlas which would define the affective space of the different cultures. We used the semantic differential method devised by him (Osgood, 1964). The gist of it is to define the location for the Evaluation (good-bad, beutiful-ugly, etc.), Potency (strong-weak, heavy-light, etc.) and Activity (rapid-slow, stimulating-appeasing, etc.) of concepts in various domains of life.I conducted this research in Romania. My surprise was the negative evaluation received for the concept of *good*. I saw with bewilderment that the characterization of one's father as *good* was an indication of the subject's negativistic attitude towards persons of authority, and of a developing personality disturbance (Krau, 1997). In order to clarify this matter I added an experiment of free associations for the various concepts, and it resulted that "good" and "tender" had a positive evaluation only when describing a woman (the associations were: mother, cup, bird, tender girl). When describing a man, the associations were: weak, timid, and appeared located at the negative pole. On the contrary, severity was linked to the traits of tough, honest,courageous, fearless, evincing force and masculinity.

In the society of today, courage, honesty and fearlessness turned into non-values, as also masculinity. Force has been supplanted by power, and perhaps therefore, the negative characterization of "good" has remained.It has no place in a culture where power is dominant with all the methods and tricks to achieve it.Like in the former Soviet empire, politics is all pervasive in the globalized

Internet society, each hiring, appointment, invitation of an expert to a talk-show on TV (on whatever topic) is an expression of party politics. Power, lies and cheating satisfy the needs "to feel good" the basic value of the new society. Reliability and loyalty to family, friends, colleagues, or simply to citizens are non-values.I have personally participated in conferences in which one or more of my colleagues, after we had in lengthy discussions reached an agreement on certain issues, came up in the final session and said, "Yes, but I have changed my mind". You cannot count on agreements, opinions, on ratings, all these are momentary acts subject to immediate change if some party boss raises his eyebrows. Even TV ratings are misused as a fa\u00f1ade and are not the democratically expressed choice of people, but a tool of persuasion in order to influence it. Democratic rating does not approve of antiglobal looting and vanadalizing, but on TV always the latter is shown and extolled. True public opinion and truth in general are non-values. To give an example, present-day Spanish movie makers always place their heroes in the Republican camp of the Civil War, but are quiet about the terror let loose also by the latter, the arson and burning of churches, monasteries, and the killing of monks and priests. The execution of Federico García Lorca by the nationalists is always depicted in the most gruesome and touching colors, the execution of Antonio Ribera by the republicans is never even mentioned.

Not only is the Internet Culture driven by politics, not only is power its basic purposive value, but it is a violent power, exercised continually, violence raised to a way of life. French movies used to present gaangssters as men of honor and deserving the love of the main actress. In a similar vein, the Geographic Channel of TV tries to endear to the public the violence of animal predators. Last but not least, the violence also appears in the tide of politically motivated denunciations made by professional denunciators against political opponents. In a great number of cases the situation is complicated by the connivance of some police officials, prosecutors or some of the judiciary. In Italy the situation has developed into a war fought in parliament and on the streets over the question of *toghe sporche* (the dirty judges' garments). The target of the legal attacks was the conservative prime-minister Silvio Berlusconi. In Germany it was the former conservative chancellor Kohl, in France the former conservative prime-minister Alain Juppé with the tendency to get to president Chirac.The persons caught in the "legal ambushes" are in a most difficult situation. They have to fight against the electronic mass-media and the printed press, and often their careers and even their lives are ruined for trifles. Even should the victims be acquitted later on in their trial, the experienced intimidation and the damage done to their image remains. It is not a certain infringement of the law that came to the attention of some journalists or public organizations, and they want to expose it. In the Internet Culture a *person* is targeted and accused on whatever grounds. If she succeeds in extricating herself, and the game comes to an end, a new game is started immediately. For the sake of the truth it has to be mentioned that denunciations and false or exaggerated accusations are not an exclusive attribute of the Internet Culture. The Middle Ages are full of such stories, but these were the

Middle Ages. Nowadays every book, article or TV show claims that we are advanced , superior, enlightened.It is true again, that in our days people are not burned at the stake or beheaded on public squares. But psychologically they are.

Thus people living in the Internet Culture must learn to live with fear and anxiety, fear from terror acts, banditism and politically (or *merely* economically) motivated career damages, all this being in concordance with society's morality. Thomas Langan (2000) entitled a book he has written *Surviving the age of virtual reality.* The title says it all on the fears and miseries engendered by this society. Besides, the flourishing of clinical psychology and psychiatry in the Western world is an eloquent proof for the ubiquitous fear.

Let us go back to the sources of morality in the Internet Culture. Curzer (1999) who is quick to establish the individual roots of morality (p. 436) also adds Ayn Rand's opinion (p. 73) that sacrificing one's interests for other people, for God, for anything at all, is simply wrong. It is also immoral, because apart from harming the sacrificer, he/she may give away money - *horribile dictu* (even the thought is fearful*)* - or renounce to some of his/her plans, and it makes the beneficiary a dependent parasite (Sic!). In order to again obfuscate the problem, an entire argument is launched around the difference between the existing psychological egoism and its acceptance as Ethical Egoism.Curzer "clarifies" the problem telling us that teachers' interests are in assigning grades more or less arbitrarily, so they can spend the time saved for publishing or partying, whereas the morally right thing to do would have been to grade the papers fairly.In this ethical essay there is no word of condemnation for the teachers partying instead of doing fairly their job. Instead we are introduced into a lengthy exposé of Nietzsche's theory on the morality of masters (strong, smart, creative, powerful, etc.) and of slaves (weak, stupid, dull, loser, need help, etc.). He states that the weak, base people manipulate the noble into defeating themselves by the postulation of God's existence, in comparison to whom they are not great, wondeful or successful. Nietzsche's Zarathustra says, "Another ideal hovers before our eyes. . . It is an ideal of a spirit to whom the highest popular standards would be a mere danger, a decay, an abasement, a temporary forgetfulness of self" (*Thus Spake Zarathustra).*

Regarding welfare, it is again Ayn Rand (*The Virtue of Selfishness,* cf. *etiam* Ronald, 1991) who states that a person in need has no legitimate moral claim on those around her. With the freedom to make decisions goes the responsibility for what happens. Rand forgets that the socioeconomic starting point of a decision to be made is not the same for all. Precisely today, a person may decide to work loyally and hard in his/her job, while the boss (manager or owner) decides he could earn more if he liquidated the whole enterprise and reopened it in Bangladesh. The worker is laid off. Should he receive welfare assistance (payments), the latter would come from the taxpayer's money, meaning the unemployed would live on the earnings of others, who are thus not able to spend the whole of their earnings. Welfare, if any, says Rand, should be on an exclusively voluntary basis. This is selfishness as a philosophical conception. I nearly said a *moral conception,* but in my view to call it morality would be a contradiction in terms drawn to its extremes. Still, this is not all, there will be more. The acceptance of selfishness as the basis of society, liberty and equality should mean that all the rights of the individual are preserved up to the end. Error again. If the individual falls seriously ill, the Internet Society presents him/her with two new moral problems: futile treatment and euthanasia. Futile is a treatment of which the physician is convinced that it will not change to the better the disease process or its symptoms. Though some improvement might be reached, it cannot be systematically produced. The decision to forego the treatment should be made by the patient, but it is nevertheless the physician who determines it on the basis of his/her knowledge. Epstein (1993) points out that if a physician decides, without consulting the patient, that e.g. dialysis would be futile in a particular case, he is likely to not even offer it, and thus allow the patient to die. The basis for such a judgement is cost-benfit analysis, valuing life according to productivity, and fearing that the treatment would impose undue burdens on other patients and on the institution, perhaps on the family. The basis of the Internet Culture appears not to be liberal individualism based on equality. This is a cover for preference given to naked power. Even if people are well-off, they cannot defend themselves when their actual health status made them weak and dependent on professional help, they have no more power and they simply will be killed. Power in the most brutal unveiled form is the main valued and general principle of what the globalized Internet Society calls "morality".

The futility of treatment question has an additional facet. It had been declared to be a scientifically objective judgement without any value judgement attached. However, precisely Epstein (1993) points out that its apparent objectivity is an illusion, and the determination of the goal toward which medical treatment aims is in fact a value judgement as to the relationship between effect and benefit. Schneiderman, Jacker et al. (1999) point out that futility is a professional judgement (we have seen that as a matter of fact it is a value judgement) that takes precedence over patient autonomy and permits physicians to withhold or withdraw care deemed inappropriate without subjecting the decision to patient approval. The argument is of course false, and false with intention. Montefiore (1967) had strenuously demonstrated that value judgement has a fundamental importance in ethics, and that all what is true of a general value judgement (on which ethics as a philosophical discipline is essentially based) has to be also true of value judgements on particular issues. Therefore, we shall add, you cannot discuss in a treatise on morality different kinds of "good" euthanasy, and eschew the problem of whether euthanasy as such is morally admissible in principle.

Thus again rises the problem of truth in the Internet Culture. If there are no universal values, as this culture strenuously teaches, then everybody has his/her own truth, and truth as such is an illusion brought and bent by self-interest or convenient beliefs that reinforce one's feeling of power. Curzer (1999) tells of an investigation of dr. Rosenheim who together with a group of students had, unbeknownst to the staff, admitted themselves into a psychiatric hospital. None of them had any disturbance, but simply because of being there, the medical staff judged them to be mentally ill, and interpreted everything they did or said in this direction. They could not free themselves without foreign help. In the much vaunted advancement of the contemporary world there is no limit to the inhumane behavior to which the feeling of power may lead.

The best example is euthanasia, the killing of terminally ill patients. Again, the mechanism of offuscation is put into high gear, analyzing the two variants of active (simple killing) and passive euthanasia when the patient is taken off from vital support apparatuses. The problem with the Internet Culture is that it never accepts self-imposed limitations. In the moment the public reluctantly accepts a hitherto controversial behavior, there will always be profit-eager individuals who will go further. The model involves advocating a change in moral beliefs enshrined in law by asking for a conduct which is in fact illegal, then somebody provocatively puts into practice what he/she preaches (be it killing patients as dr. Kevorkian did) and proudly marches to jail, while the progressive mass-media will present him as a hero of mankind. Where is the much vaunted rule of the law advocated by liberal democracies? It is respected by some circles only as long as it expresses the ideas and the desires of the most vocal leftist circles of power. In the moment of the slightest opposition, the aforementioned power groups begin a violent campaign in public opinion to change the laws "which are hindering progress". In our discussion such *progress* means the licence to kill patients, while ever new methods for perpetrating the killing spring from the creative minds of physicians, lawyers and budget-saving hungry little politicians. In the euthanatic killing the cutting off from vital apparatuses has become withholding food and liquids from the patient causing him to die a terribly painful death of inanition and dehydration, while hypocritically talking of *dying with dignity*. How would the physician feel if he himself would die under such "dignifying" circumstances?

Another problem is to bring to the open the process of deciding on such procedures and the persons who do this. It is fashionable in the Internet Culture to make reference to the history of phenomena, it gives a glamour of learnedness. Curiously, in the domain of euthanasia no reference is made to its history in the *III Reich* between 1940-1941, when the programme was stalled as a result of the protests of the Church and of public opinion (*SS im Einsatz, 1958*). So, one difference between what was going on during the Nazi rule and what is going on today in the liberal democracies, is that German public opinion was unanimous in rejecting euthanasia, while the vocal leftist groups in the Netherlands, the U.S.A., in Scandinavia are firmly behind it. True, there is another difference concerning the state planning of murder by the Nazis and the horrid application of the plan, but the facts of perpetrating euthanasia remains. I hear with the ears of my mind the righteous outcry of those who are offended by the comparison made between the present-day use of euthanasia and the Nazis, but here the comparison concerned facts. People who do not like the comparison, should not behave like those with whom they don't like to be compared. The passive euthanasia in the liberal democracies does not make the situation look better. The protracting of pain and suffering through refusal of treatment and even of sheer life sustention has led many authoritative professionals to preferring an active euthanasia, if required by the patient.

It is true that in the liberal democracies of today there is a tendency to give the victims (the patients) a say in the whole matter, while the Nazi procedure was kept secret up to the end (from the victims). There are two qualifications to be made to this issue: First, the participation of the patiens in the quest to be killed easily turns into coaxing them by appealing to their "dignity" and to "their best interest" and so on, making of their consent a sorrow masquerade. Secondly, in a number of cases the patients themselves have no word and the decision is taken by proxies, family members, who often want to save money or to sooner enter the possession of the heritage.

Even would the patients voice be a clear desire for death, i.e. suicide, and would they ask to be assisted in it, all these kinds of suicide are frequently cries of help, as attested by Church organizations specialized in help offering. If the "helpers" are people like dr. Kevorkian, then what happens is like the event depicted in the Japanese film *Harakiri* from the '1960s. In the movie a man who went plight asked his rich friend to assist him in ritually killing himself, secretly hoping that the friend would financially help him and put him back on his feet, but the "friend" simply assisted him to cut off his belly.

How did we get there? Killing people has always ben regarded by the law as "murder is murder, is murder". True, but the global Internet Culture specializes in turning over every principle held sain in society. It does it with the aid of the mass media, that campaign for allowing conducts which under the law are illegal. It so happened with euthanasia, but also with abortion, pornography, prostitution. The issues were artificially linked to existing constitutional amendments: civil rights, free speech, control over propety, and when the campaigners succeeded in finding one single judge to accept their views, the flood tore off the dam, and the cause of the majority was lost. As a matter of fact, what has pornography to do with freedom of speech or prostitution and abortion with the control of property? Also the conservatives of the Internet Society instead of considering the mother's health, have begun to speak in the same dialect of rights of the foetus, and turned a very humane question into a hateful discussion on legal paragraphs. We are told, that even should the woman have a right on her own body, she ought not violate the foetus' rights. What are these rights of the foetus? The simplest answer would be that it has the right to live, but here the liberal democrats freeze in horror. The moment such a right is acknowledged, it would require feeding famine victims and/or lazy bumps, what we supposedly do not want to do. Therefore the learned philosophers and lawyers turn instead to analyzing the relationship between the mother and her foetus. Some declare that betweeen them there is a promise relationship, but immediately other discussants state that sex being many times involuntary (and not only in the case of rape) the foetus cannot benefit from a promise relationship, which even if it existed, may be broken in self-defense. Self-defense against a weak, unarmed foetus? Yes, answers the chorus of righteous lawyers of the Internet Society, the mother should be able to defend herself from pain, anguish and the loss of life prospects.

Of course, the lack of human feelings in mothers, advocated by the "progressive" society may also be found in sons and daughters. The playwright Bertolt Brecht endeared and venerated up to this day by all "progressive" people flatly refused to mourn at his mother's death, and had instead a big perty in his rooms upstairs, while his mother's body lay in the rooms downstairs (Fuegi, Bahr and Willett, 1983). Far from stigmatizing such a horrorful behavior, it is met with understanding and psychologized in all theoretical essays on literature and theatre (Cf. Pizzato, 1998). Some would even see in this behavior a modern enlargement of the adage of Terentius, claiming liberty for the manifestation of human nature, "Homo sum et nihil humanum a me alienum puto". However, it should be plainly stated that not only is this not a behavior conform to human nature, but even animals manifest feelings of mourning.

What is disheartening in the discussion about mothers and their children, is the juridical argumentation using the terminology of commercial property rights in a matter that should belong to heart, ethics and soul. The Internet Culture has no heart, no soul only litigative interests. From time immemorial bringing a child to the world has been an occasion for joy, but it also constituted a problem, that had to be dealt with most responsibly. This meant, and should mean also today, taking into account the wishes and possibilities of the family and the moral (and legal) commandments of society. It is a cruelty to force a family to have a child when the mother is in bad health, she had been raped or if the family cannot afford the humblest conditions of upbringing (and those who force them having a baby do nothing to alleviate their situation). Nonetheless, it is inhumane to the same degree to abort a child because the mother feels it could impede a self-development she has not even defined or her plans for a vacation trip. In all these instances the law should step in. Abortion should be an option, but a much restriced one.

Besides, the whole matter of child bearing has been driven by the vocal formators of public oinion in the Internet Culture in an ominous direction. Sherwin (see Curzer, p. 443) tries to expose a hidden agenda of pro-lifers: Pregnancy and child rearing often force women to become or remain economically and psychologically dependent on particular men. The reader hears something like hatred for the building of a family, the birth and care for children. Walsh (1987) has collected the most representative opinions of modern womanhood, and among them a prominent place has been given to Carol Gilligan, whose *In a Diffeernt Voice* has been copyrighted by the president and fellows of Harvard College (1977). Gilligan's research has concerned the problem of abortion and she has dealt with it as a moral one. In the numerous cases she presents, there is much spoken of the care for the baby, but in all the cases the woman who "liberates" herself as a result of the therapy, decides to "act morally" and have an abortion on the basis of what she feels meets her neds. One of them says, "In my situation, I want to have an abortion, and if I didn't it would be self-sacrificing". The author commmends her decision, which although it might have been considered selfish, is in a differrent perspective a matter of honesty and fairness. Gilligan repeats this formulation several times, proving that this is her own conviction. In another case she presents (they are selected upon her convenience, and not subjected to any statistical treatment), the woman initially declares that in order to have the baby, she would need financial aid. She gets it, but under the wise guidance of her therapist, she nevertheless decides to abort the child. There is no one single case in which the woman, after having had the therapy, would reach the conclusion that she wants to keep the child. Roth Walsh (1987) also presents Colby and Damon's critique on Gilligan, but for a 40-page long exposé of Gilligan's, the critique has only 8 pages. It is clear where Roth Walsh' s heart lies.

The Internet Culture does not value love which is an altruistic feeling, instilled by nature into the human body and its aim is to ensure the preservation of the human race with a population of happy cared for children. The only value is sex, if possible good sex, which makes you feel good, but is irresponsible towards its results, one's partner and society as a whole. Each historian will attest that such values were held by doomed societies, which shortly fell apart as they were annihilated by the weakest onslaught.

As a matter of fact, it would not even be true to say that in any circumstance the feminist movement defends women. The major offense to what women stand for is done by prostitution and the spread of pornography. The vocal groups of the Internet Culture fight like lions for the legalization of prostitution and of pornographic material. First came the lobby of lawyers who worked for the pornographers. They received big money and fought for the acceptance of pornography not only by the courts but also in public opinion. Constitutional principles were reinterpreted, so as to suit their mandants, some even spoke of a collision of the American Civil Liberties Union with pornographers (Stan, 1995). Among other things it involved erecting the repulsion standard to the rank of supreme value: find the most repulsive person in society and defend him. In this manoeuver the values of the Inernet Culture appear in their entire glamour. Defend the most repulsive man, not the unjustly accused, the poor, the homeless, but the most repulsive person and make him/her accepted. The same transformation happens to pornography. Even accepting that it demeans women, it nevertheless symbolizes free speech and liberty, it has redeeeming value in spite of itself. Free sex, some feminists argue, has as much value as free speech.

In the '1960s Denmark and Sweden lifted their censorship laws on pornography, and amongst the exultation of the liberal press it has been repeatedly declared, that sex crimes were down in both countries, and pornography proved harmless. But pornography has developed into the third largest industry in these countries. The information released in Denmark is suspect of being covered and tampered, and in Sweden there are reports of a continuing increase in rape and crimes involving sexual violence, underground trafficking with children for pornographic purposes. Those who made research in these areas had to stop, because of the threats on their lives. The whole pornography industry is connnected wih drugs and crime (Lederer, 1980).

The world is slowly accepting child molesting, incest, sexual violence, because each product needs revamping, and few unbroken taboos have remained yet. In order to sell pornography, love and caring are negated. The widely spread journal *Playboy* presents adult men as boys playing forever, and women are their toys. Therefore the men refuse to marry and to take responsibility for children. Family members are ridiculed, wives devalued, women presented as whores, thereby removing any obligation to treat them as equals. In order to build such attitudes, the journal uses "groundbrakers", skillfully contrived photographs, cartoons and fairy tales in which the wolf molests Little Red Riding Hood, the Seven Dwarfs rape Snow White (Lederer, 1980), all is just a joke and fun, as it becometh to the Internet Culture.

One could say that these are only some extremist opinions, which in a free society cannot be censored. This is not so. In the USA a presidential commission (On Obscenity and Pornography) chose to ignore former reports that media violence can induce persons to act aggressively (Commission on the Causes and Prevention of Violence, 1969). The Commission on Obscenity contended that at worst pornography was merely harmless, at best it provided more agreable and increased openness in marital communication. Allegedly, there was no evidenec that exposure to explicit sexual materials played a significant role in the causation of delinquent or criminal behavior among young or adults (Cf. Lederer, 1980). Readily scientists prsented a *cathartic model* on pornography induced behavior whose gist was that "the more you see, the less you do", and they widely shut their eyes on reality which behaved according to a *learning model* explaining that "the more you see, the more you learn and do". Besides, the juxtaposition of violence with sexual excitement and satisfaction provides a conditioning of violent responses to erotic stimuli. There have even been psychologists who tried to help their patients overcome sexual inhibitions by showing them films on rape or encouraging them to phantasize such things (Cf. Lederer, 1980). On the kind of science practiced in the Internet Culture we shall talk in one of the coming chapters, but the issue of pornography, we were now debating, clearly demonstrates that science nowadays has lost its objectivity and in its greater part has turned into cheap venal propaganda.

Writers and thinkers are repeatedly raising the question, "Is this our century one of darkness?" There is no easy answer. The technological knowledge is advancing, no doubt about this, but not the culture as a body of behaviors based on understanding between people and on moral insight. Other centuries had their dark episodes too, even the Victorian Age, if you are looking at the Boer and the Opium Wars, or at the living conditions of the less privileged in the leading countries of the world at that time. However, these dark moments were not so pervasive, so all-encompassing and seemingly definitive as the ones of our society, whose basic functioning is ensured by the computer, globalization and the Internet. In the XIXth Century Dickens, Zola, Peres Galdós, Tolstoy and Maxim Gorki vehemently protested against the lack of justice. They denounced the existing social order in the name of ethics and of an ideal of *Liberté, Egalité, Fraternité*.Today we rarely hear voices of protest, because, even if they are uttered in private, the mass media would not spread them. Neither would any publisher take the risk of losing money with trying to sell "politically incorrect" stuff. The values of the Internet Culture ensure a much more effective censorship than could have dreamed of any loyal GPU or KGB comrade.

Chapter Four

The State Organization of the Globalized Internet Society: the External and the Internal Use of Force

In the last chapter we have discussed the values of a society driven by an advanced technology, especially in the domain of communication and by the forces of the free market. This society is not willing to enter any self-limitation regarding the expansion of the individual's material, biological drives, those of ego-aggrandizement and of acquisition. In the XVIIth century, the darkest period of England's history, Hobbes described a status of *homo homini lupus*, when everyone was a predator-wolf regarding the other. Nobody could claim an advantage which would not be claimed by any other people. The sense of equality between people gained expression in the fact, that the weakest had enough power to kill the strongest, if using the appropriate means. Life in common was made possible by the state, a monster which imposed such common existence on the citizens (*Leviathan*, 1651). There is no good of general validity, nor is there a general purpose or truth, *"Veritas in dicto, non in re consistit"*, the truth is in words only, not in the real matter, points out Hobbes

It is a pretty good description of our society in the XXIst century, but, of course we have additional special characteristics, which poor Hobbes could not foresee. The society of our time is controlled by a corporations-dominated global market, which imposes its values on the social organization. This situation has heavy consequences. With the increasing corporatization of every-day life, market values replace social values, citizenship is reduced to the act of consuming, and the private sphere has become the only space in which to imagine a sense of hope, pleasure or possibility (Bauman, 2001; Giroux, 2001).

In his analysis on the role of the state in contemporary society, Severino

(2004) refers to the definition of the state given by Max Weber (1947). He described it as a technologically rational engine, whose monopoly to force is recognized, and which allows anybody to calculate with anticipation the consequences of action performed by oneself and by others. What is asked of the state is to eliminate the risks inherent in life. However, in modern times the state and the free market enterprise go in opposite directions: the former tends to be annulled, while the latter finds itself in multiple risks. The politicians deepen the contradiction, as the right looks for lucky state "supermanagers" to guide and manage society, while the left believes in the capability of the judicial apparatus to guide the people and beware them of unnecessary risks. Severino (2004) thinks the solution lies in changing the functions of technology and of the state. Technology should no more be an instrument in helping economic activities, but its development should be the purpose, while the state becomes technology's instrument to enhance its dominance of the world.

For much such word pleases the supporters of the Internet Culture, its basis is false, and if there would be a serious attempt to implement the theory, it would lead to collapse. The state, every state, has been created to manage and solve social problems, and though technology itself is embedded in social problems, and creates social problems, it does not supplant them, nor does it solve them. The advancement of technology may hint at the direction of solutions, what ought to be done, and how social problems created by advanced technology could be solved or minimized.

One first aspect of modern technology, which has to be changed in accordance with society's requirements, is technology's enhancement of individualism and individual pastimes, while society asks for a collective engagement. We have already pointed out that in the Internet Culture collectivism and collective actions are nonvalues. The result is an atomized society of disengaged individuals who feel alienized, demoralized and socially powerless (Cf. Chomsky, 1999). Giroux (2001) goes as far as to claim that today totalitarianism resides in the thorough dislike for all things social, public and collective. The modern state is not any more the guardian of public interests, its only role should be to protect the private right to consume. Presently, such words are still exaggerations, because the state has not yet been swallowed up by technology, it still continues to exist and to ask its citizens to take collective actions, but along its own policy. The problem is to define what is the role of the state in this society and what is its policy.

Some authors contend that like the Holy Roman Empire, which according to Voltaire's biting remark, had ceased to be either holy, nor Roman, and not even an empire. The nation states of the middle of the XXth century ceased to be nations, uniformly populated by people sharing a common ethnic identity, as in the European Union, they also cease to be states with a sovereign government of a clearly defined territory (Anderson, 1997). Nevertheless, they evolve towards multinational entities with a shared sovereignty in some areas, and each of these countries and the inhabitant peoples would vehemently protest, should somebody deny them the quality of a state for and of a certain nation. Today, the member states of the European Union are haggling with the common institutions in Brussels over every inch of sovereignty, some do not even participate in the common currency, and commonly approved regulations are infringed, as in the case of the German and the French financial deficit of 2003. Still, precisely in Germany, fiery members of the Academe are militating for the institution of Large Scale Economy.Spaces (*Großwirtschaftsraum*) to take over the role of the national states. Here is again an extremist, fantasy-driven proposal, which does not take into account the people with their cultural, social, national characteristics, that no rregional superpower can accommodate. It is they, the people wo are the bearers of the economy, including the livelihood of the elitist groupos, who are playing with the ideas of liquidating the national state in favor of regional economic superspaces. Therefore, one may extrapolate that the tendency to esentially preserve the sovereignty of the nation state in Europe will continue, with or without the adoption of a downwatered common constitution - with or without the much debated paragraph referring to Christianity at the roots of the European culture.

In the last chapter we have spoken of the values cherished by the new society, now we should see how the "public space" (Giroux) is organized in accordance with them. Sassower and Cicotello (2000) see five faces of modernity: avant-garde, decadence, kitsch and post-modernism. The state of the Internet Society has all these characteristics. Modernism includes the impact of advanced technology and it stands at the cradle of this society. Post-modernism, decadence and kitsch are its main components and they have already been discussed when speaking of this society's values. On the avant-garde and additionally also on kitsch we shall talk in the chapter on the arts. For now the point is that *these* characteristics (and not other ones) appear together in the institution of the state expressing the unity of this society, which in Crary's (2001) words is founded on the ubiquity of spectacular consumption aided by the mass media and the technologies of consumption. The spectacle as such which involves all social acts, as a former specious form of the sacred, was to become the primary stimulation of cohesion and unification in today's modernity.

This way, kitsch, decadence and post-modernism have all entred the composite image of the modern state. There are, nonetheless, two things to be added. Post-modernism implies playfulness and contradictions, which are intentionally not taken seriously. The picture which catches the eye is one of blatant contradictions between a) declared values and the applied norms of behavior, b) the seriousness of the declaration and the lack of seriousness in the behavior, c) the pervasiveness of statehood in some most private sectors of life vs the lack of interference in other vital societal domains. As far as playfulness in the Internet society is concerned, it is not only a fashion of reasoning. Games are becoming culturally pervasive, to the point that they are taking dollars from other consumer entertainment options, like movies and television magazines. More than a half of the American households have some sort of game machine, a Sony or something else. Therefore analysts like Lewis (2003) speak of our society as a Video-Game Planet.

The second unwelcome thing that has to be added is that such videogames become cultural institutions which control social life. Crary (2001) has referred to Nietzsche who stated that every living thing seeks above all to discharge its strength. So, if games are central to society's lifestyle, the ubiquitous power aspirations will be discharged through them.In his book *The Will to Power* Nietzsche (1917) pointed out that modern man was in a process of decline, and only the feeling of power could redempt him.It should liberate him from the tight and anxious moral shackle. In the increment of power also lie the criterion of truth, the confidence that things should happen a certain way.

At this point we are reminded that the globalized Internet Society is a contradictory one, and although in its results the exercise of power in this society victimizes, the way and the façade how it is done, is not the one used by totalitarian régimes. In the past totalitarian régimes appeared as the naked expression of power. Lenin (1918) in his book *The State and Revolution* defined the dictatorship of the proletariat as "a most determined and ruthless war waged by the new class, a stubborn struggle, bloody and bloodless, violent, educational and administrative against the forces and traditions of the old society". There are two important differences between the totalitarian exercise of power and the one which takes place in the Internet Society.In the totalitarian exercise of power friend and foe are clearly defined. In the communist régime power was exercised in the name of the proletariat (through the party state which abused it, but this is another story), against the bourgeosie, that is to say, the struggle was between two well defined social groups, and officially recognized as such. In the former Iraq it was the Baath party headed by Saddam Hussein, who fought minorities and dissenters, in Uganda it was Idi Amin with his parasites.In the Internet Society the parties are not clearly defined, it is a struggle between haves and have-nots, but also between groups and individuals within the "haves", because it is a *homo homini lupus* society. Nevertheless, the whole war is dampened, concealed under a smiling façade, and no bloody means are being used. There are no mass graves, still the number of social and economic casualties is enormous.

Other contradictions appear in the functions of the state as such. The official policy is deregulation, but due to advanced technology the surveillance takes even stricter forms as those employed in the most feared totalitarian régimes. There is no official discrimination, but in many countries which vaunt themselves of being democratic, there are double standards in hiring and promoting on political grounds, and in schools even on religious grounds, as shows the recent head-scarf affair in European schools.

Recently the French National Assembly passed a law forbidding the wearing of any religious symbols in schools, but the intent was specifically the interdiction of Muslim headscarves. In Germany the lands of Bavaria and Baden-Württemberg were plainly outspoken in this matter with regard to teachers. The authorities labelled it a political and not a religious symbol, and so got around the constitutional guarantee of religious freedom (*Newsweek*, January 19, 2004).Perhaps, it is indeed a political symbol of ethnic identity, but this would not warrant state discrimination in a society, which in declarations stands for pluralism and nearly unlimited individual liberties. Germany should have by now by 3.3 million Muslim immigrants, France even more. For business groups these immigrants constitute a vital pillar of today's globalized economy, providing cheap labor, especially in areas where the manpower of the own population is scarce. However, it has already been said in the days of the classical capitalist economy, you cannot hire a hand, her owner always comes with. He (or she in this case) has also a head on which she puts a scarf to mark her ethnic identity. Of course, every society has the right to accept or to refuse immigration, but once immigrants have been accepeted and naturalized, the state must also accept the expression of their identity. It sounds like a bad joke seeing progressive Netherland, the avant-garde of the Internet Culture with the legalization of drugs and euthanasia, strenuously seeking to chase out immigrants. The father of this policy against immigrants was a rightwing militant would-be prime minister Pim Fortuyn, who was shot dead several days before parliamentary elections. His party still won the elections, but then shortly fell apart, nevertheless, his policy is implemented today by center-left prime ministers.

Surely, immigrants are expected to assimilate into the host society. However, it is counterproductive to try to cancel all signs of national identity. It sounds discriminatory and gives fundamentalists a good propaganda base. Says Hyman Zawahiri, one of the Egyptian theorists of Islam, "France is the country of liberty, a liberty which permits to be immoral and depraved. You are free to show your naked body, but not to dress chaste. What happens is a new sense of crusader hatred against the Islam "(*Corriere della Sera, 25* February 2004). In Italy immigrant militants and the own far left liken such attempts to the *equalizing* policy of the Nazis, this time performed with modern instruments. "They want to cancel the religion and the identity of peoples, and they also want to destroy the institution of family". Follows a quite contradictory attack of the far right on the *European masonists*",who want to exterminate the nations of Europe with the permanent immigration (*Corriere della Sera,* 28 January 2004, p.4).

There are also critics of the restrictions on immigration.The writer of North-African origin, Fatema Marissi declares that the West fears the powerful brains of the new Arab immigrants. The West preaches the free circulation of goods, but forbids the circulation of persons. The Arab countries are young, and the young move, the European countries are old, they will not be able to stop the movement rejuvenating the continent of the young, who are bringing ptogress and culture (*Corriere della Sera,* 3 October 2004). The key question is, of course, the realtionship between the new (?!) Islamic and the old, European culture. Is the intention a takeover or a covergeance and assimilation?

In such a tense, contradictory situation, assimilation cannot be achieved by interdictive decrees of governments and National Assemblies, by banning Muslim headscarves or by mob arsoning of Jewish synagogues. Otherwise, one would have to again recognize the truth in Wheeler's (1971) description of the immigrant experience, "For every second generation assimilated, a first generation spurned. For the gains of goods and services an identity lost, an uncertainty found". In my book on the immigrant problem (Krau, 1991) I have described immigration as a social drama, where the role behavior of the different actors, torn between opposite motives, is greatly influenced by the contradictory nature of the phenomenon. It is not sufficient to analyze the objective situation, because the latter is selectively interpreted and misinterpreted, every group of actors stressing real and imaginary aspects close to their own aspirations.

In the West the attitude of superiority towards immigrants is reinforced by the differences between Western and non-Western cultures regarding man's place in the world. Catani (1982) has pointed out that the West has a civilization of an individualistic type characterized by values of liberty and equality. In the non-Western cultures the needs of the individual are subordinated to the values of society, and privileged is the conformity of the group and of their members to the overall social purpose. The ultimate values are religious and /or philosophical, and they constitute a system providing an explanation of the Universe, in which people live *in* the world, and are not confronting it. In these societies the individual exists only in terms of a community member. Thus, even while assimilating the literal content of the host sociey's culture, the immigrants include this content into their general philosophical framework of thought - and remain different.

The host society tries to educate the immigrants, but with a *social status quo padagogy* (Catani, 1982), which is accompanied by more or less subtle measures of discrmination. The result is not the advancement of the immigrant population identifying with the aims of the host society, but in many cases the direct opposite.Thus, with their own hands and against their own rational interests, the host society creates militant groups, which, if not today, then tomorrow will plunge it into trouble. An unfair, discriminatory attitude, whatever its psychological roots are, forces the immigrants into a secondary deviance, which, however, may already be socially harmful (Krau, 1991). Wearing a headscarf is a behavior asserting one's different identity, but may still express the loyalty to the structures of the host society, its people and its political credo. Vocal and violent behaviors to assert the right to wear a headscarf are already signs of drifting apart and seeing in the host state an enemy.

The interdiction to assert their cultural identity is one of the immigrant's *shock* experiences: the shock of an unfamiliar physical climate, the *culture shock* of an unfamiliar cultural environment causing discomfort, anxiety, indignation, and hence a sense of loss, of uprootedness and the loss of mastery of the environment. Then comes the shock of labor market difficulties, and above all the shock of a hostile reception on the part of the host population.Employers are happy to take on immigrant labor on lower levels.However, as soon as the question of promotion arises, or of moving up into more significant areas of employment, there is a blockage.The host society wants an inconspicuously functioning group of labor hands, fully assimmilated into the host culture. However, the immigrants left their country of origin with the illusion to find a new home with freedom and understanding, offering them a life of decency and respect for what they are and what they stand for. Each group of social actors has an erroneous image of what the other is and what it should be, and the experience of shock is inevitable.

One could have expected that in a society devoted to individual freedom such problems would not arise. However, the Internet Society is a contradictory one, and as in the past, socio-cultural discrimination against *alien* immigrant cultures is superimposed on oppressional measures applied vis-à-vis all citizens . In this society the problem of freedom is much more complicated than it is oficially pesented. There is unity of opinions concerning the *freedoms from* proclaimed in 1941 in the Atlantic Charta by President Roosevelt and Prime Minis·ter Churchiill, namely the freedom from fear, freedom from want. However *freedoms of* are leding to heavy impasses when considering the relations' tween freedom and justice, freedom and security, freedom and demr tice and security are essentially limiting freedom, democracy cr hidden risk of a tyranny of the majority or of an authoritarian I leader elected by the majority. Even abiding by the slogans, a n ual liberty would privilege the powerful and rich. The Internet S to resolve these contradictions, and therefore it has also faile balance between liberty and the use of force.

All began when, as a development of computers, data on vice receivers were computerized in different institutions (r administrative). In itself this was a useful move which rr costs, and made servicces more efficient. Less customers ub-ing them became more efficient, as time losses decreasant to great inconveniences appeared: People were registeredg they social security numbers, as formerly only prison inmatrt to buy, lic institutions and then also in private ones. Today itional data order a commodity by mail from a commercial entll you John will ask you, even before you are allowed to say wh quietly abol-is your ID number. They will take down your nam of privacy, be-to your ID number, and mostly only your private e otherwise, peo-or Dan without "Mister" or any other title. The Ir ished titles. You cannot protect yourself again the interlocking of cause such is the new society, all are doing it, as were transmitted, ple are looking at you squarely. ole (were transmitted,

However, this was only the beginning. Th tor's advice, he will first computers, and the data stored on you b ther physicians in all do-sold?) to other companies, institutions. If yc ey may reject your applica-look on your computerized data, on your al, sometimes irrelevant data, mains in which you have sought medical nd the whole issue of a second tion for a driving licence on ground of su the state becomes a joke. As a refuse you treatment, medication or insy files on you, using the data medical opinion and medical aid subs profiles on you, using the data customer, commercial entrprises wilop or in other ones, with which their analysis of the goods you ordered at gorized as a customer who should be computer is linked. Then you will t served well, and consequently each day you will receive heaps of junk mail. However, if you don't respond positively to this harassment, they may decide that you should be dumped, and you will not have access to the company any more, even should you intend to buy a more expensive commodity. Nothing can help you, all is done behind your back. Big Brother sees all and knows all, and also takes immediate measures. This technology is in full progress. Enthusiatically, Want (2004) announces that *ubiquituous computing* developed radio-frequency identification tags and readers (RFID) which stand poised to take over many processes now accomplished by human toil. These systems contain small silicon chips which can identify perssonal data and/or other information, and readers that automatically receive and decode these data. RIFD tags can be molded into a product's casing and can use encryption and other strategies to prevent forgeries. They may also create an audit trail to indicate where a car was manufactured, how many times it has been sold, who were its previous owners, service history and the accidents it had. If, for instance, such tags are fixed to sumer goods, they can monitor the customers' behavior once they leave the In principle, there is nothing wrong with such data, the question is to they are handed over and what use is made of them, in other words, there is any control over them. Unfortunately, the commercial linkage computers, and especially the interlocking with the Internet prevents hility of control. The automatic computer linkage annihilates the citi-y, in flagrant opposition to what the constitution or the law may pro-'s no limit to surveillance that can be exercized with such methods. reinforces and presents in an entirely new light the thesis of im-upheld by Viorst (1998). She points out that while most of us try events of our lives to meet our personal needs, the control we over others and over what happens to us is always a highly

these
clothes
criminals.
downside w
ics. Nonethele
nology, in combi
sense and respond
whose benefit? These
possible for certain thin
the antique Roman lawye
Brother methods do not bene
corporations and by governme
and liberties. By its tacit approv
protects the misuse of technology in

practices have not been accepted smoothly. Wal-Mart in tte planned to monitor with smart tags the movements of t vehement consumer protests constrained them to drop actices. There are concerns that tags introduced into people wearing them, for the government and also for 2004) recognizes that the RFID revolution has also a ial issues, problems related to privacy, law and eth- article with expressing confidence that this tech-Internet, will extend the ability of computers to world. To sense what and rspond how, and to portant questions, now that technology makes e. *Cui prodest?* whom does it benefit, asked From what we presently know, these Big ulace, and the data are misused by greedy ies, as they infringe individual privacy g Brother practices the Internet State ringement of constitutional rights.

Governmental sources promptly reacted with a propaganda campaign trying to convince people that such new measures are necessary in order to promote security. The innocuously named Computer-Assisted Passenger Pre-Screening (CAPPS II), a fully automated system to check passenger background has the meritorious task of indicating high-risk airplane passengers. The system compares names, dates of birth, home address and phone number with private sector data bases, and here begins the privacy infringement. Airlines outsource this computerized work, using a variety of third-party software, some predate the Internet (*Scientific American*, September 2003, p.17). The computer may come up with false positives, and surely with the law-abiding "negatives" stripped naked. Thus innocent travellers are being harassed in great numbers. In late December 2003 several flights from Paris to the US were cancelled, because intelligence misidentified a half-dozen people as possible threats, including a 5-year old boy mistaken for an Al-Qaeda pilot. In view of these events, has the Administration second thoughts about inquisitive privacy infringements? Not at all, they want a more sophisticated system, and think to have found one: Acxiom, which manages 20 billion custormer records. It has enough storage space to house all the information existing in the Library of Congress 50 times over, and maintaines a database on 96% of US households, and that gives marketers a 360-degree view of their customers. Acxiom provides a 13-digit code for every person, so she might be identified wherever she goes. People are sorted by the frequency with which they use their credit card, the square footage of their homes, their interest in the *strange and unusual* (*Fortune*, February 23, 2004, p. 58-63). What a marvel, isn't it, and their stock price recently hit a 52-weeks high of $19.32!

In the middle of all this marvel, Acxiom itself was hacked by a man named Baas, who sold the data he obtained to commercial enterprises, but was tracked down, and, after pleading guilty to federal cybercrime charges (*Fortune*, ibid.) was dealt with in the court of law. Very curiously, the press is unanimous in condemning him, but has only words of praise for the blessed activity of Acxiom and other similar companies. Obviously, the Internet Society has only the interest of the companies at heart, but not of the public. Therefore, we shall be less shocked reading in the Italian newspaper *Corriere della Sera,* that at Linate airport near Milan, radar controls of the access strips have been suspended at poor visibility. According to the regulations, radar control would have allowed the landing of airplanes one by one only. This procedure would heve brought financial damage to the region, as also to the airline companies, and to those who owned and who worked for the airport. The result of suspending radar controls was the terrible air disaster of October 8, 2001, a collision which has cost 118 lives. Some readers may argue that in these events the state is not direectly concerned. This precisely is our problem. The deregulated Internet State does not exercise the surveillance requested by the need to protect the life, the property and the rights of the individual citizen, and it is deaf to all warnings in this respect. It intervenes only after a catastrophic event, and more often than not with downwatered measures, wich to many people seem like a lip service, lest harm be done to corporate interests.

Privacy invading controls are readily accepted if they further the activities (and the stocks!) of companies, and if such practices are duly marketed. We are referring to the newest Big Brother method, biometrics, which stores on the citizens' identity cards their digitized voice prints, face scanning with numerical values assigned to some of the 80 unique features of the face, in order to create a recognizable profile. An iris scan with mathematical demodulation turns the features of the iris into a digital identification, that can be checked against the database. Finally, there are the already classical fingerprints. In a number of countries (Germany, Italy) governments are issuing national ID cards and passports, which contain computer chips with biometric data. The European Union is proposing a common combination of biometrics for all travel documents. Still, John Daugman, the inventor of iris scanning cautioned that it is a flawed rationing to confuse identification with antiterrorism, and all government reports are attesting to the fact that camera surveillance had a small effect on crime, but none on terrorism. Despite such discouraging results there is a camera-surveillance histery in Britain, with 4 million cameras in position. In Lomdon a passer-by is photographed on the average 300 times in the City center (*Newsweek*, March 8, 2004). From the private sphere the surveillance mania went over into plain spying in the diplomatic field.Former British intelligence officer Katherine Gun has leaked to the press a secret US memo in which "help" was requested to spy on the undecided UN Security Council delegates in voting for the war on Iraq. Consequently, those delegates were bullied all the time, and they nilly-willy changed their voting intention. Allegedly, the conversations of the UN Secretay General have also been tapped (*Newsweek,* ibid.).

In the name of controlling it all, the state's foreign policy is simplified to a video-game of self-righteousness in which all is permitted. Says the filmmaker Errol Horris in an interview to *Newsweek* (January 26, 2004), "We've moved into a videogame era in foeign policy. The day after Saddam was overthrown, the complexity of a country was reduced to something grotesquely simple: the capturing of one man".

Of course, the problem is not only surveillance, but also a use of those data, which belies all lofty declarations on civil rights. Insurances, driving licences and travels are unrightfully denied, citizens and even school children are exposed to an atmosphere of terror. There are metal detectors in school corridors, zero tolerance for rowdy behaviors, some high schools possess many of the attributes of minimum-security prisons where the principal functions as a warden (Giroux, 2001). In the US there is a very harsh policy on crime prevention. From certain points of view it may be welcome. The problem begins when the lives of the otherwise law-abiding citizens are destroyed, because of unintended minor offenses (the cases are so frequent that the movies very often present such stories), when the rule of "three strikes and you are out" is applied in schools, and when in certain neighborhoods the population feel terror when seeing a police car. We shall see that paradoxically things completely change when it comes to punishing crimes. Would it be correct to say that the new society stands for a stronger involvement in public life? No way, the Internet society is contradictory and does not bother to have congruent views in the various problems and domains of social life. The one congruent principle seems to be the liberty of corporations to exact a maximal profit with the slightest investment. If individual citizens and foreign states accept this principle, they are welcome, the state withdraws, and they may realize all their phantasies, including drug consumption, pornography, killing the weak and the *useless*, and the utterance of all kind of blasphemies. If they do not agree to the basic principle, then the state steps up its intervention of surveillance legislation and the use of force, including military force, in dimensions seen only in the darkest totalitarian states.

In its "normal" functioning the globalized Internet Society is not another variant of a controlling and bullying bureaucracy, this society is contradictory in every one of its acts. The control is *outsourced* to automatic technological devices, and the key word is *deregulation*. The latter mainly concerns waiving responsibilities in the economic and social spheres. The result is that all levels of government are being hollowed out reducing their role to dismantling the gains of the welfare state, prioritizing penal methods over social investments (Giroux, 2001). Obtained is the privatization of the public space, linked to the corporatization of every-day life.The public sector is remade in the image of the market, commercial values replace social values, and market-based initiatives are treated as the only avenue for resolving social issues such as employment, education, housing and poverty.The function of the public space is reduced to an investment opportunity, while the former public goods are looked upon as possibilities of public disorder.

Although the Internet Society has no formal corporate governance, society is run by business. McChesney (1999) points out that society works best if business run things, and there is as little government interference with business as possible. There is a political, economic and cultural formation which construes profit making as the essence of democracy and consuming as the only form of citizenship. This way a handful of private interests control the main part of social life in order to maximize profit. Giroux (2001) expresses the opinion that totalitarianism now resides in the thorough dislike of all social things, public and collective, Gerbner (cf. Resnik, 1990) thinks that in the contemporary society the system's main function is that of protecting business from any extension of existing constraints.

Another economic function of the state is to adjust the rules of competition to fit the interests of the major players, and protect their markets from invasion and erosion as long as possible. This function also includes the ambiguous messages the system sends out in alcohol, tobacco and pharmaca abuses (Resnik, 1990) .In this sense the perpetuation of prodrug messages in the mass media is buttressed by the American society's commitment to the principle of free enterprise and free choice.

In the contemporary society such principles become empty slogans.As early as in 1940 a number of prominent Americans, like Roosevelt or Secretary of the Interior Harold Ickes, saw the things which were to come, and had serious concerns about the ability of the US press to perform its function as the guardian of democracy, when considering the undue influence on editorial policy of advertisers, financial capitalists and the *country club set*. These opinions have greatly influenced such instinctive society analysts like the great movie maker Hitchcock. In his views the press often fails to get its facts right, he frequently portrays cases when they publish the photo of a wrongly accused man on the front page. The press is not a sufficient guarantee of democracy because democracy needs intelligence as well as freedom. Journalists think more about how getting a story will benefit them, they are thinking of the rating, when their democratic mandate should alert and inform.Even the news reel, so popular in the past, had staged events and faked sound tracks.Journalists' values belonged (and are belonging also today, *E.K.*) to show business rather than to journalism, while they view their opinion as addressing an entertainment-hungry audience rather than a well informed public (cf. Allan and Ishii-Gonzalès, 1999). Today the entertainment hungriness of a greater part of the public sunk into a thorough indifference for public issues. Again, Giroux (2001) cited the New York Times writing that today more Americans care about who is going to be voted off the Island of Survivors, than who will be the next president of the USA.

In this context it is interesting to examine the models of leadership in the new society.They are no longer drawn from the ranks of heroic individuals, who in connection with social movements have fought to expand civil rights, individual liberties and democracy.The admiration is reserved to private success.The entire copy of *Fortune*, February 9, 2004, is dedicated to such leaders as CEO Terry Lahy, Mr. Big, CEO Li Dongsheng, Jamie Dimon, the new prince of Wall Street and others, while the actor-vigilante Schwarzenegger becomes governor of California, and the headlines are full of the love embroglios of the pop singer (some say the singer of pop-punk melodies) Courtney Love, of Britney Spears, who cancelled her marriage after 24 hours in Clark County U.S.A., or of Chris Noth, who is playing Mr. Big in "Sex and the City". Conversely, the Italian press desperately tries to convince that the *graffitari* who soil the cities are not heroes, but people making sometimes irreparable damage to public propriety (*Corriere della Sera*, 22 June 2003).

In the meantime the nations' true heroes are slandered and denigrated. The descriptions of J.F. Kennedy as a feeble, permanently ill womanizer are today an accustomed matter, and so are the depreciating pictures of Harry Truman or Ronald Reagan. It is interesting to note that contrary to the tendency of the press, the people rehabilitated Reagan with their affection, as he passed away in the Summer of 2004. And then come the "history" books depicting Eisenhower as unfit for the White House, Thomas Jefferson as a slave owner, or William Howard Taft as so fat that he needed a supersized bathtub. These very "educative" history books are especially published for children, so they should "have more freedom to dream of what they may accoomplish" (*Newsweek*, February 23, 2004). To accomplish what? Own slaves, be so fat that you could not enter a normal bathtub, be ill-fit to your job? Obviously the writers do not refer to these aspects, although precisely the latter are emphasized. They refer to seizing power, and the subtext reads: In order to hold power in society, supreme power, you have not to lead a model life.Only grasp power by whatever means, then you may indulge in every whim.The youth learns from this "educational" approach that you need no vision, you will not have to sacrifice anything for your countrymen, power is all, so you may realize all your most secret aspirations and fantasies. This is the picture of the state projected by the Internet Society. Of course, all great people had their imperfections, they were men and women like all of us, but not this made them great. They had the spark of dedication to their country, their people. This aspect should be emphatically presented, emulated in youth. History recordes Vercingetorix, even though he was a loser, Caesar, even though he was a kind of antique "mafioso". Queen Elizabeth I is remembered despite her dubious love affairs and frigidity, Peter the Great, despite the merciless killing of his opponents, including his own son, and Ronald Reagan despite his consulting an astrologists and despite his final senility. History records them because they had the greatness to bring a supreme sacrifice for their people, for what they saw as being right and for moving history forward. Society needs great people and this greatness has to be emphasized and not their human frailty, as the Internet Culture does. Actors, actresses, models have their greatness too in their own domain, again despite their sexual debauch, and not because of it - but their greatness does not supplant the greatness of a statesman. If some of them become leaders, it is because they feel a calling for the common good, and not becaus of their sexual or theatrical feats. History also records famous courtesans, but not because of their prowesses in bed, but because of their influence on world affairs or on the life of the country's population.

The tendency to demythologize history, so characteristic to the Internet Society is wrong. It enforces the apparent glamour of scientific research, but strips history of its pathos and exhortative influence. French history used to speak of the glorious assault on the Bastille on July 14, 1789. In his book, Prause (1966) relates that there has been no assault, the mob assembled by rumors and led by the Swiss laundry owner Hulin, was peacefully let in after promising the governor de Launay they would harm nobody. Hulin and de Launay embraced, but then the mob killed the governor and set free all the *seven thieves* and document forgers detained in this "giant, terrible dungeon" in which, as a matter of fact there were no cells but rooms only at that time. The myth was fabricated afterwards, but it is one of the most basic sagas of militant citizenship against tyranny, and it is true that the Bastille has been captured. Which of the two accounts is more useful to society and history? Let us dwell a little more on French history. On 13 March 2004 the TV satellite History Channel presented a programme on Jeanne d'Arc, the French heroine of the XVth century, who raised the people against the English occupants, liberated Reims, the coronation city of French kings, and coronated Charles VII as the king of France. In the promotional ad on the programme, the figure of Jeanne d'Arc was presented as follows: It is the story of a girl from the countryside, who at the age of 17 dressed herself in armor an rode across the battle field. She claimed to have been sent by God to liberate France from English rule and give back the throne to the king. Her visions came true until 1431, at the age of 19, when she was, however, burnt at the stake by people who feared her growing power. Her image is contradictory, she is considered both as a witch and as a saint, as a fighter and a martyr, as a counsellor to the king and as the hand of God.Her story gave birth to a myth until this very day.

What clearly appears in this story is that the brave TV correspondent takes his distance. He doesn't present a national hero, but a story of a contradictory figure, who could have simply been a witch, as the ecclesiastic inquisitional tribunal stated, perhaps a saint, as the Church decided in 1920 (!), important is that a myth was born which is now demystified. Her grandiose historical achievements for France are not given due emphasis, all is presented as the realization of visions, the very thing expected from every youth in the Internet Society.

It is true that the contemporary world is no place for military heroes to appear. In World War II some commanders rose to fame, like the British field marshall Mountgommery, the American generals McArthur and Eisenhower or the German general Rommel, but then they were denigrated and the developing legends were choked at the very beginning. There is also the pacifist stance of today's society looking warily at military personnel. Eisenhower made it to the presidency, (and is now declared as having been unfit for the job), the others were halted before they could achieve high civil functions or be entered *post-mortem* the hero Pantheon.All this does not mean that this society is peaceful and does not need heroes.First of all, in Europe a difference is made between a pacifist and a peace maker. The Italian bishop Msgr. Paglia says that the real hero is the latter, because he/she takes on great risks, sometimes they even lose their lives in trying to make peace. The Catholic Church sees Jesus as a peace maker, who has given His life for trying to make peace. Pilatus is rather the pacifist. In the name of an abstract principle he washes his hands, but does not intervene, and so contributes to the crime that is committed. Those who want to make peace cannot stay aloof, and only discuss, even vocally, and talk all the time, because it happens like in the Latin saying, "Dum Romae consulitur, Saguntum expugnatur" (while they are debating in Rome, Saguntum falls - *Corriere della Sera*, 25 February 2004).

There are peace makers also today, military persons and civilians, reporters and administrators, but their number is small, and they do not characterize the society of today. It is hard to say whether the *peace makers* who in Afghanistan throw bombs on innocent civilians gathered for a wedding, deserve this name. Surely not the UN "peace makers" who in Srebrenica (Bosnia) stood by indifferently looking as the Serbs massacred thousands of inhabitants. Pacifists exist toady in great numbers, but these are people, who only talk about peace, and are not willing to make for it the slightest sacrifice. As it were, the pacifists' continual word flood about peace is a defty political cover to let all feel good as they realize themselves in the consumption of goods, while performing their little more or less violent power games against their fellow citizens. Violence under the cover of a pacifist discourse is the face worn by the Internet Society.

Violence is the basic trait of the Internet Society, but it is not a violence fought by regular armies in man-to-man battles. Still, this society is very much ready to go to war, if its superiority in the fight is guaranteed, and if the war can be waged with technological means only, e.g. bombardments poetically described as surgical, but which, as a matter of fact, entail massive civilian casualties on the opposite side, while the own people are not hurt. This way attacks were launched against Serbia, Afghanistan and Iraq. The leadership were convinced it would not come to ground battles or to a guerila war, and that in Iraq, for instance, the chief ground operation would be tearing down a statue of Saddam Hussein by an American tank. The official statement spoke of the Iraqi people tearing down the statue, and the TV picture did not show the tank. When it came to the much more dangerous, well armed and resolute Iran and North-Korea, the same leadership writhed and pulled back, while trying to solve the problem peacefully. On the other side there is also devious violence fought by anonymous terrorists (they may be indigenous too!) who kill innocent civilians. The whole war in Iraq has taken on the look of a *netwar* fought against a multifold of loosely linked guerila groups, without a central headquarter, with no precisely defined front line, and which encompasses the whole world. The Internet Society has achieved not only a global economy, but has also awaken a global terrorist network. Fighting wars in such conditions is leading on the very problematic course of of sending combat forces into far away countries.Henry Kissinger (2004) has pointed ot that today´s principal threats are abstract and mobile. Terror has no fixed address and the survival of countries is threatened by developments taking place entirely within another state´s territory. Kissinger had in mind the development of nuclear arms, but the threat is also posed by terrorists armed with the most primitive weaponry.

Against the terrorists technologically mounted military attacks are used in which again innocent civilians are killed. It is the use of armed personnel against a population believed (rightly or wrongly) to collaborate with the guerilas. One should not exclusively accuse the Americans for this use of violence. They were by themselves the victims of a fierce unprovoked terrorist attack on Septembr 11, 2001, causing the death of 3000 people , just as Spain was the victim on March 11, 2004 with 200 people killed. More oftern than not the terorists are of an international breed. When in March 2004 the Pakistani army attacked a supposed Taleban stronghold in the province of Waziristan, the prisoners they took were Chechens, Uzbeks, and ethnic Chinese Uighurs. In Spain the attackers seem to have been Moroccans. However, one should not forget about the *indigeneous* terrorists, like the *Brigate Rosse* in Italy, the Eta terrorists in Spain or the IRA in Northern Ireland. Their common denominator is ideological fanatism. It can be of a nationalist brand (Eta, Chechen organizations, IRA), of a religious brand (Islamic Brothers in Egypt), or leftist fanatism (Brigate Rosse). At any rate it is a culture-induced modern conception that life, mainly the life of others, has no worth (even the own life is worthless in the eyes of a suicidal attentator). For them terrorism is a kind of game in which only winning is contemplated, and the casualties are looked upon like the ones of a video game.

Winning makes one feel good is the leading motive of the Internet Culture, and even the Muslim kamikadze feels good, and as the boomb is strapped to his body, he is anticipating his winning with the 71 virgins put at this disposal in the hereafter. Those virgins are for him real, his death is not. Such conceptions used to be aired in the Middle Ages, but now, in the era of hi-tech? Paradoxically, the hi-tech favors such aberrations, because it brings the all-encompassing virtuality with its video games to the fore, even in the organization of the state and its functions.

War is certainly a violent business, not only in the Internet Society, and neither only in previous wars, and then not only the Nazis committed barbarous deeds. Recently, the film industry has unearthed a horrible episode of World War II, in which on 30 January 1945 the Russians have sunk the German passenger ship Wilhelm Gustloff with 3000 refugees on board in the Baltic Sea. This episode proves that nobody can claim to have waged a war with clean hands.Coventry and Rotterdam were utterly destroyed by barbarious bombardments, but so was Dresden, and none of these targets could have militarily been justified.However, the point is not here. The film on the sinking of the German refugee ship broadcast by the satellite TV Discovery Channel on March 17, 2004, contained interviews and commentaries in which it was alluded that a feeling of sorrow for what happened would not be in place. Important is the service to history, to expose all events that had been hidden from public opinion, while the hatred remains. Some interviewees called the drawned civilian refugees a "bunch of henchmen".

A preferred jingle of reportership in the Internet Culture is that forgone events are unearthed, as they are believed to have been, and the purpose is to make the audience feel good. In the present case the authors surely felt good, and thought that also the spectators would, why would they, they should decide by themselves. Perhaps it is simply the sight of blood and violence, and death agony that pampers up people of the globalized Internet Culture. Was it not this that incited Mel Gibson to present his Passion of Jesus in the bloody manner he did, in opposition to the modern policy of the Church and the rules established by the II Vatican Council?

Terrorism is an existentialist threat in the Internet Society, it is borne out of an abysmal nihilistic hatred under an ideological cover pretext, and its purpose is simply to kill, because in doing so the terrorists draw attention to themselves, to what they stand for. It is their means of communincation. Terrorism cannot be definitively overcome or "resolved". To declare war on terror is to indulge in a dangerous fallacy (*Newsweek*, March 29, 2004). The phenomenon is bred and supported by society's culture.The proof is the "peaceful violence" within each country, indulged by the law. *You must change this culture, in order to curve the phenomenon of terrorism.*

As always, the victim contributes to the crime. In this case contributed a lax internal security, the free diffusion of radical opinions. Also contributed ideological hatred, using the privileges given by "human rights", the easy access to technology, the fetish of this society, as also access to the means to manufacture all kinds of weaponry (the duty to make business and the right to consume!).Therefore nobody should be surprised that the attacks of Setember 11 were prepared in Germany, Spain and - in the U.S.A. Lately, in Germany the condemnation to a 15-years sentence of the only member of the September 11 terrorist ring was invalidated, because of a technicality. The convicted terrorist was released. At this point the peaceful violence fought through an army of lawyers in the courts, unites with the terrorist fight against the establishment and society's failure to successfully fight crime. The fight in court is not at all peaceful, but, deluding itself, society tries to use against crime only "velvet" methods. Against criminals or terrorists such methods are absolutely ineffectual, used against honest, law abiding citizens out of political, ideological hatred they can be lethal. Therefore, what we call the peaceful violence is not less murderous than any open war, people get destroyed, maimed for their entire life. We are speaking of a society in which ten lawyers graduate for every engineer (Szasz, 1998), and they all wage merciless wars in the courts, stripping people of their possessions, in order to multiply the riches of their own and of their mandants. The Italian press calls it a war of all against all fought through the legislative and judicial powers.

An interesting episode took place recently in relation to a well-known photographer who created the myth of Che Guevara, with a beret on his head, his hair floating in the wind. The photo had been taken by Alberto Diaz Gutierrez (Korda) in 1960, and had then been given as a present to the publisher Feltrinelli, whence it landed at Reporters sans frontières, the most important organization defending the liberty of the press. Some 40 years the photo has been largely used and nothing has happened, but then they had the unfortunate idea to use the photograph in a poster criticizing human rights violations in Cuba. Immediately they were sued by Korda's heiress Diana Diaz-Lopez for not paying royalties and for infringement of a previous court order asking for the destruction of all copies. A Paris tribunal accepted her claim, and ordered Reporters sans frontières to pay more than 1 million Euros, a sum which the association could not afford, and it will have to close (*Corriere della Sera*, 25 February 2004). All the time the photo had been used en masse by the most radical leftist revolutionaries, and all had remained quiet. The instance the photo had to serve human rights, for which, allegedly, this society stands, the association whose members died or were incarcerated in great numbers in defending human liberties, is liquidated in connivation with the courts.

The courts of justice are a main arena where the violence of the Internet Society is played out, but it is not the only one. Violence is also surfacing in families and on the streets. The newspapers are full of stories on acts of violence against wives, children or about the killing of unknown, innocent passers-by. Little is done by the state power, if anything at all, to curve this situation. The state has other priorities than to protect the life of its citizens. It vows to protect human rights, but we have seen how it did it.

Giroux (2001) has pointed out that today the state's role as a guardian of the public interests is actively disassembled, though its powers are still invoked to ensure corporational privileges. Public space is privatized and every-day life is corporatized. The government is hollowed out as an independent representative of society, and its role is reduced to dismantling the welfare state. Of course, the welfare state we know from from the '1950s was economically and even socially untenable. Szasz (1998) remarked that, while formerly government was the responsibility of the people, suddenly people became the responsibility of the government. Adults are indirectly disfranchised by treating them as if they were children or mental patients, who need to be protected from themselves. In the former welfare state, in Germany, like in The Netherlands and in France, worker pay soared, while weekly working hours went shorter and shorter: In 1987 they reached an average of 38.9 hours in France (and later even 35, as also in Germany!), in Belgium 33.1 hours (except in the steel industry). In The Netherlands civil servants were hired on the basis of 30 weekly hours, and only England resisted at an average of 41.8 weekly working hours. In Sweden workers who called sick got 90% of a day's pay, and managers used to complain that on Mondadys, after a big soccer or tennis match, half of the country were absent from work (*Fortune*, December 13, 1993). However, this situation belongs to the past. Labor relations are now reigned by threats, strikes, the possibility to give perks, or at least promise jobs, by publicity in newspapers, cocktail parties, etc. The workers of a modest workshop of sewing underwear have no such possibilities. The Internet State will not defend them. In this society the survival of the strong is not an empty jingle, but a terible fact of life.

This basic attitude spills over to the state's foreign policy. At the beginning of the XIXth century the Prussian general von Clausewitz, in his book on war, coined the renowned adage that war is the continuation of politics with other means. He meant foreign policy, because he linked politics to "intercourse between governments and peoples", but now war is the continuation of a war-like internal policy vis-à-vis one's own citizens, of which foreign policy is again only a reflection.

In this context several questions ought to be considered. The first is the rapprochement between politics and war, two phenomena, which in the spirit of the founders of the United States should be maximally distanced from one another. The second question refers to the fact that statehood, politics and wars are not following from the intercourse of governments and peoples, as stated by Clausewitz, but from the intercourse of power groups. Finally, the third issue refers to the interpenetration of politics and war in the "peace time" internal setting of society.

The approach between politics and war is performed on two levels: a) the inducement of military methods into the economy, and b) the stirring up of hatred towards one's adversaries, qualifying them as Nazis and suggesting that methods of extermination be used against them. Military methods are praised as the most efficient and desirable also in business (*Fortune, 194,* 3, 2004), because of their rigid hierarchy of command, the discretionary power of commanders, and the interdiction of critique regarding their decisions. Such a management is in steep contrast to the classic "democratic leadership" proposed by White and

Lippitt, by Kurt Lewin and in all progressive works on the subject written between 1950 and 1990. I have already warned of management's tendency to shift towards a war-like attitude towards one's own employees (Krau, 1998). More and more motivating strategies are based not on positive incentives but on the fear of being fired. This means that in the direction of using power, essential to management, coercion prevails over influence, fight over attraction and offensive directedness is prevailing over the defensive one, while moral, and frequently also legal limitations tend to be waived, disregarded. Within the loci of power directedness remains the external one towards competitors, fought with the same ruthlessness as ever, while it is supported by the state. At the same time the internal power directedness towards the lower ranks in the hierarchy, including rank-and-file employees, gains an unexpected prominence, equally suported by the state of the Internet Society.

War entails the spread of hatred, and the modern society largely uses this method in their micro- and macro- affairs. Hatred recently characterizes all major and minor political debates, and the Italian newspaper *Corriere della Sera* (28 January, 2004) entitles its major article, *Politicians, Please Stop Now!* The political hatred among different groups within countries is so extensive and strong, that no common action is possible any more. Rightly, Joas (2000) points out that in this society all consensus has disappeared, even the consensus to disagree. In Italy one of the center-left parties proposed a great common demonstration on one of the central squares in Rome to protest against the 2004 terrorist attack in Spain. The center-right parties accepted the proposal, but then the leftist groups made it clear that they would not limit themselves to the commonly agreed slogans against terrorist attacks. They would present their own slogans and inscriptions against the war in Iraq, while the communists plainly declared, they are not willing to march in the same demonstration with the then conservative prime minister Berlusconi (*Corriere della Sera*, 14 March, 2004).

This incredible event does not characterize Italy alone. The Internet Society has been drawn to the verge of split. The mistrust of the people is directed towards politicians as such. No government, right, left or center, antiwar or prowar, seems up to the task of government (*Newsweek,* April 5, 2004), because the "tribal" hatred among component groups is paired with a suicidal indifference vis-à-vis common issues. As in the analysis we have made of the economy of the Internet Society, we are confronted with a *system failure also in the domain of the state organization.* Economy and social organization spring from the same roots. The denial of collective values, including collective ethics, collective democracy and compassion, and the extolling of virtuality, universal playfulness and individual pleasure seeking, regardless of what happens with others, cannot lead to anything else.

In continuation we shall see how the globalized state is functioning in the domain of rendering justice to its citizens.

Chapter Five

Criminality and Justice
in the Globalized Society

A crime is a premeditated action accomplished by a legally responsible person, an action, which is inflicting serious harm on society or/and on its individual members, or which society considers that it is inflicting such harm. Sometimes society has punished with great cruelty behaviors, which have been *considered* harmful, but ever since they have not been proven as such, like the exercise of witchcraft. Tens of thousands of people were burnt alive for such crimes. Today there are groups which proudly call themselves Wiccas, modern witches (Dunwich, 1998), but nobody complains of harm, and if medieval peasants claimed that an intervention of witches has made them sterile, such claim has never been proved. Therefore Tappan (1947) has pointed out that while not all antisocial activities are forbidden by law, neither are all the deeds forbidden by law antisocial.

The problem of what should be considered a criminal act has been complicated by the discussion on the causes of criminality. The older theories tried to reduce the problem to the antisocial character of the delinquent, which, allegedly would distance the latter from the rest of the population. A great fame acquired Lombroso (1876). On the basis of measurements performed on 27,000 offenders, he concluded that they differed from nonoffenders through some abnormal characteristics, like the assymetry of the skull and the face, an abnormal construction of the jaws, the ears; the absence of pain sensation, of mercy, of the fear of death, then lies, a reduced intellectual capacity, etc. It has been asserted also by others (Sayers, 1923) that many criminals show mental instability in various forms: an overwheening vanity, leading them to brag with their "achievements", egomania, a disproportionate sense of the importance of their offense. For them conscience could be characterized as a kind of vermiform appendix without any influence.

Although many murderers have such characteristics, all generalization is faulty, and Lombroso himself tells of a killer called Rosati who was very clever, and through his harmonious and tranquil face rather produced the impression of a contemporary statesman. Such facts have led the discussion into the area of a social causation of crimes. Even if inherited personality characteristics are contributing to the criminal behavior, people's behavior is learned and is a rection to a complex social situation vis-à-vis which they react with their entire personality. Situational factors also contribute to the delinquent behavior eliciting and making possible the actualization of certain extravagant desires, motives and instincts.

Despite all stigmata, crime is first of all a social category, because the motives and the modes of perpetration are inculcated by society. Bell (1953) thinks that in many respects crminality is a crooking mirror reflecting in a caricature-like form the morale and the behavior of society. Because of the extension and the persistence of criminality in the US, (Bell is an American author), and despite all the efforts made to eradicate it, Bell considers crime an American way of life. This is, of course, a bit exaggerated, because Europe too has its fair share of crminals, but surely modern culture contributes to it, and in a sense, America is the representative of modern culture. Merton (1938) has pointed out that modern American culture values material success, but separates it from the accessible instruments by which it can legally be achieved. As success standards become more dominant, the instruments which average people can afford to use become inefficient. Criminality is frequently linked to the use of forbidden , but efficient means to achieve the appearance of success, riches and power. Bell (1953) adds that even the gangsters strive to earn respectability, a place in American life and advancement in society.

All the biological, social and situational characteristics should be considered together, if we want to understand crime, and none should be discarded. Nonetheless, neither should anyone of these factors protect the perpetrator from punishment. On hand of letters, interviews and expertises, Ward (1995) has given a detailed description of the thoughts, the motivations and the behaviors of the serial killer Bobby Joe Long, convicted of ten cruel, premeditated murders. The defense used the story of his humiliating childhood with a prostitute mother, intending to invalidate the possibility of trying him at all, or to exact a more lenient sentence.They succeeded to retry him three times, but in all trials he was sentenced to capital punishment.At this point we do not want to discuss the legitimacy of capital punishment, but we shall raise the question, whether a humiliating childhood can shield somebody from punishment for raping and brutally murdering ten women, taking pictures of them and trophies, in order to remind and recreate the highlights of his murder feats, while he proudly declared that he is *Mad Dog* Long, who after each murder slept well and felt great.

Bad social and educational influences cannot and must not shield from punishment, but their understanding furthers an insight of how they are linked to criminality, it may help in preventing and reducing it. One should not accept at face value Durkheim's (Cf. Wolfgang, Savitz and Johnston, 1962) affirmation that criminality is not an abnormal phenomenon, because it exists in every society. Such an affirmation confounds a statistical truth (confirmed partially only, because there are societies with little criminality) with a content evaluation of values. There is also the contrary opinion of Sellin (Wolfgang et al. ibid.), and it is also incorrect, that one shoud say "abnormal behavior" and not "antisocial", because the criminals constitute a group of their own. Crime is antisocial since it harms society's members, and as such, infringes its laws and hurts its institutions, but it is also an abnormal act, precisely because it is breaking the established laws of common life. However, in our discussion the designation of abnormal should be used for actions not normal from a psychological-psychiatrical point of view, as done by tradition and convention. In legal speech modern law used to consider as abnormal individuals entering certain psychiatric categories, and who by this fact are not responsible, and therefore not punishable for their actions. The law requires their forced internation into psychiatric facilities.

Szasz (1998) deplores that psychiatrists and also the public view craziness and criminality as closely related types of deviance. Our society, he says, uses the prison system as an extension of the mental health and the welfare systems, with three meals a day, medication and job training. He also mentions the abusive *reversed linkage* between prisons and the psychiatric wards, as until 1988 in the former Soviet Union political dissenters were forcedly "admitted" to psychiatric hospitals, and treated with the most painful methods of treatment, such as electro-shock, insulin coma, convulsions, etc. Szasz (1998) asks for a clear distinction between medical patients and criminals, between prisons and mental health facilities. What he doesn't seem to see is that the linkage between the two institutions is made by the offenders with their personality characteristics, which on hand of frail criteria are distributed by the law as either falling into the *responsible* category (prison) or an *irresponsible* ward catogory. The two institutions have common, but also different features. Common is that they both serve to isolate from the public individuals dangerous to themselves and/or for society. A psychotic is a danger for all the people surrounding him, like also a crminal, and there is also the common endeavor to rehabilitate them. Beyond this, there are sharp distinctions between the two institutions. Prisons punish, and the question is which punishments are more adequate to what the law prescribes for the committed offense, wards try to cure, and the question is which cure is more adequate to the personality and the health requirements of the patient. We shall later see that our society mixes up these categories, whence appears the whole predicament of the justice system.

Criminality does not exclusively characterize the comtemporary society. The kind of crimes which are perpetrated, their frequency and modes of perpetration, the psychosocial profile of the offenders, and also society's attitude and reactions are specific and particular for each historical period. Crime appeared together with the human society, and so did society's endeavor to defend its members and punish the perpetrators. In the tribal society blood vendetta was a kind of instinctive response. It was a social activity at which the whole family or the tribe participated, and it had also an additional meaning of fulfilling a sacred duty. As time went by, punishment was institutionalized, executed by the state, and the penalty was inflicted for crimes which included those committed against the king and the state. New crimes were added to the book of laws, and the *Lex Carolina* of 1532 already asked for the death penalty in 44 offenses. In the XVIII-century France, the crimes requiring the death penalty had already grown to the number of 115, and in England people were executed for stealing objects worth more than 1 shilling, or for hewing down trees in a foreign wood.

However, even in those times enlighted people severely opposed the abuses of capital punishment. In his *Utopia* (1516) Thomas Morus expressed his steadfast opposition to put people to death for minor offenses like theft. Similar views were expressed by Grotius, the great expert of the XVIIth century in state law. Quite modern opinions were voiced in the XVIIIth century by Cesare Beccaria (1764/1939): He pointed out that the aim of punishment is not to torture and wreck people, and not to undo an alrerady perpetrated crime.Its aim is in preventing the guilty from repeatedly harming society and in deterring others from doing the same.Very significantly, he added that many people would rather be deterred by the expectation of a lifelong incarceration, rather than by a short executional procedure.

Slowly these ideas were accepted by public opinion. The jurisprudence of the XIXth and the XXth centuries begins to take into consideration the person of the perpetrator and not only the crime itself. Modern theories look at the comparability of cases, the consistency of priciples in sentencing and the comensurability of punishment in relation to other harms (Daly, 1994).

The problem of capital punishment has not yet been resolved. Contradictory arguments have been put forward, and the whole question has degenerated into an ideological-political argument. However, even the supporters of capital punishment agree that it should be inflicted only for the most heinous crimes for which no pardon and rehabilitation appears possible. Taking the lives of such individuals, we are told, makes sure that they will not repeat their crimes. Here they make a certain point, because even a *lifer* as they say in England, may escape from prison, or be somehow pardonned, go free and continue killing people. There have been told many such stories.

Then there is the argument that capital punishment is the best deterrent against serious crimes. Statistically this argument is not reliable. Starting with 1965 in Britain, in New Zealand and in other countries there was an experimental freeze on death penalty: the number of murder cases with premeditation had a slight but not continual rise. In 1965 in England there were 151 cases of murder with premeditation, there were 139 cases in 1966, 169 cases in 1968 and 174 in 1969. In 1970 the British Parliament abolished the death penalty and its place was taken by a sentence of mandatory life imprisonment. The matter is debatable for two reasons: First, we are talking about halting the deprivation of innocent people of their lives. Even if only in a few cases a would-be killer were deterred from committing the crime by the perspective of being hanged (or shot or gassed), it seems the right thing to do, because it saves human lives. It is true that this discussion is straightly leading to the question, whether the life of the potential victim is more worth than the life of a killer, whose execution deterred another potential killer from carrying out his intention. The answer is yes, without any doubt and hesitation. We shall see that the Internet Culture does not agree with this statement, but precisely here lies its moral bankruptcy.

The second problem with the decision of the British Parliament to abolish the death penalty, refers to the establishment of a mandatory sentence of life imprisonment for all murder cases, not only for those which in American law would be called first degree murder. The English judge is given no possibility of weighing mitigating circumstances, and once the jury has found the defendant guilty of murder, the life sentence is given automatically. This was part of the deal with the M.P.s. It again creates a problematic situation. It is lacking fairness, when it gives the same punishment to a person who kills *wilfully and maliciously* and to another one who has killed in a spurt of emotional outburst. The automatic life sentence also lays a heavy burden on the Treasury, who must support for years people who do not deserve to be cared for. Finally, a life-long detention may be a more bitter punishment than a quick execution. This was the opinion of Winston Churchill, who on this basis supported the death penalty (Cf. Gowers, 1956).

The opponents of the death penalty have, nevertheless, a heavy argument for which it is very hard to find an answer. It is the problem of *Justizmord*, as the German lawyers say, the people wrongly executed. After years their innocence is proved, but nothing can bring them back and rehabilitate them. In many cases even the man's family has been destroyed in the meantime beyond repair. McNamara (1969) points out that between 1889 and 1927, 50 persons were sentenced to death by error and executed in the famous Sing-Sing prison. In the US they try to provide an answer to this problem by protracting the judicial appeals for 10-12 years, but this adds a new torture to the psychological pressure in which the convicted offender and his family are living. Therefore this answer is definitely wrong. It is the duty of the entire legal system to make sure, that when it convicts somebody, the person is guilty, and conversely, that the guilty man or woman is convicted. In a protracted legal procedure witnesses may be intimidated or killed, and then their publicly made statements are no more usable in court. In such a system decisive material proofs cannot be used in the trial, if they had been obtained without the prescribed formalities, and therefore such a system does not essentially contribute to justice. It reinforces the adage, novel writers use all the time, that in modern society there is no link between the legal system, reality and justice.

Having discussed these theoretical premises, we are now equipped to analyze the problem of criminality and justice in the Globalized Internet Society in particular. Like its entire state organization, its criminal justice is also presenting characteristics of a video game, in which the emphasis is not on giving protection to citizens, but on playing by certain rules. In a serial Hollywood production entitled Law and Order, an elderly judge tells a rebelling youg prosecutor, after the judge had cancelled a guilty verdict of the jury, and set free a guilty criminal, "Here we are not concerned about right and wrong, but about doing it the right way". So, not truth is important and not to let justice prevail, but that the game be played by the rules. Nothing wrong with rules. The legal system of every country is governed by rules laid down in its Book of Laws. The problem is, the Internet Society's legal system is governed by a twisted, *politically correct* interpretation of the law, as in the former USSR. The latter was very appropriately described in George Orwell's "*1984*", where the surveillance organs are The Big Brother, the Ministry of State Security is named the Ministry of Love, and the Ministry of Propaganda, which all the time fabricates lies, is the Ministry of Truth.

The Internet Society recognizes the concept of delinquency and crime.Nevertheless, through the linkage with an utopian ideology of free and empowered citizenship, through the setting of contradictory priorities in favor of corporations, which negate the same freedom and empowerment of individual citizens, the legal system becomes contradictory and void of content. Should we be permitted to use the Orwellian method in characterizing the judicial system of the globalized Internet Society, we arrive at the certain rules:

Rule One:The games played in the Internet Society, including the legal game, must make the players feel good. The heroes of the play, the powerful for any reason, the rich, should feel a greater measure of goodness, they must have more rights than the people with less power, and these latter should feel better and have more rights than those with no power at all. Victims of onslaught, especially murder victims, have lost with their lives and their property also their power. Therefore they have no rights, and this situation sprawls to all persons who identify with them, e.g. their families, when they fight the murderer, who is a citizen with rights, and is also violent, and therefore admired for his power. All games that do not correspond to this rule must be modified or cancelled. It ensues that the death penalty must be abolished, even if is constitutional, i.e. it corresponds to the rules, but it does not make the violent hero feel good. The public will ask whether the killer-hero could feel good if incarcerated (instead of being executed). Of course he does not, and this is why the intelligentsia of the Internet Society will put up a hard fight to save him even the prison sentence. A hero must be free. Perhaps, he should get help from a diplomed psychologist.

Rule Two:The formal rules of the legal *video-game trial* take precedence over the content problems of guilty – not guilty. The trial itself becomes a game played between prosecutor and defense lawyer, in which "the best man wins", and the truth or the defendant's guilt or innocence have absolutely no importance. The judge will see himself as a football referee watching over the observance of the rules, the defense lawyers, even if they perfectly well know that their mandant is "guilty like hell", will construe a case for acquittal. They will tell everyone who wants to hear it, that it is not their fault if they are better in presenting their case than is the prosecutor. In other circumstances, the prosecutor will do the same thing.

Rule Three: The globalized Internet Society is contradictory in its construction, ideology, and sends out contradictory messages of what is allowed and what is not. The legal system accomodates and carries further this contradictoriness. The the legislation on possession of drugs, on the prescription of crimes, or the entire question of euthanatic killing are good examples.

RuleFour:The social order of the Internet Society has priorities.Corporations and people with power are on the top of these priorities, powerless little people are at the bottom, where nobody cares for them. Offenders, by the mere fact of their delinquency, by which they overpowered other people, prove that they have power. Even condemned by the courts, they are secretly admired and society's institutions will do all they are capable of to set them free. This job is usually done by the appellate courts. The first instance jury trial is much dependent on the sane judgement of ordinary "peer" people. The appellate courts have no links with the people, and it is there that all twists are done. An example could be the federal action in the US against Microsoft, at which the court decision to split up the monopolistic company was stalled and halted and retried until a placid, innocuous sentence was delivered. In Europe recently against the same company a fine of 5 million Euros has been pronounced, but it is "pocket money" for Microsoft. Analysts say that that now the market itself has taken over the punishment of the company, as the public ever more chooses Microsoft competitors (Siebel Systems, Open-Source Software) who are selling at much lower prices (*Fortune, 149,* 5, 2004).

Rule Five: The admired hero-offender remains a person with full rights, and his citizen rights take precedence over the need for measures to restrain the harm he is potentially capable of doing. Szasz (1998) reminds that inmates of closed psychiatric wards (crazy people in common language) are voting in the U.S.A.Dangerous criminals are released after only doing a small fraction of the time for which they were condemned, after a report written by a compassionate social worker or a romantic psychologist, who did it out of bounty idealism towards "the poor criminal", or because of a good pay received from his friends or family.In case the released criminal turns to be a killer again, the writer of the report is not held responsible. What are the results of such a system in action? First appears the striking picture of contradictions. We have already seen a Big-Brother-like surveillance and a careless attitude of deregulation. The compromise lies in the double standard of handing down harsh sentences (even this not always), while only a small fraction of it is actually done in jail. The consequences are catastrophic. Let us discuss some of the most famous recent cases, which happened in the most advanced democracies of modern times.

Recently, in Belgium ended the trial of Marc Dutroux, who since 1995 had kidnapped and violated six 12-13-years old girls, of which he murdered four, he let two of them simply starve to death, while he strangled the others. The man had been previously jailed for child molestation, but he was set free after a short time. Therefore, he was a natural suspect, as one after another, children disappeared in the region. The desperate parents insistently asked for police action, but the General Prosecutor refused to grant a search warrant for the suspect's house (in which the children had indeed been imprisoned and starved to death) without the recommendation of the judge of inquiry, Martine Doutrewe. The latter halted the investigation by all means at her disposal, lest the suspect would feel harassed by the police, after having sat in jail, a matter of personal rights so dear to the Internet Cuture. Judge Doutrewe was supported in her obstructionist behavior by the chief of the gendarmerie, col. Boeck, who was fighting his own private war of competencies against the local police and the professional crime investigation department in Charleroi, a little game within the game. Finally, the judge allowed a surveillance on the suspect, but it was done in an incompetent, amateurish way, like a children's game. It took placce during day time only. In the Internet Society police men have the inalienable right to sleep at night, and police budgets are too low to add additional agents to the task force. As if they would say, "Easy, dear, we are just playing". The low budget also explains the insufficient training of the agents. Twice the gendarme agent Michaux was in the suspect's house, where the two girls had been held, he heard their cries, but was unable to find the hiding place (protected by a shelf). He reported his findings to the investigating judge, who, however, did not approve or ask for more professional help. Months of wavering passed, until more resolute actions were taken, but until then the two unfortunate girls starved to death in the cellar covered by the shelf. All this happened in the same Belgium, which is the only country in the world, whose laws permit the trial of foreign citizens for political crimes committed in other countries. Belgium is eager to ask for extraditions and to start such far-fetched trials 30 years after their perpetration, this time without any delays and consideration of juridical impediments It was the intention in the case of the fomer Chilian dictator Pinochet, at that time already a feeble-minded octogenerian.

Dutroux was sentenced to life-long imprisonment. How long he will stay in jail remains to be seen. This society is unable to learn the lesson that by setting free a killer it produces more murders by its own hands. As it were, one week after the sentencing of Dutroux, the chief prosecutor of Liège (a city also in Belgium) announced that a somewhat similar series of crimes had been committed. One of the delinquents in preventive custody was Michel Fourniret, aged 62. The man had previously been sentenced to seven years in prison in France for child violations and molestations, but had been released after a very short time. He admitted to have killed since then in Belgium six girls under age. He also admitted to have buried some ten other bodies in France (the number of bodies found is 16), most of them in his castle at Donchéry. Since these killings started in 1985-1987, the French and Belgian judicial authorities are in a very unpleasant predicament, because of the prescription of a majority of these murders. The prescription law for murder is 15 years in Belgium, but only 10 years in France.

It is clear that had the authorities in the two reported murder cases been more concerned with protecting their own citizens instead of putting all their passion into political vendettas, had they respected their own laws and judicial sentences, and protected the community and not the conmen, then the lives of many innocent children could have been saved. If *murder is murder, is murder,* as an

American judge has said, and the crimes for which Chile's dictator, Pinochet was responsible, could not be prescribed, then why would the killings of Dutroux and Fourniret fall under prescription?

This whole prescription business for murder is weird, and again indicates that the Internet Society makes a game of what is not. The law makers seem to say, let the police try to find the culprits, but if they cannot do it during 10 years, and the killer has succeeded in hiding, then this episode of the Cops and Gangsters game is over, and a new game may start with a new murder. It is a new proof that for such law makers the citizens' life is absolutely worthless.

The reader must not get the impression that we are speaking of shortcomings of the Franco-Belgian justice system only. Several months ago the Swedish foreign minister Anne Lindh was stabbed to death in a supermarket as she went shopping for her household. The perpetrator, a former Yugoslav subject, was apprehended, tried and sentenced to a 15-years prison sentence. In the Summer of 2004, an appeal court revoked the sentence, and sent him to mandatory psychiatric care instead. He will go free the moment some water-eyed psychologist will write a report telling that using his so-and-so method he succeeded in curing his "patient". Other Swedish ministers should well beware! Even the murder of the former Swedish Prime Minister Olof Palme has not been solved, again because the man suspected of perpetrating the crime, a Pakistani immigrant was released on technicality grounds before the trial began.

How can all this be put in accordance with the facts attesting to a violent character of this society? Is its violence a bloodless one? By no means, the more blood and physical suffering are depicted in a movie or in a TV series, the higher is the rating. But sticking to the rules means that only the criminals are allowed to be physically violent. It is their part in the game, nobody else is entitled to play it. In order to clarify this point, let us consider one more example, this time from Italy. The second half of the '1990s saw a wild increase in criminal actvities, especially in the South of the country. There was wide spread drug smuggling with shooting on the police force, who would try to halt them. In June 1995, in the port city of Brindisi, the police sighted a smuggler motorcycle trying to escape. The smugglers had arrived by boat from the sea, probably from abroad, they had engaged in a gun battle with the police force, killed some of the agents, blew up an armored car with valuables, collected them, and tried to escape by motorcycle. A police helicopter took off, and the city's police chief, Forleo, himself participated in the action. A shooting developed, and and one of the smugglers was killed. The judicial authorities put on trial . . . the police chief for first degree murder. At the trial, experts established that it was not him who had shot. However, the prosecutor relentlessly continued the judicial action against him (notice the passionate hatred in this society!) and accused Forleo of moral participation in the intentional murder of unknown persons, in other words, not the foreign bandits were the criminals, but the police chief (*Corriere della Sera*, 25 February 2004). His trial ended in 2004 only and the prosecution asked for a 14-years prison sentence. Said an Italian Member of Parliament, "God save and liberate us from the initiatives of provincial attorneys". The min-

ister of links with the Parliament added, "This is an example of how certain judicial initiatives may burst into the social, economic and political life of the
country, like elephants into a shop of china-ware, and do so much more damage
than benefit, as they put the institutions in a crisis".

Some readers may argue that one should not draw general conclusions from
a single Italian example.The point is that such cases are numerous, and happen
not only in Italy. We are facing a general phenomenon of the Internet Culture. In
November 2004 the German prosecution put on trial the deputy police chief of
Frankfurt, Daschner, because, so the accusation held, he had threatened an arrestee with torture. Here is the full case: In the city, the son of an industrialist
had been kidnapped. The police did not succeed in finding the boy, but they
caught the perpetrator. The man refused to collaborate with the police, and
would not tell where he kept the boy. In such cases time is decisive to find the
abductee alive, and the desperate deputy police chief used the ruse of *threatening* him with torture, in order to make him talk. The stratagem worked, the man
confessed, but confessed to have already murdered the boy. Consequently, the
deputy police chief was charged with violating the arrestee's rights. This means
that for the justice system in the Internet Culture the rights of an arrestee-
kidnapper of children (and killer) take precedence over the attempts to save the
life of the abducted child, while no physical harm had been inflicted to the arrestee.

One cannot but recognize that in the abovementioned case the behavior of
the magistrates has also been violent. It was not the physical violence of a gangster, but a bloodless violence exercized through the judicial system itself, a
widely spread pattern in the globalized Internet Society. The results are the
same. By this violence through the judicial system, lives, careers and families
are destroyed, sometimes with a suicide at the end, also adding the blood. The
steady whinig about the *moral duty to renounce violence* and abolish the death
penalty is an empty word, a game of words. In the Internet Society the games
are violent.

So far several conclusions may be drawn: The justice system in the globalized Internet Society is not meant, set and organized to protect the community or
its individual citizens. The justice system in the Internet Society is not guided by
the content and the spirit of the law, by the intention of the legislator, as it was
the custom and the duty from Roman times on. It is guided by the letter of the
law, *interpreted in the spirit of political correctness*. In the process of legal action preference is given to the persons who represent the feelings and the values
of this society. Unfortunately, it is the criminals who represent the values of this
society. They are strong, violent, individualists and do not recognize authority.
Therefore they are the heroes and society treats them with special consideration.
The judicial organizations of the Internet Society and their actions form a system, acting in the spirit of the rules, which have been discussed. Therefore, even
if a criminal is convicted by one of the system's parts (usually the jury trial),
another link (usually the appellate court) will revert things to "what they should

be" and release him. As a matter of fact, the justice system of the Internet Society is only a "judiciary system", and has nothing to do with justice.

In the examples that had been given, the possible harassment of suspected killers was not weighed against the safety of children in the region (or the former took precedence), and neither was the demise of an armed fugitive smuggler and drug dealer weighed against the safety of the community. Even if accepting the Italian magistrate's action, they had to search for the officer who was the one who shot, and also this only after a conclusion would have been reached that it was not the armed gang who had opened fire. Nothing of the kind was done. The Italian Parliament voted a law aiming at bringing prosecutors under the control of the judiciary, and separate the careers of prosecutors and judges, so as to curve the continuous interchange among prosecutors and judges. The answer of the law abiding and law enforcing magistrates was . . . a strike. This shows how much importance they give to the country's laws they so passionately pretend to defend.

The problem is that modern society is not capable of deciding what kind of laws we should have regarding criminality. Should they be based on the retribution principle and punish the committed (past) crime, or on the rehabilitation (treatment) principle in order to avoid future crimes. A combination of the two seems a logical necessity (Ellis and Ellis, 1989; Daly, 1994), but the relative weight of the two components has still to be decided, and also whether the crime itself or the criminal's personality is more important in the determination of the steps to be taken. People concerned with legal theories, who are calling themselves utilitarians, seek social benefit through punishment, deterring would-be delinquents from crime, by removing them from the community or changing a law-breaker's attitude or behavior through rehabilitation. The difference between them and the supporters of desert-based sentencing (the deontological principle) is that this latter is only looking at the action of the offender aiming at the quality and comensurability of the sentences.

It seems fair that the past history of the offender should be made known to the court, for it to take it into account. However, contrary to the fashionable legal arguments of today, we consider that this is a two-way decision and does not act *pro reo* only: there are offenders who have demonstrated that for them there is no possibility for rehabilitation. W.e have heard of people who make passionate love to their wife in the night and then carry out their long ago planned plot to murder her in the morning. Many years ago Sayers (1923) has pointed out that conscience is for those people a vermiform appendix without any importance and influence. Don't bother with it, or chop it out, and you will feel all the better. As a matter of fact, all the examples we have given, Dutroux, Fourniret and Bobby Joe Long enter this category. Rehabilitation had no chance with them, and it is fair to society that they should never have the occasion to kill again. If the law admits the death penalty, then in these cases it is justified, otherwise they should be imprisoned for all the duration of their lives without the possibility of ever being released, neither for ill health, nor for psychological disturbances, and surely not out of compassion. It is also understood that never should such offenders be allowed to go on vacation from jail. Many of them have again committed murders in such vacations. In other words, the adage known from the Roman law, *Nullum crimen sine poena,* still stands, because only the punishment of the criminal rends the victim a sense of justice (remember, in our conception also the victims have rights!). It also has a certain deterrent effect on the persons with violent propensities, who are planning crimes. However, the punishment should maximally seek the possibility of rehabilitation for persons who have not commited the most serious offenses, such as criminal assault, rape, abduction, murder, and who have indicated that they may respond positively and sincerely to treatment.

This brings us back to the necessity to study the offender's personality. Such a study will always unearth some hidden internal deficiency rooted in a bad treatment in childhood, and which *may* result in an abnormal behavior, but does not so inevitably. Many abused or rejected children have highly realized themselves precisely because of their intent to demonstrate their worthiness. Nonetheless, Garbarino (1999) makes a point, when he characterizes rejection in childhood as a psychological malignancy, which may provoke in the child an addiction to the dark side of life. It is not only the child's family, which should carry all the blame. Garbarino even speaks of a *social toxicity* in the vivid and explicit scenarios of death and destruction brought in the American homes by TV as a routine fare of entertainment. Presently, there is a degradation of the social environment, social and cultural poisons are manufactured, and they contaminate the social world of children, youth and their families. As an illustration, let it be mentioned, that the Italian publisher Arnoldo Mondadori from Milano has advertised books of the "well known humorist" Antonio Amurri, which were entitled *How to Kill One's Wife and Why, How to Kill Mom and Dad,* and then, of course, *"Come ammazzare la suocera"* (How to Kill One's Mother-in –Law). Notice well: It is a serial writing, in which the killing of people's family members is involuntarily taught and induced into action by the titles and the stories of the books. Judging by these titles (to kill "mom and dad"), the author is addressing an audience of youngsters, and he lets himself be presented as a humorist, in order to disarm public resistance.

The spread of cultural poisons is favored by dangerous youth gangs with a low level of attachment to conventional society, their members have a higher than average intelligence and a sense of life being out of their control. Peer groups and the Internet are key distributors of drugs, a more material poison.In the '1970s society's message was one of clear disapproval, but today the messages are mixt ones. After each serious cautioning regarding the harms drugs do to mind and body, immediately follows a learned dissertation claiming that the meaning of a given drug to the people who use it, even the experience of the drug itself, differs considerably from one society, sector, one group or one moment in time to another (Resnik, 1990). This may be partly true, but the physiological intoxication drugs are provoking do harm in any society, any group, to any person and at any moment. Therefore in most Western countries they are illegal. However, the globalized Internet Culture spurns the legal interdiction, and praises drugs for the sense of freedom they give, for their utillity in the therapy of couples, for the stimulation of creativity and problem solving (Masters and Houston, 2000). The perpetuation of prodrug messages in the mass media is buttressed by "our nation's commitment to free speech, free enterprise and free choice" (Resnik, 1990). Thus, in many ways the American culture with the emphasis on the indulgence of the self, is a drug culture. Such an attitude is most curious in a publication sponsored by the US Depatment of Health and Human Services. It is repeatedly hinted at the fact that there should be information giving to the public, but not the criminalizing of a behavior attractive to many people. This is an open challenge and disobedience to the legal position of the US Government and the US Congress, hence to the formally proclaimed law of the state. It underlines the contradictoriness of the Internet Society, its disrespect for the law and its incapacity to do something about it. All moral and legal terminology is drowned and overriden by the new terms introduced by the Internet Culture, "plenty, play, pleasure, recreation, self-fulfillment, dreams, leisure, immediate gratification, public relations, personality, celebrity" (Susman, 1984). These terms describe a new way of life in which the pursuit of fun, whatever fun and at whatever cost is central and essential, even if it is contrary to the law. If one reads the letters of the serial killer Bobby Joe Long, published by Ward (1995), one is struck by the recognition that for this monster killing was fun. However, at the moment you are accepting the *fun morality* (Wolfenstein and Leites, 1950) of this society and the legitimacy of rebellion, any rebellion against any authority, how can you put on trial and punish the transgressions?

Let us dwell more on this *morality of fun*, on the havoc it wreaks, and how it derides the law. A report of the former American Attorney General Edwin Meese outrightly stated that the ubiquitous pornography was linked to sexual violence. Immediately, the loyal defenders of the Internet Culture gave these conclusions a double twist. The one was saying that pornography was a high expression of citizens' right to freedom of speech (Cf. Stan, 1995), the other argumented, that if pornography was morally dangerous, and a killer has been exposed to it, he was not guilty, or only partially so (Ward, 1995). We have already been discussing pornography in more detail in another chapter, let us here say to pornographers' second argument, that violence, rape and murder seen on TV may negatively influence the penchants of people, and should therefore be reduced and mitigated, overriding the chorus of free speech adherents. However, a TV picture does not constrain anybody to be violent, the choice to behave in that way is made by the viewers, but after they made the criminal choice, the offense must be punished with all the rigor of the law. TV pictures cannot and must not mitigate the guilt of an offender who took a person's life or brutally raped another person.

It is a shame how much energy and thought are squandered in order to justify pornography and violent entertainment images in society. We are told (Cf. Stan, 1995) that whether or not pornography has a redeeming (?!) value, free speech has, and free sex has as much value as free speech. Constrained by facts to see the very negative imfluence pornography exercizes on youth, on the valuation of women in society, the authors come to the conclusion that the best course is to have laws in the books against certain representations, but not to enforce them (Sic!). This is the kernel of the justice system in the Internet Society.

The general tendency of the legal procedure is not concerned with finding out the truth and sentence the perpetrator accordingly. The intention is to intimidate him and coax him into a sort of bargain game, named the Alford doctrine (US Supreme Court decision in the case North Carolina vs Alford, 1970). The defendant's guilty plea does not mean his recognition of guilt, but only the admission that the state has gathered sufficient evidence to achieve a guilty verdict. In such bargain games the defendant, which may be guilty or not, is always promised a parole release after a specified time, before the nominal end of the sentence term. In the US, but alo in other countries, a majority of law suits are dealt with by this particular procedure. The important thing is that there is a game called justice and it is played by certain rules, regardless to the guilt or innocence of the defendants.

Recently in the US new mental health courts have been set up to provide alternatives to incarceration, and in order to divert nonviolent offenders with substance abuse from jail into treatment. In exchange for a guilty plea, the offenders enter treatment instead of prison. The treatment usually lasts between 12-14 months. In California such a program has saved the state $18 million a year, incarcerations have declined by 83 p.c. and convictions by 77 p.c. (Bailey, 2003). Precisely this is the mixing up of jails and psychiatric wards against which Szasz (1998) has taken up a so desperate stand. Instead of organizing within the penitenciaries the possibility of psychological-psychiatric help for offenders convicted for infringements of the law, and who may have a personality problem (while in the eyes of the law they are still responsible for the acts they have committed !), they are poured into psychiatric wards, or even sent home to undergo ambulatory treatment. Their offense is played down, there is no more deterrence for shoplifting, hooliganism and other similar offenses. Perhaps it is true that there is a reduction in the number of arrests, because no arrests are made: the guy is under treatment. This reflects the actually promoted trend of the Justice System in the Internet Culture, expression of a passionate opposition – not to crime – but to the incarceration of delinquents. Dr. Stephen Ragusea, candidate for presidency of the American Psychological Association in 2003, deplored that the US incarcerates a higher percentage of its population than any other nation in the world. He asked that there should be new answers to the problem of crime and punishment, and pleaded, that if elected (which he was not), he would convene a national conference to address the reduction of incarcerations as a priority problem in the American Society (*APA Monitor on Psychology*, June 2003).

The Internet Culture rejects the idea of punishment for whatever deed, so there is some unclarity as to why efforts are sometimes made to apprehend the perpetrator. The quagmire begins at the moment of the offenders' conviction. We have already shown that the Internet Culture has no internal limits and halts. All tendencies are pursued until the most extreme limits. The problem is, prisons cost money, and ex-cons used to return to prisons in a rate of more than 40% within their first year of freedom. In October 2002 the New York Academy of Sciences convened a symposium on prisoners reintegration, but the underlying issue was what to do with delinquents (Crane, 2003). In this society you are interested what happens with *your* bank account and *your* PC screen but not what befalls your neighbor. The public is way ahead of policy makers, enthusiastically declared Jacobson, adding that 13 states have already closed prisons or reduced the capacity of existing ones, and 12 have delayed or eliminated plans for new prison construction. Missisipi and Louisiana have repealed mandatory minimum sentences on the ground that they are too expensive.

Todd Clean, distinguished professor at John Jay College addressed another reason against incarceration. Since prisoners tend to come from poor communities, which are already short on human and social capital, by removing more people from them, one is removing sources of social control as well (Crane, 2003). The reader could ask whether those removed bandits are the social capital so much craved for, and then who are those social controls in the eyes of our brave academicians, the mafia chieftains?

So, gangsters should not be executed, but they should not even be jailed. Then, what is the solution? The mentioned authors give no direct solution, except some confuse gibberish on local educative measures. Experience has shown that such attempts have been absolutely inefficient. Then, buy yourself a gun and try to play the hero? God forbid, not, you may hurt the gangster, and this would violate his individual rights (only foetuses and old or sick persons have no rights to live and may be killed). In the old days of the Soviet Union, some forty years ago, they told a joke on a radio listener, who asked the radio station of Erevan (the centre of all jokes in the former USSR), what could be done in the case of a nuclear war. The radio station should allegedly have answered that conscientious citizens should wrap themselves up in a white shroud and go on the top of their toes to the cemetery. However, this answer did not satisfy the listener, and he asked again, why would it be necessary to go to the cemetery on the top of his toes. "Dear comrade", radio Erevan answered, "you must go on the top of your toes in order to avoid panic" .Is this the solution the lawyers and academicians of the Internet Society propose us to the problem of criminality?

Chapter Six

Science in the Society of
the Internet Culture

Our century is especially proud of the hitherto unseen development of science and technology. The two become interwoven today. Want (2004) points out that in the simplest appliances we must configure and control dozens of devices, transfer data between them, and try to figure out what went wrong when a failure occurs. Simple tasks require an instruction manual. We need what has been called "proactive computing"systems that anticipate what we need and provide it without having to work on it heavily. New technologies can extend the abilities of computers in combination with the Internet to sense and respond to the physical world. There is a feeling that the simulation of humanity's major ills and problems requires significantly faster supercomputers, revolutionizing the relationship between the processing and the memory systems. For the moment computers ran too slowly, their cost is too high and they use too much power.

At this point there are two traps which contemporary science should avoid, but the Internet Culture falls into both of them: a) equalizing and identifying science with technology, and b) identifying science with a narrow specialty within a domain. Both dangers are very real, precisely as a consequence of the great progress made in technologies, especially in computing, and of the contemporary trend of narrowing down specialties, so as to reduce the need for reading too much in foreign domains without immediate applications in one's chosen specialty. The great scientific protagonists of the XXth century, like Albert Einstein, Werner Heisenberg, Niels Bohr, as also the "discoverers" of the DNA, James Watson and Francis Crick, have repeatedly declared that their research is not reducible to mere technology, but guided by a philosophy of perceiving the fundamental scientific problems. Henri Poincaré and Federigo Enriques insisted on the risks taken by the adherents to a single narrow specialty to shut themselves up in their laboratories and renounce the interdisciplinary dialogue and a broad philosophical vision. Science is not identical with technology. The former is linked to philosophy, values, ethics and a conception on the world, while the latter aims at designing and performing practical methods of execution, guided by science. Modern technology, if recklessly used, may even destroy scientific achievements. There is the wellknown issue of the endangered date stored on disks, today the main and sometimes only storage medium. In time, the disks get damaged, the data are destroyed. Another face of the problem is that those disks containing the research of generations, will after a certain time, be no more suited for being read by the ever new processing technologies, chiefly designed for constraining computer owners to renew all their appliances. The relationship between science and technology also appears as the relationship between fundamental and applied science, in domains with immediate possibilities of socially useful applications, but also in the more distant domains of fundamentals like astronomy, in which the increase in knowledge is our sole reward.

This situation should allow for fundamental science to emerge untainted by material interests. However, the problem is that today pure science has all the drawbacks of the culture in which it appears. Time was, the main work of astronomers was to discover new galaxies, stars, energies, black holes, etc. Now they are going for the jackpot, the theory of everything, and the best candidate is the theory of the Big Bang and the following expansion of the Universe. Both phenomena have been discussed by Hubble, Fesenkov, Hawking for some 75 years, as a phenomenon following the explosion of the matter in the Universe, which had been in a state of supercondensation. Today, Lineweaver and Davis (2005) claim that the scientific community has misunderstood the whole literature on the subject. It is not the matter that exploded, but the whole space. It should ensue that the galaxies are not receding, moving away, the space between us and the galaxies is expanding. No further dimensions of space are necessary, as the modern string theory postulates, because Einstein has said that the space can expand, shrink and curve without being embedded in a higher dimensional space. In the Middle Ages the supreme argument had been the saying, *Aristoteles dixit*, now they are referring to Einstein forgetting the words of the Ecclesiastes, *Nullus novi sub sole* (Nothing new under the sun), at least in the method of argumentation.

In this respect it is of interest how contradictory information is handled.It is well known that the Universe does not expand at a single speed, some galaxies, like the Andromeda move in a contrary direction, towards us and not away from us. Former scientists would have put forward their theory as a hypothesis only, and entrusted future observations with the task to explain and to overcome the facts that do not fit into the model. However, precaution and modesty are not the characteristics of modern science. The Andromeda phenomenon is discarded as a *local movement*, the fact that the Universe does not expand at a single speed is not explained at all, and it is peremptorily declared that the Universe will expand forever (Lineweaver and Davis, 2005). Since there has ben a status before the (unexplained) Big Bang, such apodictic affirmations are not scientific in the classical understanding of the concept, and neither is the exaggerated self-confidence in scientists' claims unsupported by solid scientifically proven facts. This astronomic episode is the epitomé of science in the culture of the Internet Our intention is not to discredit present scientific progress, but to show the negative influence of contemporary culture on the research itself and on the presentation of the results. Scientific conquests are made despite such destructive influence, and this in itself is a worthy phenomenon.

Outstanding work has been done in what has been called nanotechnology, which works with parts of the size of a molecule, i.e. of a billionth of a meter. In 2001 this industry got a \$422-million research budget for better knowing a world which is a weird borderland between the macroworld and the realm of individual atoms and molecules, where quantum mechanics rules. The nanodomain defines the smallest natural structures, you cannot find things any smaller. These structures may boast superior electrical, chemical, mechanical or optical properties, therefore fantasies of future nanomachines, nanorobots, etc., and real attempts at a new nanotechnology are appearing. As with other aspects of sientific sudies nowadays, nanotechnology is "long on vision and short on specifics" (*Scientific American*, September 2001).

Stokes (1997) considers that nowadays science has overcome what he labeled the bi-dimensionality of basic and applied science, i.e. the dualty between the need to understand basic mechanisms and processes vs. the need to know and to resolve practical problems. Basically, there is the necesssity to combine fundamental and applied research in every domain of science, from physics, metallurgy, synthetic materials to biological research in medical sciences, pharmaceutics, medical and psychological treatments. The results of the combined basic and applied research appeared in biotechnology, nanotechnology, superconductors, electronic communication equipment, and also in sophisticated weaponry. Breckler (2004) points out that even in psychology, in order to be efficient in the area of drug abuse, in their prevention and eradication, psychological therapy must understand the etiology of drug abuse, the effects of media portrayals of violence, the cognitive and emotional underpinnings of mental health, etc.There is hardly any practical advancement without new knowledge in the fundamentals of the processes. Such direction of development is also economically motivated. Only (the secretly kept) advancement of basic research can prevent competitors from introducing new truely enhanced products on the market. This, however, means that not every theoretical advancement is made immediately public, some are indefinitely withheld by critiques, which later appear to have been false or referring to a wrongly declared lack of public interest.

In the course of history discoveries and inventions have been thwarted in two ways: a) society was not ready for the new invention, neither in the general level of knowledge and culture, nor in the building of a technological basis capable of absorbing and using it. Examples are the flying machines of Leonardo da Vinci in the XVth century, and that of the Russian captain Mozhaiski in 1878.In both cases eye witnesses attested to have seen the "machines" flying a certain distance and then safely landing. However, the Russian society of the XIXth century was culturally not ready to finance, absorb and use this invention, and neither was the Western society of the XVth century. b) All material and scientific premisses existed but interested groups were opposing the new invention for fear of competition to their own product, or out of disdain vis-à-vis the inventor. Sometimes these groups used to "expropriate" the invention, using it without giving any recognition to the inventors. Many of the latter were driven into despair and took their own lives. So did the French Belier, who had discovered a new kind of anaesthesia, John Fitch, the American inventor of the steam boat, who jumped into the Delaware river, where the steamboat invented by him drove by, and many others. In 1931 Ettore Cattaneo successfully tested the first glider plane in the presence of the German aviation expert, general Udet, who congratulated him for the success. However, the backward government of Mussolini was not willing to give the inventor the due recognition and financial support. Half-forgotten, recognition was given to him only more then seventy years later – post-mortem. In the meantime, Udet took care that the Germans largely knew about the invention, and they used it in World War II, at the invasion of Belgium and Crete. Nobody has ever spoken of Cattaneo.

Society has tried to defend itself against such practices by the system of patenting.There are several problems wih it, starting with a cumbersome reviewing process, for which there is never enough time and qualified personnel, and secondly, the exaggerated claims of *intellectual property*.This roadblock to the advancement of science may be exemplified with the patent emitted in 1999 by Amyon.com. for the *one click method* in making on-line purchases. At that time this very procedure had been widely known and used, but it had not been patented, being obvious and generally known. In the US it is very difficult to challenge such inept patents in court, because the law requires a jury trial, and technological and legal intrications make it very difficult to reach an in-deepth understanding of the matter. Therefore, instead of a freely and ethically advancing science, in the Internet Society we have got a process dominated by big business and which must cut its way through armies of embittered lawyers.

The former chief technologist of Microsoft, Myhrvold has founded a firm named *Intellectual Ventures* which gathers, rents and sells ideas. They hired a group of scientists, who each month participate in "invention sessions" where scientific problems are dicussed. Lawyers transcribe the discussions, and follow up on the most promising ideas with patent applications, in the name of the firm, which using this method has already made millions (*Newsweek,* November 22, 2004). For the individual discoverer and inventor the patent system of the contemporary society brought no relief.

Everybody working in science must take as a point of depart the ideas of the *Zeitgeist,* the existing knowledge and technology. Inventors who devance them too much have the fate of Da Vinci's or Mozhaiski's flying machines. However, the moment an inventor seeks a patent based on existing knowledge, he/she is stonewalled by patents of intellectual property, issued to firms which claim a right on casually and utopically expressed ideas without any experimented technological coverage. We shall see later on that the scientific fairy tale of the future is an inseparable parasitic component of the scientific presentation in the Internet Culture. Sometimes the inventors will be offered a sum of money in exchange for their rights, sometimes even this would not happen, the invention would simply be stolen and then used or dumped and get lost, since the patent is preventing the inventor from further pursuing the matter. The inventors may peacefully submit to their fates like did Cattaneo, or rebel against it and finish the way Fitch did. To these practices resist only inventors who have the backing of some powerful company or university.

What has been said is indicating that behind a publicity façade of stormy progress the Internet Society is actually derailig the free and normal scientific development that could and should be reached with the existing technology and level of knowledge. Although there is no formal censorship in this society, the Internet Culture performs a very strict one through its priorities tightly linked to profitability and to its political values. Absolute novelties are not profitable because they require research efforts during long years, the results are uncertain, and usually there is a need for correcting them and to include the research of other teams. Therefore absolute novelties are avoided, and replaced by simply changing, often not even improving, existing products or procedures. The Windows programme 3.1 (1985-1992) for computers was a great invention, but the last in its domain. All subsequent versions, like Windows 1995, 1998, 2000 and so on, are worse, geared merely to Internet browsing, and they cause problems, irascibility and loss of time, if users want to write a text of some length. This also happens even if users additionally acquired the Microsoft Word programme, an acquisition that had not been previously necessary. The point is that the older and better versions of Windows are simply no more available and you are obliged to buy the new trash.

In computer work such a situation is very unpleasant and makes users angry, but if this happens with the drugs you need for treatment, many poeople consider it to be morally a crime. In its passionate craving to make profits higher, the pharmaceutical industry is under pressure to put new products on the market. In their greater part these products are new, but not better than the older ones. On the contrary, they come with a host of negative side effects, because their novelty is frequently in supplanting the natural components of the existing products by chemically synthetized materials. There is also a certain connivance with the authorities responsible for the legal surveillance. The authorities (the law) should ask for a proof that the new drug is better than the ones existing on the market, and not only whether it is more adequate than is a placebo pill of sugar. There would be even so an advantage in putting on the market diversified drugs, because patients respond better to some drugs than to others. Unfortunately, this aspect is not even tested, lest it raises research costs. The pharmaceutical industry justify the very high prices of drugs by the expenses necessary for their research and development. This again is not true. The industry pays less than half the sum for research it pays for promotion, and their profits are higher than in the oil industry. In 2002 the main pharmaceutical enterpises made a profit of $40 billions (Remuzzi, 2004). The producers' aim is to put on the market drugs covered by a patent, because the older pharmaca are not covered any more, and their prices go down. The highest prices costumers pay in the US, therefore there is a flourishing business of personal importation from Canada, where pharmaca prices are reasonably low (*Fortune,* March 8, 2004). This is another proof that in the US drug prices are driven high by shareholder greed, and not by the necessity to compensate for research and development expenses, which are the same for the drugs sold in Canada.

The pharmaceutical industry has lost its sense of vocation and has become a machine to turn out money, says Remuzzi (2004), director of the Mario Negri pharmacological research institute. What happens is that members of the review boards and influential medical personnel are linked by economic interests to the industry and they are exposed to advertisements and pressure, what endangers independent objective research. Even studies presented as independent are becoming suspect. The result of this policy may be seen in the fact that in this age of "stormy progress in science" no research is done for the treatment of rare diseases like pigmental xeroderma, which strikes one person in 250,000. The person is unable to bear exposure to light, and has all the time to stay in a darkened room. They are called *the children of the moon.* Such patients do not exist for the pharmaceutical industry, because they would have to invest between 500-800 million Euros during 10-15 years. The state of the Internet Society finds such a situation normal, and driven by the individualistic values of *each one has to care for him/herself,* does not even recognize to such people the status of invalidity.

Asks Leaf (2004), " Why have we made so little progress in the war on cancer?" He adds that more Americans will die of cancer in the next 14 months than have perished in every war the nation has ever fought. The proportion of cancer death is the same as in 1970 *and* in 1950.What improvement in the figures has been obtained is due to behavioral change like quitting smoking. There is a dysfunctional medical culture, which furthers this situation. Medical research goes after the tiniest improvement in treatments, but not after a breaktrough. The search for knowledge has become an end in itself rather than the means to an end. In addition, the medical research has become increasingly narrow, so much that the physician-scientists who want to think systematically about cancer as a whole, often cannot get funding. Researchers are fixed on a mouse model of cancer, because apart from the fact that no other model has been presented, the FDA drug approving authority recognizes this model as the gold standard for predicting the utility of drugs. This happens because it is a measurable goal, one can measure the tumor shrinking. However, shrinking of tumors is a lousy predictor for assessing the progress of the canceer disease. Tumor regression is not likely to improve the patient's chances of survival, if the whole cancer is not eradicated. Pharmaceutical companies don't concentrate on solving the problem of cancer metastasis (spread), which is the real killer, but on devising the more convenient drugs that shrink tumors. This is why it is hard to assess spectacular positive effects.

Cancer is not the only domain in which the absence of correctly targeted research leaves us perplex. Most irating is common negligence, which in the USA, judging after a 1999 report of the National Academy of Scienes Institute of Medicine, causes between 44,000 and 98,000 death cases each year, striking down more people than motor vehicle accidents or breast cancer (*Scientific American*, May 2000, p.18). Besides, apart from such well known cases like a doctor in Florida amputating the wrong leg to a diabetic patient, there are the unfortunately common cases of misdiagnoses, because of lack of time, feeding computers with wrong data, dispensation of the wrong drug, because it had been scribbled illisibly on the presciption. When the matter has been brought forward in a report to the President, the medical community immediately complained of too thin evidence, but nothing has been done to organize a number of serious verifications according to all scientific requirements. For one, American hospitals are understaffed, and frequently doctors have no time for lengthy examinations of the findings. On the other hand, paradoxically, the medical staff is interested in prolonging the situation, that relieves them from responsibility, and they have not to renounce the pursuit of private interests, research or amusements, so they may fel good without a time and energy-consuming attitude of concentration on the patient's problems. In the present ambivalent circumstances it is often impossible to determine (especially when the physician has no interest to do it), whether the patient died from an error or from his/her disease (*Scientific American, ibid.*).

All this does not mean that the larger society does not intervene in medical scientific research. The globalized Internet Society imposes its credo and values on the content of research, on its methods and on the communication and the spread of its results. There is an exaggerated emphasis on sex, on the search for the miraculous pill, combatting effort and fatigue, and on the methods of diagnosis, while treatment is neglected. Control and surveillance methods leading to early (and frequently faulty and phoney) diagnoses enhance the doctor's feeling of power and ego-aggrandizement vis-à-vis the patient. They also link up to computerization, and are therefore a continuation of the already discussed Big Brother surveillance exercized in this culture. In a society in which the treatment of diseases has not been essentially improved, the very advanced methods of diagnosing are a wheel turning in a void, and numerous patients shun the physicians' insistent offers for medical controls, lest they would be registered, sometimes with some exaggeratedly heavy diagnoses, in the computers of the health system, deprived of the rights linked to their former status, while a possible or incipient affliction would go untreated.

Basic research is propelled with full steam – but not on cancer, TBC, etc. The priority is on the neurophysiological basis of animal and human sex life. In her much publicized book, *Why we love* , Helen Fischer (2004) points out that in animals and humans romantic love is based on dopamine accumulation and addiction. Like the alcoholic who feels compelled to drink, she writes, the impassionate lover cries that he will die without his beloved. It is a drive (not a feeling, according to Fischer) so powerful that it can override other drives, such as hunger and thirst, and render the most dignified person a fool. What Fischer neglects is the insight, that while one of the ultimate physiological bases of love may be the accumulation of dopamine, love is a *psychological feeling*, irreducible to its neurochemical basis. This was a frequently made mistake made in the XVIIIth century by Diderot, Lamettrie, etc. in their enthusiastic rush for developing positive science. Today it proves a double ignorance : the ignorance of all progress psychology has made in the 200 years since the XVIIIth century Encyclopedists, and also the ignorance of the latter's work, despised, because it is *old trash* .

The obsession with sex breeds a kin one for a young attractive look. Research (!) has shown that more attractive people get better jobs and salaries and more respect from peers (*Newsweek,* May 17, 2004). Indeed in this domain plenty of research is done, and products like collagen injections, Rostylane and Botox are not only new, but also substantially better than older products. True, there is an immense market for them, because the culture of this society pushes ever more younger women to search for rejuvenation. While last year half of Americans who underwent minimally invasive procedures were between 35 and 50 years old, almost 20 per cent were between 19 and 34.   Such a situation entails real dangers, because all these treatments are short-lived, and then comes the knife, which leaves the face in a more ravaged state after a not too long time span.

The continual intense promotional activity has brought a yearning for a miraculous pill as a solution for every problem. Instead of searching for a better organization of work shifts, in order to alleviate industrial fatigue, especially in the night shifts, the way it had been done in the '1960s, the unanimous cry is now for the *smart pill* . The challenge for science is not a better organization of work that would start the night shift at 2 o'clock in the morning and make possible the worker's night sleep until then (Mayer and Herwig, 1961), but to transform the circadian rhythm, humans biological clock, via a pill which would cheat the body's natural need for sleep, keeping the workers alert at 3 a.m. as they are during the day.Scientists have already discovered the locus of the body's master clock in the suprachiasmatic nucleus and the genes within this nucleus. They regulate the body rhythms and flood the body with melatonin, a sleep-inducing hormone. The US pharmaceutical firm Teneka is already testing a drug that targets the brain melatonin receptors. Other firms work at cheating the cells in the eye, which respond to day light and trigger the biological clock (*Newsweek,* October 18, 2004). What all this research neglects is the insight that the body is a system built through evolution, and you cannot intervene into parts of it without destroying the total altogether. You can chemically pepper up a tired man for several hours or even days, but afterwards he may collapse. To feel tired is a biological symptom, informing of the attrition of the organism as a whole, and it will take its toll with head ache, a feeling of exhaustion and depression. For the science of the Internet Culture sleep is an illness that should be treated. It is not. Although for some hours sleep interrupts work, or *horribile dictu*, amusement, rest and sleep are inevitable for a healthy replenishment of energy.

The science of this society rests on two dangerous theses : a) drugs are an integral part of modern people's life, and b) the biotechnological manipulation of humans is capable of changing and improving human nature. Resnik (1990) points out that the gap opened by modern culture between media-nourished expectations of gratifications, and the experience which fails to to match them is filled by drugs. Threrefore drugs (I shall understand here psychedelics and pharmaca), become an integral part of the way of life, in which glamour, looking good and partying are the fundamental mental activities occupying people's mind. This way of life has a scaring reverse in the premature death of beautiful youngsters, and they are killed not by merciless diseases, but by voluntarily taken drugs, overdoses of psychedelics *and* harmlesly looking pharmaca or by starvation against imagined obesity.In a state of semi-starvation people close down physically, mentally and spiritually, as had been evinced by the classical Minnesota Starvation Study of 1944-45.The effects included depression, dizziness, slowed heart rate and the risk of sudden death. The same results are brought upon by the low carbohydrate diets, discovered long ago in Wiliam Banting's *Letter on Corpulence* (1863) and revived by Atkins in the '1970s. It is known today that low-carb diets promote rapid short-term weight   loss. The quick effects make the diet popular, but the results are difficult to maintain, even if trying to live on a low glycemic load, a measure of how much carbohydrate food delivers in a serving. In order to maintain the weight loss, people exaggerate the food interdictions, which action directly leads them to the already mentioned *starving diets.* It has also to be mentioned that the original Atkins diet of eating in parallel unlimited amounts of beef, sausage, butter endangers cardiac health. Therefore weight-loss diets are largely ineffectual in the long range. The aggressive advertising wrapped in a scientific language and using authoritative names from the world of science is made out of pure commercial reasons and reflects the Internet Culture.

Of course, the problem of endangering health by taking unnecessary and frequently noxious pharmaca is not only linked to the fashion of fighting obesity. We are referring to many of the new pharmaca only produced for the sake of competitive novelty, without leading to an improved functioning. It appears in most instances, that the existing pills or syrups, beverages sometimes in every day use are as good, if not better than the much more expensive pharmaca novelties having uncertain collateral risks. Hall (2003) tells the story of the drug modafinil produced by the firm Cephalon and approved in 1998 for the treament of narcolepsy. Advertisements produced a *barrage* on healthy people and doctors. Consequently, there has been a big demand for prescriptions of modafinil as a cognitive enhancer. This is one of the cravings of our Internet Culture, allowing people to sleep less, to stay up longer, work harder and play more. Research done at Walter Reed's Sleep Center has shown that the drug had no better effect than caffeine, i.e. simple coffee, true, neither was it worse. Therefore,

Caldwell, a scientist working for the army, proudly declared, that "ultimately there will be a place for modafinil" (Hall, ibid.).It should be well understood that it is here spoken of pharmaca consumers, who are otherwise healthy people. They are getting drug-addicted while they are using modern science in order to improve their functioning. In this respect we may mention the new scientific finding, according to which a long-standing dementia treatment improves cognitive functioning of normal people. Even were such research based on correct assessment methods, nobody has shown longitudinal research data, which could ascertain the absence of unwanted collateral damage in the long run. Until such research is performed, a drug should not be approved, and neither should the research be widely publicized. Unfortunately both events are occurring, and the wildest conjectures are spread as if they were solidly proven truth. Thus an Australian study contended that Transcranial Magnetic Stimulation might be used to unleash nascent savant skills by temporarily disabling one brain hemisphere (*Scientific American*, September 2003). So: give them the medical treatment for idiots, disable one half of the brain and you will have crated the new scientists of the Internet Culture. Seems a bit far fetched, to say the least. Later in this chapter we shall try to discover how and why such "scientific " research is done. For the moment, let us see what is on the scientific agenda of this society, and what is not.

Being a constitutive part of society's culture, the values and priorities of the globalized Internet Culture, power, individual gratification and sex, will be also the determining factors of its scientific agenda. These are the forces that put in motion the brains of contemporary scientists, loose the strings of society's grant purse, and bring the highest rewards and awards. During an entire century the mainstream scientific theory has recognized Freud's merits in deepening our understanding on the psychology of the unconscious and on its expressional phenomena. At the same time it has severely criticized his pansexual aberrations, the lack of referral to a neurophysiological basis of the phenomena he discussed, and the forced coaxion-interpretations against the patient's will and intentions. And then, E. R. Kendall, 2000 Nobel laureate in psychology-medicine, states that, "psychoanalysis is still the most coherent and intellectually satisfying view of the mind" (*Scientific American*, May 24, 2004). This statement proves that the science of the Internet Culture is not built on the devoted, painstaking accumulation of facts and the verification of hypotheses throughout years of toil, but on gratificational phantasies, the love of sex and power. It does even seem that the egregious Nobel Prize laureate has not read the original pertinent material, including the writings of Freud. How could he accept that *all* dreams express mostly repressed wishes, that if seeing a house or a cupboard in his dream, he wants to have intercourse with a woman, especially with his mother, that if dreaming he is travelling by train, he masturbates or want to rub his penis? All these are there in the two volumes of Freud's (1901/1954) *Intrpretations of Dreams,* but you must read them, if you want to make peremptory statements and not judge on the basis of information which may appear in the *Rider's Digest.* Here is one of the severest faults of science in the Internet

Culture: Older research is thrown over board, and if at all quoted, it is on the basis of slovenly compiled partisan abstracts.

It is true that every historical period has its *Zeitgeist*, its preferred topics. However, the greatness of a period is measured in the diversity of the researched domains. Therefore the Renaissance appears as populated by giants, and compared to it we are dwarfs. Many of our scientists simply revisit existing research, adding useless information on sex and the like. In a lengthy experimental study, M. Bailey from Northwestern University documented that gay subjects had an erectile response to pictures of nude men, while heterosexual men reacted to nude pictures of women (*APA Monitor*, April 2003, p.51). Did such a banality known to everybody justify the energy, time and funding that goes with a research? Is there any novelty in its results? Not more than in the renowned case recorded in the XVIth century when a printer from Leipzig by name Balhorn, made a great fuss about a *new* school reader he published, in which the only novelty was an egg depicted under the hindside of a cock. For the sake of a more recent example, the very frequent renewed analyses of the mutiny on the HMS *The Bounty* in the XVIIIthe century may be mentioned. As widely known, the ship had anchored in the islands of the South Sea, where the crew members had the occasion to mate with native women. As they were ordered to sail off, they mutined. These days a "deeper account" of the events is offered by Shermer, author and publisher, in which he links the mutiny events to the oxytocin secretion during sex, a phenomenon newly (!) discovered by Uvnäs-Moberg. It induces a couple to stay together for a longer time. This staying together should have been impeded by the order to sail off.Shermer declared that "the ultimate reason of the mutiny was evolutionary adaptive emotions expressed nonadaptively with irreversible consequences" (*Scientific American*, February 2004). In fact the causes of the mutiny are well known, and they are social and psychological, including a tyrant cruel captain. Now in the new high-tech era we are told that it is a matter of biochemistrry. We may wonder why not search for the sex-bound enzyme, which sparked off the French or the Bolchevik revolution.

Even if hard work is done in science, it is too narrowly conceived, reflecting the narrow specialization and knowledge of the scientific personnel. A good example is the research on cancer, the war, which in Leaf's (2004) words we are going to loose. He reminds that in the last years 150,855 studies on experimentation with mice cancer have been published, but very few have led to human treatments, mainly because the reaction of a mouse is different from the reaction of a human being. Leaf points out that the search for knowledge, any knowledge, has today become an end in itself, rather than the means to an end, yet the research stays increasingly narrow. This is so because of a wrong funding policy rewarding a narrow perspective.

For the same reason fundamental research is less and less done in industrial and economic organizations. In the past decades engineers at AT&T's Bell Labs invented the transistor, the laser, the optical fiber, the touch-tone phone and the fax machine. Xerox' Palo Alto Research Center came up with the computer mouse and the basis of today's computer operating systems. These innovations made lots of money, but typically not for the companies that spawned them or for their shareholders (Sennott, 2004). At such horror the ax of downsizing struck the zealous researchers, and the golden age of industrial research was over everywhere, except, partly at Microsoft.

The narrow focus of the scientists' specialty and research promotes the values of the Internet Culture, but contradicts the wholesomeness of reality and of the human person, be it a patient or the doctor and researcher himself/herself. After many years modern medicine again comes to appreciate the mind-body linkage, but gives it a twist in the sense of narrowing down the medical specialties, in order to reduce responsibilities. Since it can be proved that the mind is capable of influencing biological processes, let psychologists and alternative medicine deal with it. It is not the doctors' job, and not their responsibility, not even the old doctor-patient relationship. In the past, the necessity of such a relationship semed self-evident, and healing was inconceivable without it. More than half a century ago the psychoanalyst M. Balint and others have pointed out that the patient needs a dose of the strongest drug of all, the doctor, the reviving of the old relationship known for centuries (*Newsweek*, October 4, 2004). Like with many other scientific problems having social and health impact, for the time being, this battle seems lost. The physicians and the scientific workers of the Internet Society, addicted to their computers, have no desire to let themselves be burdened with all kind of problems, which disturb their marvellous duo with their computer, in which they enter all kind of symptoms and diagnoses. This gives them a feeling of control and superiority over the patient. The moment the doctor entered a diagnosis into his/her computer and made a prescription (or refused to make it on Medicare budget grounds), the doctor considers that the case is closed.

The physicians of the Internet Culture see as their duty to submit the patients to all kind of control procedures, wanted or not wanted by them. Then they send them to all kind of specialists, to prescribe a medication, allowed by Medicare authorities or recommended by a pharmaceutical firm, but they do not to speak with the patient about his/her illness related anxieties. They recognize that there may be a need that should be cared for, but they refuse to do it, lest they got emotionally involved. They think, the talking should be done by *specialists*, psychologists who are paid for it. The problem has become especially acute in terminal illnesses, where the patients cannot be "deinstitutionalized", sent home, in proper English, to be cared for by their families or by persons specialized in preparing people to die. Therefore within the American Psychological Association a Working Group on Assisted Suicide (?!) and End-of-Life Decisions has been formed. In 2000 they presented a report with numerous recommendations (*APA Monitor on Psychology*, November 2004). Two things are bluntly striking in what has been published from this report. First, they are using a rude language, lacking any trace of human compassion. Second, as already seen in this society, the proper treatment issues are eschewed, and the center of stage is occupied by problems of diagnosis and control. While until recently we used to speak of coping with fatal or terminal illnesses, the psychologists of the new generation speak of *the end of life and the quality of the death experience*, for both patients and their families (*ibid*. p. 53). Psychologists would explain to all conerned the expected level of psychological deterioration, and would prepare the family for the difficult decisions, such as whether to withhold expensive treatment (although it could extend life) in patients with a poor quality of life. The patient is not asked in this matter. The same recommendations regarding family decisions are made if the patient is a child caught by a terminal illness. For a family which cares for their loved one fallen terminally ill, and for the concerned people themselves, who crave for a bit of hope even in the hereafter, such blunt, insensitive and heinous words are a slap in the face.

Some of the cases require the communication of medical knowledge, but even then it is not the physician treating the case, who is talking with the patients and their families. To this purpose a separate narrow specialty has been created, the bioethicist, who "forthrightly and with courage", and today this jargon means bluntly and in a detached manner "explores the information and the ethical issues surrounding difficult, often life-threatening decisions" (*ibid*. p.56). These issues concern ethics, don't they, and not human compassion. Here appears another system failure of the Internet Society in the outsourcing (the concept is known from the economy) of medical care too. The patient is whirled around from one doctor to another, while the human aspects are left to personnel, who does not have medical knowledge, and is merely paid to give a simulacrum of human warmth. We are conscious, we do have mental states, thoughts, experiences, feelings (Harnard, 2001). Unfortunately, this is a cry in the wilderdnis. The Internet Culture holds a reductionist view on science similar to the mechanist materialism of the XVIIIth century with La Mettrie's *L'homme machine* (1748). Its science does not conceive nature as a system with hierarchic layers of a different quiddity. The Marxists correctly said that there are qualitatively different forms of movement in matter, and each domain belongs to a different science. Therefore the psychological phenomenon is irreducible to biochemistry or to physiology. The researcher who has painstakingly searched the biochemistry of sexual arousal has not found or explained love, has not satisfactorily explained the mutiny of the Bounty, the self-sacrifice of a father or a mother for their children, or the self-sacrifice of a soldier for his comrades or his fatherland. Nor has a map of genes or a concoction of enzymes been able to satifactorily explain, whence prevent, the events of the Stanford Prison Experiment (Haney, Banks and Zimbardo, 1973) or of the Obedience Experiment of Milgram (1965). In these experimental situations students formerly behaving considerately towards their colleagues, turned out performing brutal, hateful actions vis-à-vis them, if they perceived the latter being at their mercy. They interpreted in this sense the orders given to them. Such things happened not only in university experiments and not only in the past, it happens right now in our days in the Abu Ghraib prison in Baghdad vis-à-vis real prisoners.

The reductionist stance in science induced by the Internet Culture is false. Each science conerns a domain existing in its own rights and cannot supplant the other domains. It may introduce some clarifications, but it cannot solve the problems of the more complex and therefore hierarchically higher energy structures. Biochemistry can contribute to the understanding of some physiological processes (which exist in their own right), and the latter can contribute to a better understanding of the higher order psychological processes, but again, without supplanting them.

At this point some readers may object saying that the moment we succeed in changing the manifestations or the basic underlying biochemical process of a disease, we have altered the physiological or psychological processes. Led by such theories researchers have begun to uncover brain chemistry that most addictions have in commmon. Some drugs, like topiramate, have ben found to work for several types of addictions at the same time: alcohol, obesity, smoking. Similar results should have been obtained with prozac in states of depression (*Newsweek*, December 6, 2004). It is clear that in a hierarchical system the basic components (here the biochemial ones) do influence the superior structures and functions, but only as far as biochemical deregulations hinder the normal processes in the superior structures. When it could be established that in many situations of craving an abundance of the neurotransmitter glutamate has an important role, medication reducing it inhibited the craving. *However,* craving is a psychological behavior. It may include or not a genetic *predisposition,* it certainly includes certain biochemical phenomena, but it is triggered and maintained by psychological factors. Already for one hundred years somatopsychology (Cf. Uexküll, 1964) has again and again demonstrated, that if a pharmaceutical intervention interrupts one of the links of the process chain (like the glutamate-bound transmission in the psychological manifestation of craving), the basically psychological phenomenon finds another way of expression, weird as it may be. Our behavior is based on genetic and biochemical premises, but it is neither genetic, as we nowadays frequently hear, nor is it biochemical. A particular genetic structure is favoring behaviors of a certain type, but humans are conscious social beings and the ultimate factors which cause behaviors are rooted in the human psychological structure which is including consciousness. It also has to be added that psychology is a theoretical science with practial applications and not only a collection of practical procedures, whereas the task of the theory would be to constitute an entitlement for dispatching logo- or behavioral therapy according to the indications learned from some guru. More and more this sems to be the case in the Internet Culture. It is a second aspect of the scientific reductionism practiced in this culture, the redution of a theoretical science to a collection of applicational techniques, the theoretical basis of which is neglected and forgotten.

To complete the picture of reductionism in the Internet Culture, we must add a third form of it in which inferior evolutionary biological structures are assimilated with the highest ones, a reduction of inferior to superior. There had been an older discussion whether animals have conscience like humans.   Animal psychologists, like Köhler, and even Pavlov, the physiologist who abhorred animal psychology, have agreed that superior animals are capable of a rudimental intelligent behavior, but they do not have the characteristics of human conscience, which includes self-reflection, conceptual thought and language *in the absence of the situational setting*. Nor have animals higher moral concepts and feelings. Consequently, conscience is a human evolutionary characteristic. Such a discussion bewilders the scientist of the Internet Culture, accustomed to the absence of limits and limitations. They feel so attracted to predators, so close to them, that it is a must that animals have a conscience, a culture (?!) and values. The so-called "mirror test" is declared by some to deliver the proof for ths contention. In 1970 G. Gallup Jr. painted a mark on a chimpanzee's face, while it slept, and then put the awakened animal in front of a mirror. The chimpanzee touched the mark on its face. The majority of scientists considered the gesture as a situational reaction to a perception, and the story was forgotten, until the glorious days of the Internet Culture, when the mirror test was again used with dolphins, elephants parrots. Theories on the evolution of self-awareness were emitted, but none has been proved. Logically, there should have been an experiment verifying wether the animal is capable of remembering the mark in the absence of the mirror image, but nobody has tried to do it. Apparently nowadays scientists do not trust their own evolutionary jingles. The mirror test with the mark on the face reveals no self-awareness in animals, but a situational reaction to the perception of a change in the memorized image of the environment, the image of a (fellow) chimpanzee.

Self-awareness is not the only human characteristic bestowed on animals by the science of today. Goodall (2005) even speaks of a religious behavior in chimpanzés. She has allegedly witnessed it when the monkeys saw enchanting and frightening natural phenomena like waterfalls. Their hair stood up, and they started a rhythmical dance. Goodall sees in this behavior fear, awe, which she, a most politically correct figure, interpretes as the origin of religion. Therefore she thinks that those animals manifested a religious behavior. Going by this logic the maximal cowardice should be the summit of a religious experience, an utterly false idea. The death-defying courage of saints has marvelled people for hundreds of years. The *error fundamentalis* of Goodall lies in the fact that she identifies the fundamental inner cognitive and emotional religious experience wirth an accidental behavior of fear, which may appear, but to which the religious experience is not necessarily linked.

The same errors are made with values. Hechter (1993) cites natural selection as one of the sources of value genesis and explicitly applies the concept to animals as well, based on their stable orientations. Out of ignorance, or again, out of his orientation to reductionism, he is omitting the essential difference between instincts proper to animals and the conscious orientations of humans. Juan Toro, a neurologist from Barcelona, went one step further, claiming that animals differentiated between human languages in an experiment, where 64 rats could distinguish between Netherlands and Japonese (*Corriere della Sera*, 10 January 2005). Formulated this way, the conclusion of the experiment is false. It had been demonstrated one hundred years ago in Pavlov's laboratory that animals are capable of differentiating between sound complexes and of elaborating various conditional reflexes to them. This does not mean that those rats understand

Japanese or have the same linguistic abilities humans have. They differentiate between sounds of various qualities, say high pitched or in a low frequency, but they do not understand the conveyed sense, as humans do, and they usually cannot reproduce the sounds of a language uttering, which is an essential human activity. Even a parrot's utterings are situationally conditioned sound complexes, and do not constitute a conscious use of language.

Having clarified the reductionism of science in the Internet Society, let us turn to the other scientific procedures in use. Time was, scientific publications had to put forward well established, verified and replicated facts only. Not any more. Goodstein (1996) points out that in the past, science was only bounded by the limits of imagination and the scientist's creativity. Now it is primarily limited by the available amounts of research funds. What has previously been a purely intellectual competition, has now become a fight for scarce resources, with an undesirable effect on ethical behavior. Even the institution of peer review is in danger. Journal editors send manuscripts submitted to them for publication to referees, who remain anonymous to the authors. Funding agencies do the same with research projects. According to scientific and ethical rules, those referees should judge and report scientific merits or faults, but given the competitive situation, more and more misconducts appear, senseless verbal aggression, only aiming at causing psychological harm. For such misconduct the referee is never called to account. Robert Sternberg (2003), the former president of the American Psychological Association, tells the story of such a hostile reviewer, who suggested Sternberg "should find some other line of work more consistent with his limited level of mental abilities". I don't know of which article of Sternberg's it was spoken, but whichever it was, the referee (he should have had scientific credentials if the article was sent to him) allowed himself a despicable expressional mode, which civilized science cannot tolerate. This reviewer is the example of the degeneration of science in the present time, of the all-encompassing violence spreading in the Internet Culture. In parallel, scientific misconduct becomes all too common. The National Science Foundation (cf. Goodstein, *ibid*.p.34) defines it as fabrication, falsification, plagiarism, or other practices that seriously deviate from those which are commonly accepted within the scientific community for proposing, conducting and reporting research. Let us add to this list violent *ad hominem* evaluations in lieu of a constructive critique. Of course, there is also the fraud proper, with intent to deceive in research reports and in evaluations. We read scientific (?) papers which describe investigations as they logically should have been performed rather than how they had actually been done. It even occurs that results are in some way knowingly misrepresented.

In his conclusions, Goodstein (1996) himself appears tainted by the Internet Culture, when he declares (page 37) that scientists are not disinterested truth seekers, they are more like players in an intense winner-takes-all competition for scientific prestige, or merchants in a no-holds-barred market place of ideas. Why this indulgence for "common human conduct" by scientists? Joas (2000) has pointed out that modern society sets the origin of values in the individual, and liberals even advocate a complete freedom of values (as accepted external norms, *E.K.*). If the only value you are adhering to in science is a behavior that makes you feel good, the way is open to fraud and violence. Should science not be about truth? If the value source is the individual who feels good, there is no objective truth any more. Barasch (2000) points out that we are living in a media bombardment surfeiting us with prepackaged ghostly icons of consumer culture. Imagination becomes "image". We increasingly live with technology-mediated half-realities. Crary (2001) adds a physiological fundament to this theory, when he points out that the functioning of vision becomes dependent on the complex and contingent makeup of the observer, rendering vision faulty, unreliable and arbitrary. It can no longer claim an essential objectivity or certainty. In other words, what we see is is what we want to see. Former scientists had always added the social correction of practice to the subjective distortion of vision. Not any more. The social is devalued and the individual him/herself stays the sole arbiter of truth. I am not convinced that the deformation of scientific truth in the Internet Culture is merely the result of a not supervised and ill-controlled physiological process on the loose. Referring to Nietzsche, Joas (2000) remarks that the genesis process of ideals in intentionalist images emphasizes the deliberate nature of the deception. Therefore behind the deformation of scientific truth there should be a plain "malicious" intent. For causes that have already been discusseed, in the Internet Society the scientific production of verified facts is poor, and its paucity is covered by falsely presented or interpreted phenomena and a falsely used terminology. The separating line between scientific results and wishful thinking is vanishing, as it also vanishes between science and advertisements. Let us discuss this phenomenon in the very broad research on Alzheimer's disease. It concerned not so much the treatment, as the statistics of symptoms and post-mortem examinations. The problem with these methods is that their conclusions are uncertain in principle, because a non-specific symptom may be caused by another disease, or both diseases may have a common cause undiscovered yet. So, it has been pointed out that the risk factor for heart disease tracks with those for Alzheimer's. Post-mortem examinations revealed amyloid plaques, and they also appear in people with heart disease. Then, scientists added high blood pressure (especially diastolic) and obesity. There is nothing specific in these conclusions, which have been promptly criticized, and all is back to square one. In this age of tremendous scientific development there is no new therapy. In the Edenham Centre in London the latest treatment for Alzheimer's is garden therapy (gardening in plain English). It should not only improve the quality of life for people suffering from Alzheimer's, but also help alleviate the anxiety that comes with dementia (*Newsweek*, January 26, 2004). Of course, this "new" therapy does not cure, nor even does it halt the disease. In turn, we are compensated with elaborate fantasies of what physicians will be able to do some years from now. In the meantime, we are told that the causes of Alzheimer's are probably genetic, the universal excuse for medical incapacity.

Doctors speak of the gene presenilin1 in chromosome 14, indentified in 1995 by Schellenberg, Kostik and Gate. Its mutation (there should be some 50 possibilities of it) should inexorably cause the early onset of the disease (*The Sciences*, July-August, 1999). Then would the steadily progressing knowledge of our genomes lead to the eradication of the disease? Nope. Firstly, all research is oriented towards mapping the genes and not towards curing diseases. Ten years have passed since the discovery of the presenilin1 gene, and there has not been the slightest advance ever since. Either the published results have not been reliable, as it so often happens in recent years, or, after gaining publicity the three researchers were not interested to invest hard work in order to pursue the matter further.

On April 14, 2003 scientists announced that they have finished sequencing the human genome, logging the three billion pairs of DNA nucleotides of a human being. The number of genes in humans has been estimated at between 30,000 and 50,000, a figure higher only by 50% in comparison to the band worm. Evidently, the problem is not in numbers, but in structures and functions. This aspect received a true "Internet Culture twist" and was derailed in the direction of bioengineering, the genetical transformation of plants, and of nuclear transplantation resulting in cloning, a "copying procedure" of human beings. It is happily linked to the domain of sex, it may be linked to feminist politics, negating the family and especially the necessity of a father, and it also gives a delusive feeling of power and of the possiblity to play God. Some venture the occasion to use organs of the clone for transplants. Such diversified possibilities of use make cloning popular in the key strata of modern society, and above all, it make it a very profitable business.

So far the best results with manipulating genetics have been obtained with bioengineered food, although there are problems with it too, mainly following from the fact that we yet do not know the consequences for the user organism in the long run. Therefore many people refuse to buy such products. Nonetheless, cross-breeding was also hitherto largely known, it is also an intervention into genetics, and in principle at least, the results should not be different. The cross-bred produce did not harm people, so neither should do this the bioengineered ones. The trouble is that the scientist of the Internet Culture does not stop after passing a very controversial barrier, he is driven to change things for the sake of change and regardless of consequences, in the hope of making more money and sticking out, becoming famous and powerful. It has been made known, e.g. that human genes have been introduced into apple trees, strawberries and fish (*Corriere della Sera*, 3 October 2004).

Such news may cause people to smile at the insensate jokes they are today doing in the name of science, but at a deeper look, the ultimate aim is not a joke, but a terrible abuse of science. In 2005, WADA, the World Agency of Antidoping in sport, has published a desperate warning given by Dr. Friedmann, director of genetical therapies at the Univ. of San Diego, Calif. He said that in a number of laboratories methods have already been worked out for genetically transforming athletes by inserting into their DNA genes allowing for an increment of their muscular capacity and of their resistance to efforts. Such a manipulation cancels sport, as we know it, transforming it into a biotechnological exercise, a competition between laboratories instead of one between people. At any rate, American and Canadian laboratories have already succeeded in composing two anabolizer steroids, the THG and DMT, which cannot be traced with current check methods for sport doping (*Corriere della Sera*, 13 February 2005).

Today it is impossible to know what consequences the addition or the exchange of genes will have on people. The possibilities are scaring and it is hard to shield the scientists working on such tasks from the reproach of Frankensteinism, the intent or at least the indifference towards creating monsters. Perhaps it is not an intention, but it is a possibility, which they slovenly or knowingly overlook. This reproach sticks with much vigor on cloning.

In his book on "posthuman future", Fukuyama (2002) claims that biotechnological manipulation of human beings may move us into a posthuman stage of history, change human nature and erode the bases of society. Human genetic engineering could adversely affect our mutually interactive social and also political lives. If we would not ban reproductive cloning, Fukuyama says, we shall legitimize far more wide-ranging biotechnological manipulations on human beings, which are posing a threat to human dignity and well-being.

What happened with cloning illustrates well Fukuyama's opinions and fears. All started with the correct and progressive idea to repair damaged organs using cells from a donor with the same biologial construction (family members) in order to avoid rejection by the host organism. This procedure known as therapeutic cloning, aiming at generating, for instance, pancreatic islets to treat diabetes or nerve cells to repair damaged spinal cords is distinct from reproductive cloning, which aims to implant a cloned embryo into a woman's uterus, leading to the birth of a cloned baby. The purpose of the procedure may be also here to gain organs to treat adults. This would mean that you "produce" a human being with the explicit intention to kill it, in order to treat someone else. Besides, it has been established that reproductive cloning has potential risks to both mother and foetus (Cibelli, Lanza, West and Ezzell, 2002), and therefore in several countries a moratorium/prohibition legislation is in place. In the USA there is a total ban, in some European countries, like recently in Britain, the law admits research on stem cells. Cloning as such stays illegal, because of the infringement of every moral precept and also of the criminal law. Behind every successful clone there are incredible numbers of failures, beings done away, and even the successfully cloned beings die very shortly. Harry Griffin, director of the British Roslin Institute, where in 1996 the sheep Dolly had been cloned (it died shortly afterwards), had pointed out, that the majority of animal clones live for a short time only. They suffer from severe dieseases, even if at their birth they are looking quite normal. T. Dominko from the Research Center on Primates from Oregon, has told that she tried to clone 300 apes, but has always failed. The Italian writer Giuseppina Manin has rightly pointed out that behind every birth of this type, one has to reckon with hundreds of failed attempts, a real massacre of foeti and aborti. (*Corriere della Sera*, 30 December, 2002). Should they live, they would be caught in the most severe questions of identity and emotions. Besides, research has found that clones are not genetically identical to the donors, and sometimes exhibit dangerously different patterns of gene expressions (*Scientific American*, September, 2001). Contending that it should be possible to build and police barriers between therapeutic and reproductive cloning, the editors of *The Scientific American* (October, 2001) vehemently oppose the then planned total American ban on human cloning, putting forward the key arguments of the Internet Culture: The advocates of biotechnology have predicted a brain drain of scientists fleeing to countries where therapeutic cloning is legal, and the US biotech industry would suffer. After this terrible "stick" comes the Internet Culture "carrot": developing treatment for Alzheimer's disease, Parkinson's, diabetes or paralysis with the aid of therapeutic cloning.

There are two problems with this kind of statements. One should not tolerate massacres and débâcles in the present in exchange for fairy tales about the future, and the basic premise of the statement is false: the vocal scientists of the Internet Society do not push for therapeutic, but for reproductive cloning. The underlying cause of this endeavor is the curious aspiration to be God-like and to create things in the mandant's own image, be him a rich entrepreneur, a politician or a sect follower. Biologists-experts and philosophers see here the greatest threat cloning is posing to mankind, causing havoc, which surpasses that of an atom bomb. I. Nisand pointed out that while the latter kills people, perhaps through several generations, cloning destroys the essence of the human species. The damage is sudden and collective. The uniqueness of the individual is threatened as a bearer of the principle of random gene mixture between father and mother cromosomes. Therefore reproductive cloning should be considered a crime against humanity without prescription limits, and punished by an international court of law (*Le Monde*, January 2003).

It is perplexing that when the twisted values of the Internet Culture are involved (infringe all taboos and traditional morality, be God-like), the same values are used in order to put a hold on human progress in the technological domain of atomic energy. Because of ever-soaring prices, oil is a twindling reserve, and the solution would be to conceive and build better atomic plants. The problem has been solved by France, a country with no major petroleum reserves, which has made the world biggest bet on nuclear power (*Fortune*, May 17, 2004). Today France derives 75% of its energy from nuclear power, far more than any other country other than – Lithuania. France is the world largest exporter of electricity, and has Western Europe's cheapest electricity prices. It would be logic for the world to unite with France to give nuclear energy a second chance, but this is forbidden since the "peace movement" of the long-ago writer Ilya Ehrenburg and his protector, Uncle Stalin. Both are dead now, but their movement went over to the West. Its name is now Greenpeace and the slogans are the same. You cannot have a scientific argument with them, they shout and destroy facilities, as they had been taught by their great two teachers, even if such behavior is not legal. *Tant pis pour la loi* (Bad for the law).   Warnings of moral or even legal nature had never made any impression on the brave scientists of the Internet Culture, including those concerned with reproductive cloning, to which we are returning. A former singer, rallye pilot and newspaper man,

Claude Vorilhon, founded the Raëlian sect in 1977, which in turn founded the Clonaid company for the realization of cloning programmes. In December 2002 the cloned baby Eve should have been born. It had been "ordered" by two lesbians. Brigitte Boissebier, the CEO of Clonaid declared that in the (then) following weeks 20 other clonings would be made by her laboratories (*Corriere della Sera*, 30 December 2002). Very curiously, nothing has been heard of them since, but the physicist-journalist Michael Guillen whose task it was to form an expert group for the DNA analyses of Eve, has declined comment and declared that "there are scary prospects".

If a conclusion is to be drawn from this use of science in the field of biotechnology, it surely is a positive attitude towards research on stem cells for therapeutic use. Scientists largely consider that stem cells are "activated eggs", cell blasts and not an embryo. When embryos are involved, the problem arising from cloning becomes very severe from an ethical and social point of view. It is hard to argue with cardinal Alfonso Trujillo, pesident of the Pontificial Council on Family, who states that fertilization should be a human act originating in love, and that embryos should not be treated as objects. This position induces two questions: Whether an embryo may be "produced" only in order to harvest organs needed to cure somebody, and whether prior to the assisted implant of a fertilized egg a genetic examination of the cells should be allowed. Were the morality of the scientists who are performing the intervention ensured, there would be no problem, but in this society things are more complicated. The need for organs easily degenerates into premeditated killing, and the pre-implant DNA analyses of "ordered" babies may lead to a kind of dr. Mengele life-death selection, where the criterion could be gender, the color of hair, of the eyes, etc. Both are not uses but abuses of science. Therefore, the existing legal interdictions seem very much in place. The problem is not only for the law to punish the abuses of science, but for the science practitioners themselves to internalize professional ethics, and to oppose abuses.

In the conception of this society, science is a commercial enterprise like a big store, which should ensure huge earnings. Therefore, scientific ethics are done away and replaced by a) open deceit b) research with nonpertinent data c) the emphasis in the research report is on future fantasies and not on present results. For the open deceit, let us first consider an example from the already discussed cloning hysteria in the Internet Culture. Publicity-hungry scientific workers have sinply put forward false data. The natiional science hero of Korea, Dr. Hwang, has repeatedly announced successful clonings. He presented an allegedly cloned dog, and there were rumors of a baby cloning. On December 23, 2005 all these "scientific achievements" finaly collapsed, ans were exposed as a fraud. Of the 11 lines of stemcells he presented 9 were fake. The man publicly presented his apologies and resigned from his position at the university, but it is not sure whether he was reproached a criminal act of deceit or the plumpness of his faking methods. In another domain the *Scientific American* (January 2004, p.25) gives the example of laundry ball manufacturers claiming that their scientifically designed product works on quantum mechanics with a method called

Structured Water Technology, or in another case they claim using infra-red waves that change the mollecular structure of the water, all this being pure and obvious bunk, like the snake oil advertized in past centuries. More subtle are other methods of creating a positive judgement towards certain products or research activity by using nonpertinent data or fantasies of the future. For the sake of illustration, we shall refer to the presentation of a research on a vaccine against cancer and research on drug addiction. Recently a proposed vaccine against cancer has been presented, which allegedly has led to a survival prolongation of 8.4 months in comparison with patients who received a placebo (*Scientific American*, July 2004). Already at this point two criticisms are in place. This society dares to expose patients to a treatment with a placebo, knowing that it will lead to a more rapid death. Previously, such a research would have been considered highly unethical and unprofessional on the verge of criminal. Surely, the doctors would have lost their licence, and in all probability they would have stood trial. Then, secondly, you are asking for millions of funding and are putting on the market a very expensive drug, and all what you get is a delay of 8.1 months ?! However, the best is yet to come. Scientists have objected that a vaccine tries to teach the immune system to go after cancer cells, something it hasn't been able to do in millions and millions of years of evolution, therefore a "smart bullet" like monoclonals would be a preferable research target. No, say the marketers of the Dendreon vaccine, a long-lasting immunity (which has not been proved, *E.K.*) might turn cancer from a terminal disease into a chronic one, that stabilizes and allow patients to live out their lives. Such a presentation, a fairy tale about a desired future sent the company stock raising with $150 milion in January 2004 (*Scientific American,* July 2004). It has been a fairy tale, because soaring stocks or not, nothing has come out of the vaccine and patients merrily continue to die. Seemingly, fairy tales do not make impression on children only. Geoffrey Colvin (*Fortune*, 151,1,29) considers that the whole future American economy will be based on imagination. The very basis of value creation is shifting from the disciplines of logic and liniar thinking to the intuitive nonliniar process of creativity and imagination. It represents a leap of faith, but that's how it has always worked. We are falling behind in science and math? Hey, says Colvin, we are awsomely good at creating games, humor, design, story and other elements of hypothesized future. This means, if modern science fails, (as it does), we can always imagine big successes, we have the fairy ytales. Let us therefore continue with fairy tales told on geniuses.

In 2005 the world comemorated the anniversary of the publication of Einstein's articles outlining his theory of relativity. Festschrifts and homagial papers on Einstein were published, e.g. a special issue of the *Scientific American* (September, 2004). There is no doubt in anybody's mind that Einstein has been a genius, the problem begins when someone sees him as the only genius brought forward by mankind, or comparable only to Newton. In the quoted special journal issue, Lightman writes (p. 90), "If we journey back through centuries, passing such towering figures as James Clark Maxwell, Ludwig Botzmann, Charles Darwin, Louis Pasteur, Antoine Lavoisier, we must travel all the way to Isaac

Newton before finding another human being of comparable scientific achievement. And before Newton there might be none". The excerpt evinces ignorance and arrogance, and indeed, the readers of the Scientific American have severely criticized the author (January 2005, p.6) for the omission of Euclid and Archimedes. Lightman remained adamant and, though admitting that the ancient Greek scientists were "powerful thinkers", he reiterated that we must reach through the centuries for any comparison to Einstein. The idea is again false and proves Lightman has only an unclear notion of what a genius is.   In the dithyrambic appraisals on Einstein appears a more fundamental flaw of the science in the Internet Culture, reflecting the game rule "winner takes all". They see Einstein's proclamation of certain theories only, and forget the fundament wrought by his predecessors. Sir John Maddox (1999) pointed out that Maxwell's theory admits the possible unification of electricity and magnetism, whence at the propagation of electromagnetic disturbances time would pass more slowly on an object moving relative to an observer. Thus a basis was created from which, via Henri Poincaré it was only a small step to Einstein's theory of relativity. This statement does not belittle Einstein's merits, because it was *him* who took this step, but it demonstrates the fact that geniuses are embedded in the gradual process of developing material and spiritual civilization. It was Galton (1869/1978) who in his way-opening theory on geniuses has drawn attention that genius is continuous with near-genius with lesser degrees of eminence. Eysenck (1995) states that we must accept that genius is the top of the iceberg, and not qualitatively different. There are no "towering figures" appearing from nowhere, like messengers of the gods, or a "big white uncle" to the Indians.

In order to reduce the polemic, I am ready to accept the definition given by the editors of the *Scientific American* (Sept. 2004, p.4). Avoiding the word genius, they point out that "every list of the 20th century's most outstanding figures must include Albert Einstein, because that era and our own is unimaginable without him and his influence". Nonetheless, cannot the same be said on Louis Pasteur, Marie Curie, on Charles Darwin, Ivan Pavlov, Max Planck? The editors say that Einstein attained a wider renown, but this is a matter of political and publicity conjunction. The mingling of science with politics and publicity is a distinctive trait of the Internet Culture. So is the trend to give the highest evaluation only to scientists working in the fields of mathematics (and astronomy perhaps), which is linked to computing, the "baby" of this society, as it is also to the pervasive trend to find a "theory of everything" and to play God. I wonder whether the celebrators of Einstein know that he firmly believed in God and in that the final answer to the Universe is to be found in religion. Of course, they would not take notice of this information. They prefer a tale of supposed events instead of real, occurred ones, which would hold up the philosophy and the opinions of the present-day culture, atheism among them. They tell that he would have fought for Arab-Israeli peace and *would have* spoken against the war in Iraq. The editors of *The Scientific American* are saying (page 4, ibid.) that scientists have a moral responsibility to explain their work, including political implications, and that to say otherwise would mean that science does not matter.

Here again is a twist characteristic to the Internet Culture. What is the link between the theory of relativity and politics, between it and Arab-Jewish relations or between it and the invasion of Iraq? As any other person, scientists have the right to political opinions, but these latter should not influence the appraisal of the scientist's activity. The problem is that political opinions may backlash on the scientific activity, influence it. It happened to Carl Jung, one of the "towering" psychologists (the concept is theirs not mine) of the XXth century, who enthusiastically welcomed Hitler and Mussolini for their strong personality, etc. Jung's political opinions are never mentioned. So, have scientists the moral duty to explain their opinions, or don't they? I think science should not mingle with politics, and I explained this point of view in relation to Jung (Krau, 1989). Today, it so seems, participation in politics is a condition for people to be recognized as scientists, but only left-wing politcal opinions give this entitlement. We have here another of the Internet Culture's fundamentally false ideas. Then, of course, not only mathematicians are geniuses. The latter appear everywhere and speak every language and not only English. Einstein himself spoke German during the greater part of his life.

We are here tapping one of the essential issues involving geniuses. It was Galton who first defined the genius in terms of achieved reputation, but until this very day there is no consensus as to the qualities for which reputation is given. Is it achievements, originality, creativity, asks Eysenck (1995), and he states that it is in this sphere that an interference of the *Zeitgeist* takes place. In order to support his affirmation, Eysenck leans on the mid-century surveys of Farnsworth on 100 composers, and on the ones made by Moles of 250 composers (only 100 are mentioned by Eysenck in each case). The ranking of composers differs in the two surveys, but none mentions e.g. Paganini. Why? He seems less known in the US, but is it a reason for denying his unrepeatable geniality? It results that genius cannot be without social approval. But, what is it that ensures social approval: achievements, originality, creativity? Here Eysenck introduces a very interesting observation, saying that genius is known for certain unusual behaviors or accidents in life. Byron is famous for his lifestyle, Hölderlin, Van Gogh for their schizofrenic breakdown. Einstein had an unusual early history of careless grooming and a nonconfformist social behavior. He frequently appeared without socks, and pictured before reporters pulling out his tongue. This has given him an appearance in conformity with the popular notion of "genius" in the culture of the Internet Society.

If some consider the above statements to be an unfair accusation against modern society, then tell me, please, why did nobody mention Copernicus among the giants of mankind? His revoutionary thought put the Sun in the centre of our stellar system, and thus set the basis of modern thinking about the Universe, influencing science for centuries. Here is a quiz for the causes why scientists and the historians of science in the Internet Culture nonchalantly chose to bypass him: he was a monk, he believed in God, and has dedicated his book to the pope he did not write and publish in English, he had no left-wing political views and did not reprove the invasion of Iraq, which had to start some 450 years later,neither Lightman, nor any Internet bird has ever heard of him, all the above answers are correct. If trying to give a serious consideration to these questions, one will have to admit that all what we have said on science in the Internet Society is correct . Now let us return to Einstein and see how modern society has dealt with him, apart from empty phrases.

Einstein passed away in 1955, as he was coaxed to allow an autopsy to be performed on his body "for the sake of science". There are today conflicting views as to whether he donated his brain to science, or dr. Harvey, the performing pathologist, took it out illegally. At any rate, he put it into a glass jar with formaldehyde, and slices of the brain were given to all those who asked for it. The rest stayed in the jar for some 40 years, catching dust as the jar would be tossed from one shelf to another or under laboratory tables. When finally dr. Harvey reached the age of 80, he put the jar into the trunk of his car and traveled to Einstein's grand-daughter to give her back the family propriety (Harvey, 2001). As a matter of fact, it had been a violation and dishonoring of the great scientist, in fragrant contradiction with the hymns of praise sung today in his honor. Instead of publicity, the perpetrator of this misdemeanor should have had a serious discussion with a district attorney, in order to clarify what has happened. As to those 40 years, time and again researchers would examine the brain in the jar, but they did not find anything uncommon. Only lastly, M.C. Diamond found a larger than normal number of glia cells. They lack the membrane properties to propagate their own action potential and rely on chemical signals to convey messages. Fields (2004) pointed out that the firing of neurons *somehow (?)* induces glial cells to emit ATP, activating a communication, whereby various genes should be induced to switch on in the cell nuclei. So far these are surmised facts which are only hinting at the *possibility* of a short-range connectivity between astrocytes (glia cells). Even if the phenomenon is real, it involves a quite large number of factors and processes. However, as things are presented, the whole story looks as if we had already entered the era of producing geniuses. If neurons are like telephones, so we are told, astrocytes may be like cell phones, communicating with chemical signals. Perhaps a higher concentration of glia, or a more potent type of glia is what elevates certain humans to genius (Fields, *ibid*, p.33). Nevertheless, all this contention is wishful thinking, science fiction without any fact coverage. The above-mentioned astrocyte research has nothing to do with Einstein, the genius-producing fantasy is pasted on it to achieve more credibility and publicity, while it is enthusiastically presented as the newest progress in the science of modern society. There is no proof to link glia functioning to human geniuses. The advent of a genius has a very complex causal texture in which a biophysiological facilitation of associations (if it were ascertained !) is only one component, and not less decisive are personality characteristics, a propitious social-cultural environment (Krau, 1997), and last but not least, there are also meta-psychological factors which escape human control (Krau, 2003).

The same unscientific simplification also appears in the research on the addiction phenomenon. We have already mentioned the work of Resnik (1990), where the emphasis had been on the social factor, whereas Master and Houston

(2000) had underlined psychological descriptive factors. Now in thorough isolation from these works, there is a biochemical attempt (Nestler and Malenka, 2004), which using the most advanced technology of functional magnetic resonance imaging (fMRI) and positron emission tomography (PET) scans, described the activity of nucleus accumbens receiving a flood of dopamine in cocaine snoring addicts. It is mentioned that the same activity appears if the addict is shown a video of someone using cocaine or a photograph of white lines on a mirror. The same regions of the brain (the accumbens, the amygdala) react in compulsive gamblers, who are shown images of slot machines (*ibid.* p.54). In itself the research is meritorious, but it fails to address the *psychological* problem of addiction it purports to resolve. This is so, because it does not link up with the addiction research in other domains (physiology, psychology, sociology) and neither with research done in the past. The trigger of behavior by repetitive conditions acting as reinforcers is a conditional reflex, thoroughly studied in Pavlov's laboratories one hundred years ago (Pavlov, 1924/1951). In this case the whole biochemical picture is of a secondary character, the behavior is elicited not by the direct biochemical stimuli, but by their past associations, i.e. by physiological and psychological factors. The scientists living in the Internet Culture are not capable to fathom this linkage and causal structure. They work in the isolation of their specialty, and they do not know what others are doing or what has been done in the past, even in their own field. In many cases the scientists do not read books and their knowledge is based on the digests from the Internet. They do not know languages and they do not know, or do not want to know research done in other countries, especially if it had not been published in English. This disdain for the past, even for their own American, English or French past, absurdly goes so far, that some American TV programmes call a hoax the American landing on the Moon. 20 per cent of Americans have doubts whether they really went there, and in 2002 NASA had to spend $15000 for a public relations campaign to convince public opinion of the reality of this historic event (*Scientific American*, February 2003).

A great deal of valuable research has been done in the past in Europe, e.g. in the domain of hypnosis, of rockets, etc., and is now reinvented in the US through a great effort of the American taxpayer. The ignorance spreads even to terminology. Speaking of hypnosis, we have recently read on hypnotherapy, what should mean therapy through hypnosis (*Scientific American*, January 2004, p. 20). In Europe the term has always been used for therapy through sleep, because the original Greek meaning of *hypnos* is "sleep". What does such a confusion matter? The antique Greeks are dead together with their language, the past does not count, nor do foreigners who are not publishing in English. In his empowered mind, the scientist of the Internet Culture considers that no other scholars have addressed the problem, which is reduced to the characteristics he/she is capable of seeing. Therefore a very partial research (even if meritorious) is falsely and presumptuously presented as the ultimate word of science.   There has been, for instance, for some years a modest reseach, which started in Zürich and continued in the USA with the purpose of "enhancing" DNA through adding artificial components, "genetic letters" to the four existing ones. No one has made genes from them, and the problem with an engineered cell is that it is constantly changing within hours. Nonetheless, a new science of *synthetic biology* was heralded, with the aim of "designing and building living systems that behave in predictable ways, that use interchageable parts, doing things that no natural organism can" (*Scientific American*, May 2004, p.49). There is no correspondence between the setting of the research, its obtained results, the real perspectives, which derive from them, and the bombastic name and fairy tales regarding the future which are fed to the public and obfuscate the real picture.

The same also happens in computing technology, where legitimate and meritorious research is done in order to increase computing speed. At present the efficiency is low, and little of the processing capability can be brought to bear on real world applications. This does not stop scientists from declaring that the next generation of hypercomputers will offer an important tool for exploring the world's most pressing problems, including global warming, disease epidemics and cleaner energy (*Scientific American*, July, 2001). Not only that a tale on the future is served again as solid science, but it is also surreptiously inserted that the solution of the urgent global problems is a matter of computers, which it is not. The world problems cannot and should not be reduced to computing. They have social and psychological-emotional aspects, which a computer without any human feelings and consideration cannot, and mainly, must not handle. The word "considerate computing" does appear today (*Scientific American*, Jannuary 2005), but its context reflects the video-game Internet Culture. The word refers to computer programmes that would not allow mobile phone ringing during a concert, or a loud-voice proud computer message of the type "your batteries are fully loaded" suddenly proclaimed during an important conference. The kind of consideration *we* have in mind refers to the content of decision making, and not to formal characteristics. If you programme a computer to principally abide by efficiency, cost reduction and the increment of wealth, then given the increasing financial crisis in caring for old and sick people, a computer will come up with the solution of liquidating them or of letting them "going away" quietly. One could object that a computer could also be programmed in a more "considerate" direction, but it never could have the compassion, the consideration, the feeling needed to resolve individual or group cases with special problems. If science in the Internet Culture is leading towards handing over the decision making in social matters to computers, then it is again the wrong way. The more so, that the expected results of the victorius "considerate" computer of the future can be only obtained by increasing its surveillance skills. The programme must sense or infer what the owner is and what he is doing, and then weigh the value of the message against the cost of disruption. This attentive system is always watching and has come to know the owner and his/her work habits better than he/she does (*Scientific American*, January 2005).   All this does certainly not mean that there is no scientific progress in this culture. Throughout history science has steadily advanced because there have always been people who fought for the enlargement of human knowledge. The important characteristic of present-day science is that it is based on the most developed technology history has ever known. However, the way things are done, this strength turns out to be its undoing. The research technolgy (its material basis) overtakes the research, and a situation appears in which the use of technology seems to be an aim in itself. We have largely quoted biomedical research done with the newest equipment (functional magnetic resonance imaging, PET scans, etc.), but one gains the impression of a fishing expedition set up to try out a new fishing hook with an upgraded rod. There is no new knowledge, and no new conception, and no new treatment. Thanks to the new equipment we penetrated deeper into the understanding of biochemical processes and phenomena in the body and especially in the brain, but this did not enhance a deeper understanding of psychological processes and phenomena, nor the possibility of correcting and healing disturbances on the physiological and psychological level.

Several years already scientist work hardly to measure with greater precision the height of Mount Everest and of K-2.The original measurements had been performed in 1856 by a British team and showed 8846 m. for Mount Everest and 8611 m. for K-2. The results were confirmed by Italian scientists in 1992 and 1996 with a difference of only a few centimeters. Now 19 Italian university departments with 49 scientists are working on 9 projects wich include the repetition of the measurements by a new georadar technology and are part of a fresh new science of "geomathics", a combination between geology and mathematics (*Corriere della Sera*, 26 October, 2003). The whole issue has already widely and wildly been published, although even the modest expected correction has not been ascertained yet. Even if it were, does it justify the many year investments of energy and money? In older days there used to be a redoutable "so what" test of scientific research. The globalized Internet Culture has apparently abrogated it.

There has been great progress in telephone communication through mobile appliances, which recently are enabled to transmit video-pictures of the person with whom one speaks. This is a very useful thing, but new advancement in the same direction, like turning the phone into a computer, a TV set, or enablling airline passengers to speak on he phone during air flights, as it is envisaged now in the US, bring more danger and damage than benefit. A TV-enabled phone will be used during classes by youths annoyed by school science, and who are desirous of amusement, it will be used during theatre spectacles, or when driving, until the driver lands on a tree. Phone converastions during airflights present great dangers for flight security. In the year 2000 a Crossair flight Zürich – Dresden crashed at landing, causing the death of 10 persons. Experts established that there had been an interference of a little handy-phone with the board instruments. Apart form such dangers, a majority of passengers try to repose during the long hours of a flight. Imagine that other 20-30 passengers try to cope with boredom by a loud-voice phone conversation. Clearly, nobody would be able to get some sleep. Against this inconvenience stands, of course, the substantial profits of the phone companies. In Europe they speak of a new market of

6 milliard Euros. Here is the whole problem of science in the Internet Culture. It is designed to benefit corporations, not the public.

There is, for instance, the issue of vaccines and antibiotics, both very potent means to fight diseases. Vaccines may have a huge advantage over antibiotics, they knock out the bacteria before they can develop resistance. But vaccines have not been profitable for business. They are harder to create and harder to prove, because you give them to healthy people. The US government, through its FDA agency towers funding difficulties and bureaucratic impediments making the approval very difficult. Therefore few research and development is done in this less profitable domain. In 1999, after successful preliminary trials, the Nabi company started the final tests with a vaccine against the very dangerous *Staphylococcus aureus,* largely present in hospital settimgs. The cost rose to tens of millions of dollars. The declared aim was to reach immunity for 54 weeks. When the results came out, the patients presented an immunity for 10 months only. The company asked for an approval as a 10-months vaccine, but the FDA refused , and in 2001 gave a ruling, that, since the original nominal goal was not met (54 weeks), a new trial should start with the beforehand declared goal of a 10-week immunity (*Fortune,* September 30, 2002).Ridiculous? Yes, and the comapany refused to invest again tens of millions in a needless supplementary trial. As a result, the victorious *Staphylococcus aureus* remains to cause wide spread so-called hospital infections with a lethal outcome. It happens that experimental outcomes are embellished, while negative results, which are vital to the continuation of the reaearch are not published at all. So it came to the lawsuit in which the State of New York sued Glaxo-Smith Kline for suppressing data showing that the antidepressant Praxil increased teens' risk of suicide. There is a new move requiring all clinical trials to be registered from the get go, and considered for publication. Registration in the National Institutes of Health is already mandatory for research on serious diseases, but the enforcement is lax. The association of pharmaceutical manufacturers opposes mandatory registration and instead proposes a voluntary results database – one may conjecture why. The editors and the authors themselves are also contributing to the problem, the former only vie "for the best and most exciting papers", the latter don't want to appear as losers in a society in which only winners have legitimacy. When Reysen started a journal for articles "in support of the null hypothesis", virtually no articles were submitted (*Scientific American,* December 2004). It has been reported by the Public Citizen group that drug firms wield a great deal of control over their research, and they allegedly are frequently manipulating their data or withholding unfavorable results entirely, while in other cases the results are not presented according to scientific norms, inducing the conclusions the firm wants to be acknowledged. They plot percent change instead of absolute figures and thus make the effectivenes of the drug appear larger. The time intervals in which the drugs had not been effective are simply omitted, and so are negative side effects. The problem only appears if patients die of them. (*Scientific American,* February 2003). Lastly, there is a trend to supplant research with real human subjects with virtual computer models. The firm Entelos created the model of a virtual patient "swallowing" pills, which then get metabolized, subjected to a series of differential equations in digital organs ranging from the pancreas to the liver and the brain. Weight, age and sex are taken into consideration. Johnson & Johnson signed up with Entelos to test an obesity model, which it then has surprisingly declared to cover diabetes (*Scientific American*, February 2003). Modelling the efects of drugs is a good money saving idea *on condition* that the results are looked upon as preliminary, because there are many factors influencing the complicated processes within the human body, which the computer programmer, even be he a physician, does not know. The mere presentation of such results modelled on computers, as it is done with great ado, is therefore misleading. Especially today, when science is linked to technology, there is another queer phenomenon regarding new technologies. Enormous sums are spent, in order to avoid using inventions which already exist, but had not yet been applied, because what exists is "old and traditional". The automobile industry is investing billions of dollars in technologies that promise to make the internal combustion engine obsolete. But there is a vast reservoir of existing inventions for new car models that innovate on traditional lines. Decision makers would not accept them, because they wait for the revolutionary new technology to appear and sweep the market. This does not happen, and the solution to the fuel problem is the hybrid car, already presented nearly two decades ago. The Clinton administration spent a billion dollars to reach the same conclusions published seventeen years earlier (Wonk, 2001). It did not solve society's problems. Consequently, there had to be another factorat wwork. We have considered that it was the production of wealth through additional cost reduction and profits, also using illegal manoeuvers, but in the light of the aforementioned case of the fuel problem this conclusion also seems incomplete. There is, however, another additional basic motivation, which even precedes immediate financial profit, and this is the political motive. In a scientific journal Partha Dasgupta, professor in Cambridge and Eric Maskin, professor in Princeton (*Scientific American*, March 2004, p.65-69) express their ire and revolt against a voting system which allows G.W. Bush and J. Chirac to be elected against such "people's candidates" like Al Gore and Lionel Jospin. Nota bene: The authors use science to devise methods allowing to circumvent the popular vote, and bring to power, what in the former Soviet Uniion had been called "the Party candidates". The authors performed an in-depth analysis of the elections in France and in the USA in the year 2000, and found that they have been influenced by additional candidates (Buchanan, Nader, Le Pen) who stood no chance of finally being elected. Numerous models were elaborated in the search for the one which would ensure the election of the "right" candidate. After considerable toil and comnputing, they came up with their "scientific" proposal. When more than two choices are presented to the voters, the latter should submit a ranking of candidates, and majority rule should determine the winner. This addition is necessary to avoid the fallacy of the Condorcet paradox, in which again an "inappropriate candidate" could win. Here we have the science of the Internet Culture in its full splendor and motivational background. This science is openly put in the service of a political ideology, and it has no problem with acting against the democratically voted constitutions and electoral laws, which ask for electing a president without "scientific" manoeuvers. Once scientists were portrayed as heroes, who painstakingly sought answers to society's problems, now contemporary science devalues the questions it cannot answer. It again and again repeats the jingle launched by Stephen Hawking that physicists may soon construct a theory that will unite all the forces of nature into one mathematical equation, which can be written on a T-shirt, the formula of the theory of everything. Rightly, Overbye (1993) points out that scientists are partly to blame for the mess of today's science, which in lieu to solve the problems linked to everyday life, searches for the theory of everything, in fact pushing people to look for the Tarot cards more and more. There is no reason to think we know the right questions yet, e.g. why the Universe exists, let alone the ultimate answers. Even in finding solutions to modest problems science is handicapped, because, in the words of Ignacio Martín-Baró, a social scientist and clergy man, the predicament of science and of scientists nowadays lay in that they work in a setting in which they are frequently challenged to speak truth to power. It may be a dfangerous undertaking. They find the truth about the country, the social actors, the social forces, and look for reasonable solutions to their problems, but are thwarted by political forces (*Psychology International*, 2004, 15, 4). Shortly after he said these words, Martìn-Baró was killed in El Salvador. Many people think that groups adhering to the pro-corporatist culture of the day had been involved in this tragical case. So much on the freedom of science in the globalized Internet Culture.

It is only now that an answer can be given to the question of why science and the arts in the Renaissance and later in the Enlightenment era were driven by giants, while we, with our satellites and mobile phones, are the dwarfs. First, the cause lies in the lack of width and richness of the investigated issues, but there are also problems with the low quality of scientific work, the vanished love of truth, the ignorance of past scientific research, and the failure of delimiting science from bare fantasies and wishful thinking. Cicero (*De Officiis*, 1, 19) has said that science separated from justice and from the other virtues should be rather called scoundreldom and not wisdom: *Scientia quae est remota a iustitia et a ceteris virtutibus, calliditas potius quam sapientia est appelanda.*

Chapter Seven

The Educational System in the Internet Society: the School and the Family

The education of past times has always been accused of being ill-adapted to the needs of society and to the needs of the students for a smooth absorption into the socioeconomic web of the environment. The incriminations referred to allegedly useless matters taught in schools, like Latin, and to methods based on memorization, which again, allegedly, did not develop independent reasoning in students. Notwithstanding, it has been a permanent preoccupation of educators to put forward new proposals in theory and practice, in order to enhance the achievement of a multilateral education, linked to the developmernt of the personality and to a better social insertion .

Back in 1834, in his *Guide to German Teachers,* Diesterweg differentiated between material and formal education. While the former referred to the acquisition of specific knowledge and skills, the latter aimed at developing thought and verbal expression, observation and analysis, as well as moral qualities, like a strong character, who knows what he/she wants in life. Scientists and educators have ever since debated, whether the emphasis should be on the material education (Dörpfeld) or on its formal aspect (Niemeyer). The majority embraced Humboldt's *utraque* rule (the"both rule") meaning the inclusion of languages and history on the one hand, and mathematics ands physics on the other. In the XXth century moves to the forefront the development of the child's cognitive forces according to its interest. John Dewey asks that the point of departure in the educational process should be the child's expressed interests and its practical experience. This theory led to the Decroly project of *Interest Centers* and Evelyn Dewey's (John's daughter) and Helen Parkhurst's *Dalton Project.* The system of classes, the age bound formal groupings of children were dismantled, and

the teacher's role was reduced to a consultant. The student chose which laboratory to enter, when, and what to do there.

However, the educational process is not an automatic one. An instruction
material cannot be appropriated and evaluated without a teacher who is transmitting it, and without students performing a special activity of learning (Bruner,
1967). The learners must identify the material as a problem, but they should be
guided in this undertaking, in order to make the right identification and evaluation. Therefore it is wrong to give up the classical understanding of the school
and the teacher, even if in modern times their notion and definition is enlarged.
The Dalton Project disorganized the educational process and was abandoned,
but nonetheless, this *active method* proved a great benefit in developing the student's intelligence and their faculties, as they acquire the necessary knowledge
and skills indispensaable for their future integration into the world of tomorrow.
The method furthered the student's desire and capacity to engage in a process of
permanent education, necessary in a society in which the technological progress
made history advance at an accelerated pace. This means first, that education is
not only an action performed on others, but also one performed on ourselves,
and during our entire life span (Dottrens, Mialaret, Rast and Ray 1966). Today
this saying is true more than ever. Secondly, there are changes in the educating
institutions and the educating staff. While school and family preserve (should
preserve, at least) their role as factors of education, television and the Internet
legitimately join them, TV anchors, actors and actresses, models and football
stars today complete the "pedagogical collective".

All these changes have to be taken into account, but they do not alter the
scope of education and its final aim to provide a multilateral development of the
student's intellectual, moral, aesthetic and physical capacities, to offer the bases
of human knowledge and more special knowledge and skills in a domain chosen
by the person for his/her vocational activity. Another aim is to provide knowledge and skills in social and recreational activities. Our purpose in this book is
to investigate how the present-time education copes with these tasks. From the
beginning on, difficulties are towering, when it comes to decide on the contents
of education, i.e. which are the desired capacities, which are the desired basic
knowledge and skills? At the allencompassing influence of the market, the educators of the Internet Society are eager to introduce the principle of consumer
satisfaction into the educational process. A worthy idea, but who is the consumer? It is the student, they answer, but is this really so? Even be it, educators
forget that their task is less to offer entertainment, good feelings and fredom
from boredom, but to shape the future member of the social community, as a
citizen and a performer of a vocational activity. In this sense, the consumers of
education are not the pupils, as the persons who they are today, but society, the
persons who these pupils will be tomorrow with their future needs, determined
by society and expressed by employers, parents and the community at large.
Only educating in this perspective are young people able to prepare for the competitive challenges of socioeconomic life. However, we have seen that there has
been an attempt to let the child decide what it wants to learn, and which capaci-

ties it desires to develop. While the child's aspirations have necessarily to be taken into account, society is always present in the educational process. People are living in society and the values and opinions of the social environment take their toll.

The problem is that not always society represented by its public opinion, acts in favor of a better educational system, which would give the students higher knowledge and would better develop their abilities. In the chapter on values we have seen that the Internet Culture breaks with the past, it dismantles the teacher's authority and the frontal methods of transmitting knowledge, including the obligatory reading. The immediate educational purpose of this culture is to instill individual momentary good feelings, freedom from learning efforts and from boredom. It is a kind of *"Pinocchio Principle"*. The preparation for the future is seen under the same characteristics, since work has been devalued, and careers *de facto* terminated by an instable economy, relying on continual employee retrenchments. The obsessive shunning of effort and of all sort of rules, in order to fel good, free and capable of devoting oneself entirely to leisure, creates a sort of *vocational anorexia*, a psychological rejection of work and its conditions. Plump leisure activities have risen to the only coveted pastime. Some analysts thought that acquiring a higher qualification would shield the individual from such a perspective. However, the recent trend to offshore even high-tech activities to developing countries, has confirmed the dire reality, that there is no escape from the all-destroying money greed of the Internet Society, veiled under slogans of free competition. Such a lifestyle deeply influences all social activities, including education. It creates a doomsday atmosphere of "let us live now, tomorrow all will be gone", whence the acquisition of knowledge, especially knowledge gained in the past, seems futile from a double point of view. First, the propaganda drums are hammering that only modern theories realized through new computer programmes have any value, and secondly, the young student is prevented from seeing that knowledge does help people be happy and satisfied in their adult life. Why bother to learn, if time can be better spent in sport or sex ganes, in revelling with drinks and drugs.

Pointing out that today specific knowledge has become *déclassé* and that students have only to be taught to think, Lefkowitz (1996) lists another much more troubling reason why instructors and students place less and less emphasis on the acquisition of factual information. They are led to believe that there are no such things as facts, because today facts are manipulated and misinterpreted.

The twisted educational conceptions of our time must account for the heinous disfiguration or destruction of the world's most appreciated art works. Recently a bomb has been placed in the Uffizi palace in Firenze, where the great art works of the XVth-XVIth centuries had been exposed. Pictures were damaged in the Louvre, the statues of the Basilica del Redentore in Venice were severly damaged, and so was the renowned Fontana dei Fiumi in Rome. The perpetrators were three boys, and a 28-years old man who wanted to take some pictures from an unusual angle. He climbed on the Neptune statue in Firenze's Piazza della Signoria, and broke the hand with the trident of the statue into 32 pieces (*Corriere della Sera,* 4 August 2005). It was not a crime with malicious intent, as with the bomb in the Uffizi, but it was a criminal disconsideration of famous art monuments, and it had been instilled by faulty education, by a perverse deformation of aesthetical values. We get a hint of all this in Gross (see Gross, Levitt and Lewis (1996), when he says that today the conviction is stronger than ever, that inculcating correct attitudes towards big questions is far more important than conveying actual knowledge. Thus all teaching must be indoctrination.

Indoctrination is achieved by: 1. The *content of education* through: preference given to certain school matters and curriculum contents

1.1 A biased description of the transmitted facts. Education becomes an instrument of the economy, and for the expression of the values of the Internet Culture.

1.2 The monopoly of English over other languages, just as the Soviets also achieved their indoctrination by using Russian as a monopolistic language for scientific contacts

1.3 Aspirations regarding the students' vocational future in a game-like world.

1.4 The content of the advocated lifestyle Crooked moral-spiritual values

 2. *Antipedagogic educational methods*

2.1 The loosening of the instructional-educational framework of the school

2.2 Emphasis on independent discovery not guided or sustained by the teacher or by reading the relevant material

2.3 Reading and homework is discouraged

2.4 The emphasis is on leisure activities, which reduce the effort and the time budget that should be used for learning

2.5 The anti-educational content of favored leisure activities, like violent gangs, violent computer games, drugs

2.7 The active fight against religion, using an ethic of self-contention

2.8 Promoting estrangement between children and their parents

2.9 The lessening of controls on the persons accepted as educators. Colleges, which release false diplomas, become a mass phenomenon.

In school there are matters on which there is a special emphasis, like computer technology and mathematics, but an even greater emphasis is put on sport and sexual knowledge. It is not a sexual education as such, which would teach students to defend themselves against STD (the now fashionable expression for Sexually Transmitted Diseases), but picantesque information about arousal and pleasure. The April 2003 issue of *The APA Monitor on Psychology* had 30 pages on this subject (The Science of Sexual Arousal, Sex Differences in Rerelationships between Arousal and Orientation, Women and Sex, Sex Research Faces New Obstacles, "Outness", Key to Social Support for Gays and Lesbians, etc.). The same publication had explained in its August 1999 issue that androgynous sex roles were widely furthered. Sex as a lead to build a family is definitely deemphasized. In such conditions one should not wonder if nativity is shrinking in proportions which scare national leadership in the U.S.A. and in most European countries. Britain's population is stagnating, Germany is expected to lose 11 million people by midcentury, and the number of Italians may fall from 57.5 million to 43 million inhabitants (*Newsweek*, May 30, 2005). This also happens in India and Iran. As to France, which does not experience a demographical low, she greatly cares for families and allows them to better reconcile their professional and private lives. The same may be told of Denmark. Countries with the fewest family supports, like Italy and Spain, also have the lowest birth rate. One could also see a link between this fact and the recently voted Spanish law legalizing marriage between gay people. It is not this union as such that has negative consequences on the cultural and demographic phenomena. Unions between gay people had existed all along. It is the spectacularly handled legalization, with drums and "parades of love" through the big cities and the recommendation of androgynous sex roles. They all seem to supplant the heterosexual family, the principal source of children with the lure of a new experience and excitement of an alternative sterile sex orientation.

It is true, the worrying about the declining nativity balance is not shared by all. International demographic institutes, like the International Institute of System Analysis in Laxenburg (Austria) predict that the world population will peak at 9 billion and then start shrinking. This means, that the world population, now over six billion, is unlikely to double ever. For Longman (2004) this is an occasion for jubilating. A slowdown in fertility rates brings economic benefits, as the number of children declines, resources are freed for investment in adult consumption. Children have become costly impediments to material success, people who are well adapted to this environment will tend not to reproduce. Many others who are not so successful will imitate them. As a result there will be fewer children to look after, which leaves more resources for adults to enjoy (are all adults shareholders and investors?). However, the perspective of an everlasting enjoyment is clouded by the fact that the declining nativity causes the phenomenon of population aging, an imbalance of older people. Longman (2004) who full of apprehension raises the issue, does not state his preferential methods for solving it, but from all what the Internet Culture does and thinks, it is obviously euthanasia. Prevent the birth of babies through a furious propaganda against the family, for a gay lifestyle, or kill them through abortion, kill the elderly, and then enjoy yourself. This is the credo of the Internet Culture, and this is the future they are preparing for us. In these conditions to speak about an educational system seems caricaturable.

A true educational system is erected by society and for the benefit of society, and therefore it must have also a collective and not only an individual perspective of self-improvement (Giroux, 2001). Teaching has to deal with the transmission of knowledge, the facts of nature accumulated by scientists throughout centuries. In parallel, education should build the students' personality, and their social and vocational capabilities. Through its value system the Internet Culture constructs two difficult hurdles preventing the attainment of these objectives. It develops a "passion for ignorance" (Felman, 1987), and then it mystifies the facts that should be transmitted. A few decades ago the French psychoanalyst Jacques Lacan had suggested that ignorance is a "passion". Education had hitherto taken for granted the quest for knowledge and has designed methods to fill the void created by ignorance, but in the new world this void is desired and consciously created by the media. Therefore, in the first place, teaching has to do not with the lack of knowledge, but with resistance to knowledge (Felman, 1987). Society has created it with its own hands by drumming in everybody's ears the disdain towards tradition and scientific knowledge acquired through hard work and through the sacrifice of private enjoyment. What is today transmitted is not the mass of phenomena and events which took place in nature and society, but what is said on them (*Scientific American*, April 4, 2000). It is argued that also the personality is construed through the use of language by the social environment. Every civilization created its own concept of self and of the desired personality. The post-modern self-concept is decentered, multidimensional and in continual change (Anderson, 1997).

In provoking permanent cultural and psychological changes, globalization also takes its toll in education, which becomes an instrument of the global economy. In each country there is an invasion of the culture of Coca Cola, McDonald, rap and other such benefactions of the present time. The risk is that the young generation will not know the culture and the history of the nation to which they belong (Luca, 2001). This trend is reinforced by the overgrowing monopoly of the English language, and by the massive arrival of immigrants in Western countries. France is the only country, which fights for their assimilation, and seems to be aware what multiculturalism will mean for the national culture in the future. The problem is exacerbated by the overlayering of English on the national languages as a language of business, technology, and increasingly, of empowerment.The Italian *Corriere della Sera* (26 October, 2003) published a desperate call to save the national languaues, *Salvate le lingue dal monopolo dell'inglese*". Ironically, the same process also destroys "the Queen's English", as *Newsweek* (March7, 2005) calls it. The new English speakers, who outnmber native ones 3 to 1, are not just passively absorbing the English language, they are shaping and modifying it. New Englishes are mushrooming the globe over, from Hinglish, a mix of Hindi and English, Spanglog, a Spanish mix in the U.S.A., Tagalog in the Philippines, etc. Instead of trying to keep English pure, here too the brave researchers and educators of the Internet Culture give in to the level-reduction trend. They propose to renounce grammar and approve expressions like "she *look* very sad, a book *who*, *tree* instead of three, in order to avoid the difficult "th" sound, and so on.

Educational authorities are waiving control not only on the language in which the teaching is perfomed, but also on the educating staff. In September 2005 the Association of European Teachers presented to the European Commission a report regarding corruption in the academic institutions of Romania. At the University of Iassy, diplomas were sold in a considerable number, while the professsor, who led this practice, became the rector of the university. At the Faculty of Medicine in Bucharest professor jobs were given to people with very low scores in their contests. In a smaller university (Targu Jiu) one of the professors recognized in public that he does not know the title of his doctoral dissertation (*Magazin,* 7 July 2005). What education can such educators give to the students, if they have neither the knowledge, nor the educational ethos, which should characterize their profession?

In the US national goals in education have been published in 1989, but teachers said that they are not relevant, because the students are below the admissible level. The school offers several levels regarding skills, pace and assessment forms in Mathematics, English, in the biological and the social sciences. However, in some schools exams are made with open books, and are repeated until all students will pass, in other schools students are promoted even if they fail to pass the examination (*The Educational System in the US,* 1999).

The result of the "new" education in the U.S.A. is that 44 million adults are functionally illiterate and an additional 50 million people cannot read and comprehend texts above an eighth-grade level. Some muse that this situation is indicating that it is easier and cheaper to have children educated abroad, and then import the semi-finished product, college freshmen (*Newsweek,* February 23, 2004). What has been said is not astonishing, because the knowledge level of US colleges is constantly sinking towards mediocrity, the teachers are offering the knowledge which the students want and how much they want of it (Henry, 1994). It has to be added that in the US the national average of students' homework is less than 4 hours per week (Booth, Crouter, Shanham, 1999). Also the above-mentioned survey (*The Educational System,* 1999) has established that only a quarter of American high-shool students spend daily 1-2 hours at home work, the others spend under 1 hour or nothing, Even teachers used to prepare their classes for the other day during one hour only. Such situations are appearing in other countries too. In Israel the last decade has seen a massive opening of colleges, branches of universities from other countries (e.g. England, Latvia, etc.) which offer diplomas of B..A. and M.A. in management, for instance, after courses of three months, once a week, during which students are taught to answer the set of questions they will be asked on the final exam. For more safety, the exam papers are written by the students at home. It is very characteristic, that in the branches led from England, the teaching staff is called tutors, whose task is to propose, read loudly before the class or dictate the answers to the, say, ten exam questions, using the manuals arrived from the center in London or elsewhere. The consequences of this diploma industry are apparent in the bad shape of the Israeli economy, organizational management and public administration.

In whatever country, even if the school is not a fraudulous institution, the faltering surveillance, which causes cheating at tests becomes nearly institutionalized. In a recent huge study conducted with 50,000 college students by the Duke University Center for Academic Integrity (Vencat, 2006) 77 percent of the interviewees admitted to having cheated (in 1993 there were 56 percent and in 1963 only 26 percent). In the author's analysis, first of all, technological advances have made cheating easier than ever, through picture messaging cell phones or "outsourcing" via the Internet to experts even in India, to get an "original" essay. The fierce competition, which is also flooding the school is another cause of the surge in cheating, as educational credentials are seen throughout society as the only vehicles to success. I should like to emphasize, however, that the entire culture of the Internet Society furthers cheating. It is the lack of moral principles, which gives the O.K. to the cheating intention of students and makes supervisors look the other way.

In Western Europe the situation is not much different. Still, in Germany there is emphasis on imparting vocational skills and on helping students at all levels, not only the gifted ones. There are, however, special classes for the gifted (*The Educational System in Germany*, 1999). In the Internet Society the issue of fomenting gifted children, instead of staying a partial educational task, becomes a destructive social problem, because every attention is given only to them, while the instructional level of the masses of children plummets. High-profile educators seem not bothered by this situation, and argue that the main purpose must be centered on creativity ensuring the continuation of the technological innovations needed in a competitive market. Forgotten is the formerly much quoted saying of Edison that genius is one percent inspiration and 99 percent perspiration. Therefore Eysenck (1995) speaks of the absurdity of modern eductional methods, which stress the alleged natural creativity of children, but refuse to impart the necessary knowledge, without which creativity cannot function. Highly creative people always used to be opposed in society and creators had to have very weighty arguments in order to convince the public. Once Oscar Wilde has said that the public is wonderfully tolerant and forgives everything except genius. At all levels, even on the level of the endowed genius, who "seeks regions hitherto unexplored" (Lincoln), knowledge is needed to solve problems.

Highlights from the US Department of Education test on mathematics, issued in August 2001, show that more than one third of all high school seniors and more than two thirds of all black seniors don't have even a basic competency in mathematics. They do not understand elementary algebra, probability, and cannot make simple measurements of the kind required of a beginning carpenter. A simple study on reading showed that 23 percent of high school seniors lacked rudimentary reading skills and also the basic knowledge of science, history and geography (*Scientific American*, October 2001, p.15). An international survey made by the Organization for Economic Cooperation and Economic Development on real problem-solving among the 30 most industrialized nations found that the American 15-year old students ranked 24 out of 39 places. The four nations which occupied the first places were Finland, South Korea, The Netherlands and Japan (*APA Monitor on Psychology, 36 ,3*, 2005 ,p.11). We must not forget that these surveys targeted not general culture, but the most basic knowledge necessary at any place of work, and in a normal average social life.

There is a curious reaction to this situation from the leading strata. They see that there is a problem, but they do not want to accept it for what it is. Hoff Sommers (cf. Gross, Levitt et al., 1996.) disclaims the "pathological science", which sees dangers, where there are not, and "pathological journalism" which spreads such illusory dangers. In the same vein, Gibbs and Fox (1999) speak of the "false crisis in science and education". They quote Rickover's book from 1963, in which he called the American education a "national failure", and predicted that the "Russians will burn us", because of their more rigorous science and math coursess. The same had also been said on Japan in the 1983 publication "A Nation at Risk". Both conclusions proved premature, the authors say. They, and also others, like Porter (see *ibid.* p.67) remind that the competitiveness of the American economy is based on dozens of variables, from trade policy to the zeal of antitrust prosecutors. "Adequacy of schooling" is low on the list, beneath "port infrastructure quality". Quality of scientists and engineers falls even lower. Nonetheless, there had been about 1000 laws passed since 1970 on school reforms in the U.S.A., but with little impact.

Today high-school graduation in the US is virtually automatic W.A.Henry III (1994) points out that 63 percent of the students continue their studies after high school at an annual cost of $150 billion covered in 2/3 parts by state funding. Statistics show that 20 percent of job holders are overqualified for the jobs they are doing. There are much more diplomed managers and journalists than needed. We are speaking here of administrative statistics based on diplomas, not on factual skill qualification. Really imparted skills are low in the US school system. Colleges do not raise the cultural level of students. They downgrade it to the level of mediocrities.

Obviously, we are in need for fewer students, but of a higher quality. All this is true, but it is a problem of the educational system, which in the Internet Society churns out educational and cultural refuse. The former Soviet Union and Japan had shools with a much higher level of imparted knowledge, but their clout has been broken by outside economic and political circumstances and pressures. The same campaign is now under way to bring in line the German school system, which some years ago was a world beater, and prided itself of its egalitarianism. Today in Germany universities are overcrowded and underfinanced. Tuition payments and selective admissions had been abolished, in order to foster egalitarianism. Professors and staff became civil servants, earning the same pay at every university (*Newsweek*, February 23, 2004). Chancellor Schröder vowed to create a new tier of elite universities. As very timid steps of budget raising are under way, some universities with special links to American universities are performing their own "revolution". At Munich Technical University, president Wolfgang Herrmann is actively reorganizing his institution *along American lines.* He has toughened admission standards, and introduced professional managers. The aspiration is that such elite universites will be "Harvards", teaching the elite, habilitating the elite, being the supplier of an elite destined to dominate. On the horizon a twofold schooling system appears, one for the scions of families capable to pay the tremendous tuition fees, and the other for the masses of people.

The instrument for creating a double-railed school system is tuition fees and psychological testing in schools. Contrary to all pledges of culture fairness, and of a rigorous scientific basis, intelligence tests in the world are biased towards language-based media. Even the non-verbal intelligence tests like Raven's Progressive Matrices, which rest on categorizing and systematizing abilities is tributary to a culture where such operations are prominent. Besides, several types of intelligence have been described (Sternberg speaks of three types, Gardner of seven), and each life activity requires another type. Tests have been elaborated for each intelligence type, but validation measures are poor, and therefore in the US the President's Commission on Excellence in Special Education has proposed that the use of intelligence tests should be discontinued (*APA Monitor on Psychology, 34,* 2, 2003). The proposal was not heeded, and testing is merrily further on used for peremptorily deciding the fates of pupils who are sent into the one or the other path of the educational system. If also taking into account the "stereotype threat" produced   by cognitive and emotional burden (*APA Monitor on Psychology, 2003,* 34, 2), then a decision based on intelligence tests, which would deny a youngster access to a certain school, and relegate him/her to an inferior school type, or to one for the disabled, appears a most doubtful decision. It has to be emphasized that the problem is not the tests, but the use made of them. As an informational educational device tests are excellent instruments. However, the tests are tools for sustaining an unfair culture.as a control device, which cuts careers, and sends some of the subjects to a life of success, while others, are dispatched to an inferior type of schools, and are allotted to a fate of poverty, without giving them the chance of proving their capacities,

The aim of the Internet Culture is not to be fair, but to give legal sanctioning to the economically dominating social stratum to transmit its status to its scions through a privileged path of the educational system. The elite system of education, which is today already existing, imparts highly specialized narrow skills. The broad outlook and comprehensioon is missing, as a result of the values and the antipedagogical methods imposed by the Internet Culture. Meanwhile the "common" education makes out dioplomas, but fails in transmiting even basic knowledge and skills. Only much too late the students would realize that these diplomas are worthless theoretically and practically. They are only leading to the "catch 22" of overqualification, giving the prospective employer the legal justification to reject the job application.

The performance of both educational systems (including that for the elite) is low, as compared to the shools of past times. In the classic school the curriculum was established by society through its empowered organs of administration and education. Educators frequently criticized the system, but the process surely resulted in a systematically presented ensemble of contemporary knowledge and needed skills. True, many superfluous things were taught, much effort wasted, but those who later in life needed this knowledge, could securely rely on it, and creatively develop it further.The modern critics of the traditional education methods are right in so far that traditional curricula were indeed fragmented. Today there is a growing need to relate and to make choices, more complicated ones than did our grandfathers, and mainly, there has been a shift from an industrial to a technological society, which creates more information that the human mind can readily digest. However, the critics draw the wrong conclusions, when they ask that the traditional model should be cancelled in its entirety. First, they are asking that the distinct disciplines should be done away and (in Fogarty's view, 1995) that the curriculum should be composed of themes chosen by the students: The American Dream, The Ice Age, The Pyramids, Spiders, Wisdom, Shoes, etc., etc. Such themes are chosen by groups of students, different groups choose different themes. They analyze them, bring together information from various sources, discuss it, and stay with the conclusions *they* draw, not the ones put forward by science. Here is an excanple of how such teams tackled the problem of dinosaur extinction, a key subject for the Internet Culture (*see* Fogarty, *ibid.* p.49): Well, our group thinks, that the continental shift brought with it a colder climate, which affected the food supply". "Our team thinks, declared the representative of another group, that the plant-eating dinosaurs ate poisonous berries, and they died off, the meat-eating dinosaurs soon had no food source". "We think the dinosaurs were caught in a plague of some sort. . .". And then, as a dramatic high-energy finale, each group creates a rap song about their theories.

Notice, that in the whole procedure, the opinion of science on the issue (meteorite impact) was not even mentioned, and the rap song has probably immortalized the pupils' own fantasies. Secondly, such a few chosen issues cannot embrace the volume of knowledge modern men and women should have about natural science. Let us see how this kind of learning system went over to Germany, eager to catch up with the new culture. On September 20, 2005 the German state-sponsored television station Deutsche Welle, in its programme on the progress of science in Germany, reported the new achievements of pedagogical sciences. Primary-school children were shown learning a lesson of natural sciences in a park as the teacher gave each one of them a hazelnut and asked the kids to hide the nuts, so they could not be stolen. Later on, the pupils were given the task to retrieve the nuts. The comments underlined that the satisfaction caused by retrieving the hidden hazelnuts would ensure the learning, as the occipital and the deeper zones of the brain would send to the frontal lobes dopamine linking up nervous centers and opiumoids which cause pleasure. This felt pleasure would ensure the learning of the imprint. There are two mistakes in this modern "scientific" learning. First, one wonders what the kids have actually learned. The answer is: nothing. They simply hid away some hazelnuts, and then retrieved them. They have learned nothing about the nuts, where and how they grow, nor on squirrels which used to eat them. Perhaps they had a good time in the park, but in school they should also learn something. For entertainment there are other places and times. Another very serious problem is that in Germany, it so sems, the officially touted perspective on learning negates the pedagogical process based on psychological laws and phenomena, and tries to establish a direct linkage to the biochemistry of the brain. The biochemical process surely exists, but it is not the cause of the psychological-pedagogical processes, it is its consequence. The art of education is to provoke pleasure by the knowledge itself and not by artificial means of rap songs and hiding hazelnuts. Educators do not intervene directly (and they also should not!) in the biochemical brain process, they do it through pedagogical methods influencing the mind and the student's emotions, and this is well known, precisely in Germany from the time of Wundt, Herbart, Fröbel and Diesterweg. Apparently, they are "oldies" today. Modern schools transmit a gallimatias in crumbles, hoping it will produce opiumoids, which automatically would ensure learning. Only a clear knowledge can be learned, when it is involved in a purposeful action and integrated into a knowledge system. This is known long ago as the *law of learning (law of effect)* elaborated by Thorndike (1911/1932), and it holds that a living being will retain and reproduce those actions that have led to success and have been rewarded. A detailed application of this law to human learning is to be found in Zintshenko (1961), who emphasizes the link between the purpose of action, its instruments and the learning imprint in memory. An action is memorized which greater efficiency and rapidity if it is a purposeful behavior. Second in efficiency come the actions that are instruments in achieving the purpose. Best results are obtained if the subject performs a *mnemical action, i.e.* with the special purpose to learn and remember the behavior for a long period of time ("for all my life"). This means, that in order to learn something effectively, there has to be a clear orientation to do this, and a clear subject matter, representing a link in a certain scientific wholesomeness of knowledge, expressed in a logical consecution. Such a request has already been made by Comenius in the XVIIth century. There is also a need for a system of pedagogical methods guided by the teacher and which allows for the appropriation of the knowledge from the simple and easy to the more complicated and difficult (the psychological consecution).

In the school instruction of the Internet Society, even when the intention is to learn something, and not simply to amuse the kids by finding hazelnuts they had hidden, or roaring rap songs on dinosaurs, the system of science gets lost. This is so, because the subject matter is fragmented into themes interwoven with other disciplines, like literature, physics, history, and so on. It has also to be repeated that the enthusiasm for dinosaurs seems queer indeed. Society seems obsessed with these predators. When the "famous dinosaur researcher" Robert Bakker found the carcas of a new specimen, he allegedly whipped off his hat, fell to his knees, and tears welled up in his eyes. "It was", he said, "like seeing the Pietà" (Sic!) (*Newsweek*, June 27, 2005). Yet, the enchantment with dinosaurs cannot make known the history of English literature, nor the universal literature, human society, or its spiritual evolution. The fragmentation in knowledge produced by these curricula of chosen themes is worse than the one caused by the traditional method. Here we have to state that the traditional education made efforts to alleviate the effect of fragmentation. Says one of Fogarty's pupils (*Ibid.* p.6) "A subject is something you take once and never need to take again. I've had my shot of algebra. I'm done with that". In the traditional method, in Europe at least, you *take* subjects only at the university, not in high school, where the acquisition of basic science is obligatory. According to the system of each science, its subjects are developing during the school, progressing in a linear form or in concentric circles, thus ensuring the best chances of knowledge acquisition. No student can say he/she has had his/her shot of history or mathematics and is done with that. Educators who want to bring abreast the curricula with present-day requirements, must simply build into them linkages among various disciplines, and the school authorities should insert into the curriculum disciplines reflecting the technology of modern times, like computer work. It is a soluble question of time budget.

It has been repeatedly reported that industrialists have misgivings that they have to teach their employees what they should have learned in school. The issue has two faces. Mostly such complaints are referring to the inability of young employees to read elementary instructions, write a simple report or make a simple calculus of arithmetics. In this precisely the "new" teaching methods are guilty, which for the sake of "attractive" themes and rap songs neglect the basics. The managers' complaints could have, however, another source, the demand that school give vocational instruction, as was the tendency in the former Soviet Bloc. Again, the modernizers are on the wrong tack. Primary and high school must give the basic instruction and general culture needed by the future citizen at work, in the family and in his/her public roles. High schol is not, what used to be called a "trade shool" and a substitute for on-the-job training. Business managerswho want to lower production costs and are asking for job training in schools at the expense of general culture, should meet with a decisive rebuff. It should be however, clarified that while the purpose of high school (middle school in Europe) is not to train computer clerks, carpenters or travelling salesmen, it positively is its purpose to develop the love for work, the desire to embrace a vocation and to do hard work in it. Such purpose sharply opposes the "anorexia" regarding work and careers propagated by the media of the Internet Culture. Instead of the rap songs on dinosaurs we should like to hear a rap song on work.

As a matter of fact, work is not entirely absent in the preoccupations of this society, but as usual, it comes with a twist that deprives it of effort and supplants the quest for a general culture. Fogarty (1995) tells the story of a 5th grader, who has an exclusive passion for Indian lore, because since his toddler days he had played cowboys and Indians. The author likens him to the immersion of *aficionados* and graduate students in their field of studies. The two situations are different. The post-graduate students have already acquired their basic general knowledge in school and their professional immersion is a welcome specialization aided buy their general culture. The "specialization" of the toddler or the fifth grader, without any general culture, creates preposterous ignorants, who with their *a fortiori* wrong conceptions can only bring harm to science, to their environment, and also to their own future careers.

The learner-centered focus has to mean that room is given to the self-realization of the personality, who has interiorized the basic material and spiritual facts created by mankind. It cannot and should not mean that the pupils choose what they want to learn, because they do not have the experiencce and the expertise to decide what they will need in their lives and what society needs from them. It should also be mentioned that most recent research has stressed that direct instruction is more efficient than discovery learning (*APA Monitor on Psychology*, June 2004, p.54). A learner-centered focus also cannot and should not mean, that school has to be a place providing entertainment, which abhors effort. Lastly it should not mean that, acording to what Fogarty (1995) proposes, that the teams of learners compose a sociogram with the staff members they prefer and those, whom they feel, are unable to work with them on a long-term basis. Such a model does not apply, neither in the army, nor at the places of work. School must forge unity, friendship and the integration into an institution, even if the individual has a critical attitude towards it. People falsely educated in the rejection of such desired behaviors, may later on be candidates for vocational failure, because of disadaptive behaviors, or in some cases for suicide.

Paradoxically for his own theories, Fogarty stresses the need for students to learn how to learn, as the key survival skill for the XXIst century. However, he does not seem to understand that learning is a specific work activity, directed towards not always entertaining contents, and also performed as an obligation, under the tuition of an authority figure. When he declares that the focus in the class room will change from the teacher, as a store house of wisdom to a facilitator of student thinking (note the non warranted certainty!), he is proposing the wrong way. The teacher must develop the student's thinking, as a formative face of school instruction, but in order to do this, he shall stay a storehouse of wisdom. He is not only a facilitator, but a developer with responsibility for leading the whole process, as an empowered representative of society.

In this context we should discuss the problem of teaching machines and the role of computers in learning. The idea of instruction by automatic devices was first launched in 1926 by the psychologist S. L. Pressey, who constructed a machine, which presented knowledge items and verified their acquisition by the students. In 1954 B.F. Skinner succeeded in bringing the *programmed instruction* proposed by him to teachers' attention. He and other scientists created the theoretical framework for a new didactic procedure based on the following principles (Lumsdaine, 1960): The programme is presented in small steps, which can be easily learned, and each step asks for the student's active response, containing an application of the enounced knowledge. The students are receiving immediate feedback on their answer, and usually they are led through auxiliary questions to correct their answers. The students work on the programme in their own rhythm, the more capable ones are progressing in larger steps, the less capable are presented more explanations and more intermediary steps.

The educational experience has especially favored the creation of programmes in the exact sciences, based on the teaching of concepts, like physics, mathematics, but we have achieved good results also in the programming of history, based on the learning of facts, on condition to increase repetitive questions. The use of teaching devices (machines or manuals) had also to be accompanied by oral lessons of the teacher, in order to produce the emotional impact history should have on the young student (Krau, 1965).

After booming in the '1960s and '1970s, programmed instruction by teaching machines is today taken over by the computer. The outfit is of a more complex nature, the information that may be presented is richer, yet the basic problems remained. First, if the purpose is the acquisition and the correct understanding of the computer-presented information, then the learning programmes with verifying questions and correcting items are a necessity. In the Internet browsing this aspect is neglected. The Internet Society does not value acquisition of accurate knowledge and their memorization. Secondly, the machines, the computer can at best instruct, but not educate, in the words of the Spanish philosopher Savater (2005), it can give *"infomación"*, but not *"formación"*. Savater (2005) continues: Education is tightly linked to ethics, it is a necessary preparation for entering the world of citizenshhip. One cannot merely train people to press computer or machine buttons or to make money, without forming their capacity to live together in a community, to cooperate and to be citizens. This is not a task for a computer, the "human link" has to step in, and again the human teacher must have also control of the instructional process. Of course, teaching should not be done dogmatically. In Sweden and in Canada the teacher discusses the curriculum with the students. "The topic is energy, tell me what you want to learn", he asks. As the discussion moves ahead, the students invariably realize under the guidance of the teacher that they have to know certain basic facts and principles. The first step in discussing a subject matter used to be to get the children's believes. Teachers then use some of the students' ideas as starting points for experiments or presentations, and help them understand why scientifically accepted explanations are better (*Scientific American*, October, 1999). In these advanced teaching methods students are *participating* in the process of their own instruction, but the teacher is *leading* them on the way to enter a highly motivated learning of the basic knowledge, foreseen by the curriculum. However, it is not them who are deciding on it. One must definitely resist the quest to create a school of fun and entertainment. Good schools prepare strong thinkers, but they care to give the thinking mind a broad basis of facts, the right facts, from which skills needed by society are derived.

This aim of the educational process is obstructed in the Internet Culture not only by using wrong, pupil-centered methods for choosing what will be "learned" and how, but also by the unavailability of a correct, unbiased exposure of the facts. Here is what an Italian history textbook for high schools (Juridical State – Economic State) says on the events of the Berlin wall: "In 1961 the Western powers succeeded in putting into practice the material separation of Berlin into two zones by constructing a wall . . . Only on the 9 of November the East-German president Krenz, in an understanding with the Russian president Gorbatchev, announced the demolition of the wall and the reunification of the two Germanies" (*Corriere della Sera*, 10 April 2005). Every word in the quoted fragment is false, and one wonders, whether the ignorance of the writer or his bad faith is greater. Obviously, the freedoms proclaimed by modern society have been used to create citizens with a leftist-communist perspective on the world. It is the Jacobin model of scholarship (Giroux, 2001) in which an attempt is made to destroy the other person or group in order to establish one's point of view, and then prevent their possibility of exercizing their rights. The wrong teaching methods support such indoctrinations, because the young students believe the printed words of their textbooks, from which they gather their information, as the teacher stays a sympathetic bystander only. The students have no way of knowning the monstruous falsity of what they have considered as "independently found information".

To these reproaches the modern educators answer, that their aim has been to liberate the school system from every constraint, in order to further the realization of independent personalities, who make independent choices. Here again we are offered the solution of pouring out the baby with the bath water. There has to be some control on the learning contents, on their scientific correctness, on their systematic character. Do we want to have masses of ignorant rogues in school, whose sole memory from their school years is a rap song on dinosaurs with a blasphemous, abhorrent comparison between these animals and Michelangelo's Pietà? In the name of free choice of teaching materials do we want to grow a youth indoctrinated with cheap political lies, like the one told on the Berlin wall? The key word is poised judgement, and in it even rote learning has its place (e.g. learning the nation's anthem or paragraphs from the Declaration of Independence). The learning of a foreign language, with its grammar and literature is also welcome in an age when one deals with globalization and multiculturalism. On both sides of the Atlantic such knowledge would promote the dissolution of hatred, and a mutual understanding. And if speaking of languages, the real languages (not the Pigeon-English) and even Latin are real facilitators. Those who had to learn several languages, and not only Roman ones, know that an elementary knowledge of Latin grammar made their task a much more easy one. It saved them years of toil. There are also the Latin proverbs, famous quotations, so precise, suggestive, you will never forget them. Beyond this, Latin literature conveys a life conception with people ready to make sacrifices for one's friends, one's community, one's fatherland. Research tells (Drumann, Mommsen – cf. Cauer, 1911), and it is true, that the masses of common people may not have always behaved that way. The point is that the arts and the literature of the antique world, including the Indian and the Chinese, show us examples which have educated generations in the best traditions of the Western World and of the East. They made possible the spiritual advancement of humanity and presented images for imitation to youth throughout the centuries up to this very day.

The problem has also another very inportant face. Even should you give school children the right to decide on learning contents, this is not an absolute liberty, as it is presented. There is always the influence of the cultural environment, of peers, mass media, significant adults. The moment school authorities with their peadogical expertise withdraw from exercizing their right and duty to supervision, it is the aformentioned factors which strengthen their influence. Concretely, doubtful values of egoism, pornography, disdain of the weaker and violence will have more and more influence on the educational process. Anderson and associates (*APA Monitor on Psychology*, July/August 2003) asked more than 50 stiudents to listen to a collection of violent songs ("Shoot 'Em Up, "Hit 'Em Hard") and nonviolent ones like "Finger Lickin' Good", "Love vs Loneliness." Then tested the subjects with word associations and word completion tests, and with the State Hostility Scale. The results indicated a relationship between violent song lyrics and increased aggressive thoughts and feelings of hostility. Violent song lyrics increase negative emotions and thoughts that may lead to aggression.

Similar information comes from all parts of the world, and also beforee 9/11, 2001. According to the data of British Telecom and Research International, 60 percent of the multiplayer (concomitantly playing with others) stay connected to the Internet up to weekly 14 hours. One of four players is female (*Corriere della Sera*, 22 Octobr 2001). The paper finds this age normal, because, in order to become a champion, you need years of training. This means that the game addiction and the participation in violent games take place during the high school years. Among the plays are "First Person Shooting", the Conspirators Game Majestic, in Italy Grande Mela, where the hero makes his way through explosions, or Quake III Revolution, a terrorist game. All these games are considered dangerous for fomenting violence, but nothing is done to put a halt on them.

The Internet addiction to violent videogames has bad consequences, which derive from the desire to be like the heroes of those games, and actually live the game situations. The latter are frequently linked to amusements including alcohol and drugs, while also fomenting violent behavior. In October 2001 the New York Academy of Sciences invited Dr. Miczek for an overview of research regarding violence (*Academy Update,* Jannuary/February *2002).* The speaker declared that the most important general insight of recent years has been that life experience can shape brain chemistry, and the mere anticipation of a fight increaes dopamine levels and reduces serotonin, preparing the actual fight bahavior. The picture is completed by alcohol consumption. About 60 percent of all violent acts, murders, child abuse, family abuse, assaults are associated with the consumption of alcohol. Here it has to be added that the antisocial behavior of children may have its premisses in the correspondent behavior of the mother during her pregnancy: exaggerateed alcohol consumption, drug addiction, emotional loads deriving from addiction to violent TV programmes. Therefore some researchers say that the basis for aggression is laid down in the mother's womb (*APA Monitor on Psychology*, August 1998). Nonetheless, a key factor to antisocial behavior is direct incitation to violence, also without any alcohol. Even reading "professional" war correspondences may constitute such a factor. In a revealing interview the renowned photographer Ferdinando Scianna (*Corriere della Sera*, 16 January 2002) describes war photographers as addicts to their vocation, frequently also to drugs, and who "sleep with phantoms". They are construing the picture they take by "arranging" the real situation and they do it, because a reality told without strong overtones does not have the necessary emotional impact on the public. Today the photographer is not an invisible witness, and when he/she arrives, the people by themselves "arrange" an event. Scianna tells the case of the lynching of two Pakistani prisoners in the war faught by India for the *i*ndependence of Bangladesh from Pakistan. The bloody scene occurred at *and because of* the arrival of a picture thirsty war correspondent, who for this "corrageous correspondence" has later on received the Pulitzer Prize. The effect of such "news breaking" may be catastrophic violence, but behind every picture taken, Scianna tells, may always be the truth, but also lies. The fabricated photographs enter the schools through the newspapers as documentary material for the independent research of the students, and "educate" them in the spirit of a bloody revenge ideology, of burning hatred and violence. Nonetheless, all would have been based on a lie, stirring up the wrong feelings and in the wrong direction.

Basically, the trend for violence roots in educational experiences with violence, including media watching, Internet games, and "fatal friendships", says Sageman (2004). He analyzes the profile of modern terrorists, and reaches the conclusion, that, contrary to what had been thought, the suicide bombers are not brainwashed youths, indoctrinated into religious zealotry, but happened to become fast friends with existing memebers of the jihad, who recruit them for terrorist activities. Of Sageman's sample 68 percent joined the fundamentalist movement because their friends were already involved, another 20 percent became acquainted with the movement through a family member, over which the family had little control. This clearly means, terrorism spreads because of the lack of control by school and family over the subject's peer groups, while the attraction towards violence preaching peers is acquired through addiction to violent video games, or simply by watching violence on TV, again not controlled by family and school. It then depends upon the peers, whether the violence of the group will be directed towards common gangsterism or terrorism with a religious-fundamentalist nuance. In Naples (Italy) the police has been surprised to discover a regular alliance between students from the most respected high school of the city with the Camorra (the Mafia of Naples). The object of this understanding was the theft of motorcycles and handy-phones in return for drugs. The school authorities had remained silent, entrenched in their endeavor to liberalize the educational process, and this meant to them not to intervene into the lives and the behavior of their students. Then arrests have been made, and the concerned parents have brought the whole matter before the public (*Corriere della Sera*, 16 January, 2002).

What is curious in the great ongoing debate on pornography is that the participants are silent about the role of the educational system. Their silence furthers the antisocial consequences. The connivant refuse to take a stand, to spread the right moral values and to enforce them is a key propagating factor of the wrong cause. Moles (1967) compared the diffusion of "cultural representations" with the spread of an epidemy. Scientifically, this is not true, although in this special case pornography may be likened to an outbreak of the cholera. The diffusion of cultural phenomena, "cultural representations" as Moles calls them, is only feasible with social support, the desire to be adopted, what cannot be said on diseases. An educational system voicing strong resistance to the spread of violence, pornography and drugs, would substantially reduce these negative social phenomena.

Pornography is not the only cholera of the Internet Culture, whose spread is impassibly watched by the educational system. Another problem is the fashion of dirty language evoking the Tourette syndrome, usually considered a malady, whereby sufferers bark, contort their faces, and without any provocation yell what is called coprolalia and offensive epithets. While learned medical people debate whether Tourette's is a neurological condition or a mental illness, its culture-bound characteristics are known for centuries (*The Sciences*, November/December 1999). A visitor of a modern high school will be impressed by entire classes uttering coprolalistic shoutings, and it is clear that this is no disease, but a phenomenon supported by a dysfunctional and misfunctional educational system. Neither the family, nor the school did take any measures, persuasional or punitive, to stop the development of such a scourge. Four-letter words like shit, f... and other appear in every sentence, while the teaching staff lends a deaf ear, or is secretely enjoying it.

What can be said on the fascination of the American society and of its schools with serial killers? When in the early '1990s a man named Wine Potts was arrested as a suspect for committing over 14 murders, trucks and cars filled with smiling adults and children were streaming into Estillfork to catch a glimpse of Pott's cabin. "There'll probably be a movie about it" they said. Television viewers were tuning into interviews with Jeffrey Dahmer, the Milwaukee cannibal, who dismembered 17 young men (*Time International*, April 4, 1994). Experts blame the formation of serial killers on the breakdown of their family and on their abusive childhood. However, it is the public fascination with them, which reinforces such tendencies, and we shall add, that it is the indifference of the ongoing educational activity, or the quiet acquiescence of the teaching staff which reinforces the public's fascination with such monsters. The same may be told of the vocal complaints if killers are sentenced to death. Often, in their classes, teachers loudly excpress their opposition to killers' execution. They even participate in night watches in front of the gates of penitenciaries, when the punishment is to be carried out, but do not even mention the monstruous killings, and the disrespect for human dignity,which the convict evinced. In vain scientists say these men are "failures at life at every single level (*Time, ibid.*), the media make of them heroes, and the youth are absorbing this wrong image. "People built me into something" said the convicted murderer Lucas, "I became a monument. I got fans, mail, friends, people that would die fior me". Has anybody recently heard a person say that he/she is ready to die for America?

There is another point to the story. True, the school must be seriously accused of sending the wrong messages, but even if it were the right ones, they would not get through, as it happens with smoking and protected sex. Says Tom Coates, director of AIDS prevention studies, "People do a lot of dangerous things, like smoking, dangerous driving. It shouldn't be a surprise that they don't act on information they are given" (*APA Monitor on Psychology*, April 2003, p.58-60). The article continues telling that today people with AIDS is no more seen as dying and scary, because they live longer and reasonably well with antiviral medications. Then they are always moral messages in the discussion about sexual behavior, and this can lead teenagers to distrust the information they are given (Sic!). So, the educational system has played down moral values up to such a point, that introducing them in a discussion, even a vital one for the person's health, will lead to discarding the entire information.

In the Internet Society the messages in educational matters are wrong, but also the whole content and ways of communicating the information are inadequate. First, it is the Internet itself, with its uncontrollable information (or manipulative disinformation) spread, which undermines the receipt of societally useful knowledge. There is also an unfairly imposed preference for this medium, marginalizing the printed information in books and journals. Jane Healy speaks of "endangered minds" as she writes, "Fast-paced lifestyles, coupled with heavy media diets of visual immediacy, beget brains misfitted to traditional modes of academic learning. Finally, the future generation may be unable to concentrate long enough to finish a novel" (*Newsweek*, October 3, 2005, p.95). Precisely, because books take more time for perusal, they can give richer information and a more convincing argumentation. Above all, the Internet is ephemeral, the printed book will last. Surely, the rapid understanding and the fuzzy thinking promoted by the Internet texts are valuable qualities, but they should complete the thorough argumentative thinking based on a rich knowledge of past human achievements, and must not supersede them. The European countries see the coming débâcle. Galli della Loggia (2005) points out that Italy has left her elementary and high schools to decay. They had been the flowers of society. Now Italy is a country which *does not read,* which is addicted to television, which already for years has not produced a great movie or a great novel, which only ruminates what has occurred 10, 30, 60 years ago. Italy has become a nation of a middle class with exaggerated dimensions, which is incapable of inventing something new, of elaborating value syntheses and new ideas. It should be added that the same could be told of every other contemporary society, Germany, France or the US. No really great movies, no great books, even if commercial publicity is trumpeting otherwise. The much vaunted "Lord of the Rings" is slightly better than, say Blade 1 or Blade 2, but it presents the same exaggerated graphic, loathsome, counterproductive violence. The same appears in Mel Gibson's Passion of Jesus, intended to be the film of the century, but it turned out blasphemous and rejected, because of its depiction of violence and ideological undertones.

All this happens as reliable reseach repeatedly proves, that young people who are reading books, literature, are more active than those addicted to TV (*Newsweek*, June 21, 2004, p.56), that TV addiction deturnes from acquiring the necessary information to succeed in learning tasks (*Scientific American*, 286, 2, p.62), that the information acquired through books is richer and more precise than the one offered by the electronic media (*Scientific American*, March 2000, p.7). Internet publications, the cinema, talk shows and picture news-reports have surely their role in society, but it should not be the key role, while supplanting any other source of information. Giving exclusivity rights to the dinosaur barking from the TV screen, and reducing history to a comics show is creating people of self-righteous ignorants with inflated Egos, that prevent the absorption of any differing information.

However, it would be wrong to only accuse the electronic communications of this state of affairs. Especially in the last years, numerous books, which this society has produced, are not better than its electronic communication output. Indeed, it seems the book market is adapting to the new ideology. Graphic novels without text have leaped from $75 million in 2001 to $207 million in 2004, have finally broken out of humble shops thanks to Spider-Man and other graphic literature, which requires no effort to read and reflection. Academics in the US and in Europe are teaching comics as literature in the classroom (*Newsweek*, August 22, 2005). Manuals are looked upon as commercial items only, without any thought given to their educative value. Their aim is not to give the most precise presentation of knowledge at the school level. It is to be entertaining at the level of the lowest buffoonery with stories on fornicating kings, (the latter are described as if this would have been all what they did), corrupt priests, weak, immoral presidents, even if history had mainly presented them with positive qualities. Examples are the king Louis XIV of France, queen Elizabeth I of England, the cardinals Richelieu and Mazarin of France, the presidents J.F.Kennedy, and D. Eisenhower of the U.S.A. On Eisenhower it is said that he was ill-suited for the White House (*Newsweek*, January 26, 2004, p.34). On J.F.Kennedy we are told that he was weak and frail, he had to take medication in order to hold a speech, and he was not able to memorize the imporant sentences from the speeches written for him (*Corriere della Sera*, June 22, 2003; November 18, 2002). The writers of the Internet Society are elated with throwing mud on great leaders. "Reading about imperfections of famous people gives yougsters more freedom to dream of what they may accomplish", reads an article in *Newsweek* (February23, 2004, p.8). To dream of slave ownership, of cheating one's wife? It seems that what some writers are proposing as chief materials for educating American youth in the spirit of patriotism is to be unable to memorize a few words in a foreign language, to be so fat that one doesn't enter a bath tub. At any rate, these are the traits emphasized in American presidents.

"Power is a game", declares Greene (1998) in his "educative" work for the young generation and adults. "You must learn to wear many masks and keep a bag full of deceptive tricks. Deception and masquerade should not be seen as ugly or immoral"(p.XX). He then continues his nearly 500-page book with the exhortation to give up character, as a chronic, stable mode of reaction (p.423), and also sincerity, because oinly a bad actor is sincere (p.196). "Never promise a gradual improvement through hard work, rather promise the moon. . . luck, self-sacrifice and time in one fantastic stroke, bypassing work (p.266-67)". Greene presents an entire gallery of heroes in order to support his "educative" theories. The summit places are occupied by the world's con artists and deceivers, Yellow Kid Weil, Count Lustig, robber baron Jay Gould and the circus director Barnum, but some politicians also appear. To judge by the number of quotations, his chief hero and example for mankind is Mao-Tse-tung, mentioned a record 8 times wirth "enlightening" episodes. True, F.D. Roosevelt is also mentioned in 4 episodes, one of them praising his ability to answer critics of his insensibility to the money waist on his dog, Fala, while so many Americans were still living in poverty. His speech in defense of his dog was one of the most popular he ever gave, says Greene (p.306). This case should exemplify the greatness of the president and exhortate the younger generation to imitate him.

The conclusion of what has been said on the education in the Internet Society, is that its deplorable situation is not caused by the inadequacy of this or that curriculum or method of teaching. It is again a systemic failure of this society with its value system and driving forces. In the realm of education the flaw bgins with a negativistic attitude towards the family, where the foundations for the education of the future citizen are laid. Therefore, at this point, we should take a closer look on the attitude of the Internet Society towards the family. In the past hundred years, the family, as a social institution, has undergone changes in its size, cohesion, in the content of its activities and in the essential links among its members. The extended family declined, and in the industrialist and post-industrialist eras, the tendency had been to reducing it to the nuclear family. Even this process had weighty social and cultural consequences. The day-to-day contact with the older members of the extended family declined, an so did their influence and their authority. From a position of honor they arrived to a stance far less valued. Lieberson (2000) has followed up this process in the names given to children, and has shown that, while in earlier times child names used to be those of their grand-parents, this custom vanished to give way to the influence of existing fashions in naming. The erosion of the family influence continued in the Internet Society, which is leading a concentrated attack even against the nuclear family. This happens, because being a social institution the family has (or had) some authority over its members, it could put a hold on some ways of amusement or try to introduce some oldfashioned ethics, aesthetical conception or even religion in its lifestyle and into the education of their children. It could also try to impose savings and refrain from uncontrolled money spending, harming thus business. Finally, the family used to give to the education of their children a certain direction and content. All this is not acceptable to the present-day society. Nevertheless, the family cannot be negated frontally. There could be resistance. Therefore, the attack has not been led against the family as such, but against its essential, central institution, marriage, against its rights, authority and activities. Marriage cannnot be defined, declares Sperber (1996) and goes on saying that marriage is merely a bundle of locally defined rights, hence all its universal definitions are vain. In this he leans on Lévi-Strauss (1956) who has said that everywhere a distinction exists between marriage, a legal group-sanctioned bond between man and woman, and a type of permanent or temporary union resulting from violence or consent. He concludes that marriage does not denote a precise type of cultural linkage.

From here the way is open to introduce into the concept and the practice of marriage contents which are contradictions in terms and actually negate it. The demolition concerns several key issues. Since time immemorial, marriage has been the union approved by the group between a man and a woman, frequently also accompanied by a religious ceremony, a relatively stable union, that should further the procreation of the next generation, and the material and legal protection of offsprings. Hitherto public opinion, its leaders, the artists, educators and the media would declare such a union as a desirable goal for youth. Today all these pillars of marriage, and with it of the family, have been destroyed. In Spain the new Zapatero law admits marriage between same-sex partners, with the right to adopt children, obviously from people who do not want them. It is not my intent to make value judgements on homosexuals and lesbians, but they forcibly have another world picture on human relations, and it is this different world picture, which they, again forcibly, pass on to their adopted children. At best, the result would be an androgynous lifestyle, incompatible with a stable, heterosexual family.

American lawmakers have seen the danger and in the last years have taken measures to promote marriage in its classical conception. Promptly, they were attacked by a choir of Internet Culture birds. The marriage-promotion funds, the latter told, would be better spent on more effective strategies, helping poor women equip themselves to better support their families and move out of poverty. Others chirp that increased domestic violence is also a concern, if women of the low socioeconomic level are encouraged to marry (*APA Monitor on Psychology*, 35, 8, 2004, p.42-43). There are several points to be added to this issue. Violence and a negativistic attitude towards children are not exclusively linked to a low socioeconomic level, and are not specifically appearing in the US. Every day we are reading in German, French and Italian newspapers, that women from all social strata are arrested as supects for killing their children. In these days France sees in then town of Angers the trial of 35 parents, who lended their 45 children as sex slaves. A guilty verdict was given on July 27, 2005. On August the 1st started in the German town of Brieskow the trial of a woman, who killed one by one her children, as they were born, nine altogether, and buried them in the backyard of her house. Researchers found violence towards children also in Finland, despite her greater support systems. General economic difficulties, unemployment and budget cutbacks correlated in all social strata with spousal hostility, lack of support, answered by aggression and by the disobedience of children (*APA Monitor on Psychology*, 35, 6, 2004, 14).

In the U.S.A. interested organizations are vesting the whole issue in an ideological clout. The Administration desperately tries to keep out of this, and to implement a sound policy based on evidence, but it is under a constant tremendous "politically correct" attack. The marriage-promoting measures the Administration took, were based on research showing that children are happier in two-parent (low-conflict) biological families, regardless of their socioeconomic level (*APA Monitor on Psychology*, 35, 8, 2004). Although there is reliable research evidence attesting to the beneficial effect of orderly family life on children, the data are ignored and prominence is being given to the "politically correct" opinions rejecting married families. This ideology does not center on the child's life happiness, but on the feminist idea, that the mother should feel good, free and sexually satisfied, happen what happens. Therefore lately, adoption and artificial insemination by donor have risen to prominence in media coverage. Anderson (1997) points out that these practices mark the start of the new *modu-*

lar parenthood, and are essentially influenced by globalization. Prospective parents range about the world in search of adoptive children. The latter become modular commodities, as also do various body fluids, organs and secretions for insemination. We can give them and receive them, buy them and sell them.

Even if some women are bearing their own babies, the high-tech Internet Society is present, women receive epidural anesthesia and other drugs to facilitate labor, and they want to have a say in scheduling delivery at their convenience, instead of the baby's. Therefore more women are asking for high-tech delivery, C-sections, and doctors are quick to perform them, one in four deliveries, stastistics say. The procedure wastes money and makes childbirth less safe. It slows recovery, requires more rest, and later negative influences on the child's psychology are probable. These influences join the inherent child-rearing difficulties, and those added by a less as expected collaboration by the husband. A negative influence is also produced by the desire that the child be ahead of the developmental curve, involved in artistic and athletic acitivities, fed with a "healthy" diet, which the child loathes and vocally rejects, etc. Studies suggest that one third to one half of new parent couples experience as much marital distress as couples already in therapy for marital difficulties. The 2004 National Marriage Project at Rutgers University concludes that children seem to be a growing impediment for the happiness of marriages (*Newsweek*, May 16, 2005).

Or are they? It depends on how you would like to see the happiness of your family. In the traditional family the child had its well defined place within the family and the parents were proud of it. Indeed, research attests to the fact that such families are happier. Married couples tend to have more assets, live longer and are better adjusted emotionally than their single counterparts. Children thrive when reared in stable two-parent families (*Newsweek*, March 1, 2004). Introduce the Internet Culture and all changes. There is a wild propaganda against marriage, spearheaded by "artistic" productions, TV shows. The result has been an attitudinal decoupling of marriage, sexual activity and fertility. Women are pressured to put career and "outgoing" needs before the familly. In Western countries this attitude is leading to a drop in nativity. The feminist ideology devalues men. It rejects their biological role as fathers, of founding a family, of procreating and educating children. Under the cover of (legitimate) demands for equality between genders, feminism is leading an unfair vocational competition against men. Here again we are seeing the characteristics of the Internet Culture, which is incapable of setting limits. The basic ideology of equal rights in the family and in the socioeconomic domain is undoubtedly correct, but the following rejection of the family, of marriage, of children and of the masculine gender are wrong and are leading to catastrophic developments. In the 1999 The *Scientific American* (October, p.22) alerted that the number of men receiving a bachelor's degree from US institutions has remained the same for 25 years, while the number of women has steadily increased. Analysts suggested that men's failure to keep up with women traces to stress earlier in life. Boys have fewer role models in recent decades, because of the decline of two-parent families. They have poorer grades because they disproportionately suffer from culturally acquired learning disabilites, and are attracted by peer groups despising school education. Women now are receiving 55 percent of a master's degree, and they outnumber men in bachelor degrees in a 104 to 100 ratio. Thus educated women have a harder time finding a comparable educated mate. In ever greater numbers men are prone to depression, but they would not acknowledge it, and would not ask for help. Levant (1997) developed the theory of normative alexithymia (the inability to express emotions) but instead of the change of culture, he proposes to coax men into accepting psychotherapy. Such a procedure would destroy what is left of the traditional model of a man, in which professional psychological help is accepted only in most severe situations. By the way, psychotherapy would not improve men's social standing in this culture and their educational record with all its consequences. Statistics show that in the US some 50 million people cannot read or comprehend above an eigth-grade level, and the majority of them are men. All this reinforces the feminist-propagated rejection of marriage and of children who seem to hamper women's career advancement.

This attitude seems to have recently gained support from the "gospel of joy" that men are no more needed for conceiving children. The Lilavati hospital in Mumbai, India, as also the "famous" (some say ill-famed) dr. Severino Antinori from Rome, working in a "Mediterranean" country, care that every woman , be she even sexagenary. Also the lesbian couples can conceive their own genetic offspring. Says Tiger (1999) in his book *"The Decline of Males"*, more women are having children without men, and therefore more men are without the love of families. Women as a group are working more and earning more, while men are working less and earning less. Women are voting in patterns distinctly different from the voting tendencies of men, a trend that affects government and public dialogue. If in the past we have seen vocal demonstrations of women for equality, we are seeing now men organized as "Angry Dads" demonstrating before Parliament in London for more fathers' rights in childkeeping. When the journal *Newsweek (*April 11, 2005) published an unbalanced article about mothers' difficulties in childrearing and asked them to behave like perfect mothers without time to themselves, angry readers (rightfully) objected (*ibid.* August 15, p.13) that the article marginalized the fathers, as if they had a secondary role in children's education. All the solutions to give mothers and the families a break excluded the fathers. The article has presented a situation where the woman had to take care of every detail in her husband's life as if he were handicapped. Described is a dominance of women which does also wrong to themselves.

The rejection of children is known to have catastrophic consequences, but in the modern world new disastrous manifestations appear. In more and more countries rings of rejected and abandoned children are roaming the streets in criminal gangs or serving as soldiers in rebel armies in three quarters of the world's conflicts. Singer (2005) points out that in the past there had been an unwritten "law of innocents", that has longly exempted children from armed conflicts. Today conventional armies have to accept killing child soldiers, while hopefully creating escape corridors for the kids.

What escape corridors? It is the new culture, which bars them, and a charity of several million dollars cannot solve the problem. If you destroy the family and the welfare state, there is nobody left to open corridors and keep them open. The Internet Culture has done all it could to destroy the family. In a congress of social psychologists, held in Israel in January 2004, it was proudly declared that the family is in the process of transformation from monogamy to an open marriage. Of course, one could object that one should not give prominence to the wet dreams of every congregation held somewhere in the world. The problem is, precisely the Internet takes care to give them a global circulation. Fortunately, even in Israel the issue is only partly true, but were it, the family as a social unit ensuring a common life with the procreation of children, would have ceased to exist. There are few women who can love their husband and their children, when they every day or night are in bed with other men, and there are few men who are disposed to accept such bahaviors. In such case it is not only theoretically, as in the antique Roman law, but also practically impossible to know who is the father of their children.

There is another group of women, who simply loathe living together with a man, a stranger with all inherent frailties, and they are convinced that they are much better off living as single mothers with their test-tube babies. How will such a child be later on capable of thinking to marrry? It pleases the propaganda media of the Internet Society to present the status of women today as the achievement of freedom. Craik (1994) shows that they remain enslaved by the ideological-cultural fetishism of the present society. As women moved from the constricted family-dominated culture to the more individualized values of modern society, the form and content of domination changed, but new authorities replaced the old ones. In the name of freedom from tradition, they trapped women in fresh forms of sexual objectifications and bound them to the consumerized and sexualized household.

It should be noted that in the abovementioned opinion it is spoken of a household, not of a married family, which society strives to supersede using all its economic and ideological means. Booth, Crouter et al. (1999) point out that there used to be a mismatch between desired goals for work and family and the limited opportunities in modern society for fulfilling them. The first result is the postponement of plans to marry, which looks innocuous, but has very negative consequences. In fact, after all postponements, many plans to marry will be cancelled. Then the family must cope with the decreasing chances for men to get a job, which favors the already discussed depreciative attitude towards men. On the other hand, the postponement of marriage has not induced sexual abstinence, thus leading to a rising nonmarital birth rate. The latter is furthered by the increasing fashion to use nonmarital alternatives, like cohabitation. Interestingly, it is not linked to those who face the least secure economic futures. The support for cohabitation in lieu of marriage is quite general across the population, and differences by social class are generally not significant. Especially young men who value their leisure pursuit are drawn to cohabitation, while among women such a solution is sought by those preferring lots of money and career goals

(Booth, Crouter et al., 1999). The quoted authors think that the current slow-down in the achievement of career stability could be partly seen as result of a lower interest in marriage instead of its cause.

It may be therefore concluded that there is a positive link between career maturity and marriage, but mainly at the start of the vocational activity. The research recorded in Booth, Crouter et al. (1999) brings two important facts to attention. First, young men's career maturity has a strong positive effect on marriage plans, but although current earnings constitute an important variable of career meturity, the latter is not a function of the earnings they produce. The research variables tend to form a package. Low education, stop-gap employment, part-time work tend to go together, as does the reverse, more education, career employment, year-round full-time work and higher earnings. In this sense it appears that the youth of today is in need for a longer period of preparation for their vocational careers, and a delayed transition to adult roles are increasingly becoming likely. It frrequently appears in a prolonged dependency of adult children on parents. Premature transitions to the labor force, to residential independence, to romantic unions or to parenthood may handicap the ability of young adults to establish economic independence and maintain a family (Booth, Crouter et al. *ibid.*). This phenomenon has also existed in the past. What is new, is that, while women's early earning position has a positive influence on marriage decisions, a woman's later stable job and good earnings may have a weighty role in her decision to divorce. The prosperity trend for women foments the dissolution of families. There are cases when it from the start on impedes family formation.

The consequences of a life in poverty have largely been described. Depression, disobedience of children and the antisocial behavior in adolescence and later on, have been frequently mentioned. Much less attention has been given to the educational syndrome of the inexistent father and/or the contempt for the masculine gender, both of actuality in the new culture. I have come to study these phenomena during long years, as a side-component of vocational maladjustment standing in the way of self-realization (Krau, 1997). I found that among the factors for achieving adjustment at the place of work and trough it self-realization, there is one which seems naive and banal, but is deeply rooted in the personality and has far-reaching consequences. It is a negative attitude towards authority figures at the place of work. A careful scanning of the data has proven, however, that eventually such an attitude led to maladjustment only if the subjects characterized their father in denigrating terms, or they came from an disintegrated family. It appears therefore, that frequently such attitudes are not induced by events in the employing organization, but reflect a deeply rooted personality disturbance, which seriously hinders adjustment and self-realization. Curiously, it is a one-way influence. The more negative the attitudes are, the greater is the obstacle they represent for career realization, but high degrees of positiveness do not increase the chances for an enhanced career path.

The second curious phenomenon is that for both genders the "malign" influences of negative attitudes are produced by the father's image, and this after decades of changes in the structure of the family. It ensues that the father's presence in the process of child rearing has an especially weighty importance, and not only in the classical family structure described by Parsons and Bales (1955). In this family structure the father concerned with tasks termed as instrumental, provided a role model of vocational behavior, while the mother's role, termed as expressive, centered on caring emotions. The father provided the guidance necessary to materialize the offspring's career behavior, the mother offered supporting love.

Today it appears that for the child's future career development (where career is the sequence of jobs occupied in a person's life) importamt is the model of a father conforming to norms of guiding the family. He should have steady work habits, physical prowess and openness to the community of men, while respecting women, and especially his wife. This is also true when speaking of the "new father", increasingly nurturing and involved with the caretaking of children and housework (Lewis and O'Brien, 1987).

In order to deepen the insight into the constituents of attitudes termed as negativistic, I subjected the characterizations given to fathers to a free association experiment with the subjects who participated in the research on vocational adjustment. The characterizations had been expressed through adjectives, such as severe, tough, tender, helpful or through short case reports that could be reduced to the same adjectives. The latter were later used in Osgood's Semantic Differential method. The whole research was in fact done in collaboration with Osgood in his planned International Psycholinguistic Atlas, which because of Osgood's ill health could not be finished. The results of my research in the domain of attitudes showed that adjectives like "tender" and "soft" had for boys a connotation of feminity and weakness being associated with mother, cat, China porcelain, bird. The subjects associated "severe" and "tough" with worker, friend, father, good teacher and they got a highly positive rating. In the Semantic Differential method each concept is rated in the dimensions of Evaluation, Potency and Activity (Osgood, 1964). Subjects rating their father as severe or tough (but not a tyrant) had positive attitudes towards authority figures at the place of work. However, those having characterized their father as good, quiet or tender saw in him a weak, inept character, and developed negativistic attitudes towards authority figures at the place of work. The result was maladjustment to the job, which later on embraced their whole vocational and also their personal life (Krau, 1997). We may therefore conclude, that the father's presence is necessary in the family as a (masculine) role model for the education of both genders, and that people later on react with personality disturbances if such a father model was missing. One may figure out the consequences of forcing on children a hermaphrodite lifestyle. This contradicts Bem's (1987) fighter declarations in which she accuses a repressive society for forcing compulsive exclusivity in one's sexual responsiveness, homosexual or heterosexual (p. 207). But then she had declared (p.206) that her interest in sex roles has always been frankly political, and that her hypotheses have derived from no formal theory, but rather from a set of strong intuitions. No comment is needed.

This is not to mean that one has to idealize the traditional family, which forced women into the role of superwomen trying to do it all, juggling an incredible number of roles: career woman, student, volunteer worker, homemaker, wife and mother. Often they got a superwoman syndrome instead, with a range of physical, psychological and interpersonal stress symptoms (Schaevitz, 1984). Obviously, this too is a receipt for the destruction of the family. Therefore in the '1980s much has been achieved to correct and revise the division of burdens in the family, to increase the fathers' participation in the household. Schaevitz (1984) acknowledges the progress, which has been made, but states that men need help in learning how to achieve role sharing, and be more aware of and expressive of their feelings, a claim which we can fully support. However, it has to be emphasized that the father is and has to stay a man, and must not be transformed into a eunuch servant, as also the mother should stay a sensitive, caring woman and not become an Amazon warrior in the office or at home. Unfortunately, the Internet Culture has given the problem quite another twist. The self-conscious Internet woman does not waste her time to gently teach men sharing burdens. To hell with them! She does not need a man as a companion, and neither as the father of her children. Fatherhood is not reassessed, as it had been in the '1980s and '1990s, it is cancelled. If the mother is too busy to care for her children, there are foreign workers, immigrants to educate them. They are cheaper. Then, very early, the child is taught to switch on a computer and to click the mouse. From this moment on let the Internet do its education. There are enough attractive sites. Of course, also pornographic ones. Then there are the new toys, killer videogames, or the play "Liar-Liar", especially designed for "dialoguing" with the child. Later on the Internet will also supplant the school, first of all the homework. It will also be the key source to "independent research", on which the learner-centered education is based. The circle has closed. The Internet has emerged as the main educational institution of this society, the only institution with prestige. Teachers have none, because they have become occasional consultants and directors of rap songs on dinosaurs. The family has been dissolved, the norm-enforcing father has been removed. The mother nilly-willy, this time through feminist constraints, has entered the superwoman status. She feels good, because there is nobody to oppose her will, and voice other opinions, but soon the chronic fatigue sets in, leaving her little time and energy for educating her children. They stay alone with the Internet of their computer, with their peers, who may introduce them into antisocial ativities, and if the child feels lonely or unhappy, the drugs are there, and they cure all bad felings, including the foregone self-realization. In a novel published in 1985, Bret Easton Ellis, with a scary lucidity, described the modern youth subject to such an education. The title of the book is "*Less than Zero*". This is not about the youth of poverty-stricken strata, but about the offspring of a well-to-do generation, they have all the money they want, they have got all they had wished for, they had had premature sex experiences, and there is nothing left for which to make an effort. They are delusioned and nihilists, without any feelings for another person or the community.

More and more this situation is seen as alarming. Asks Colvin (2005), can Americans still compete in the global tech-driven struggle for business? We are not building the human capital we used to, he answers. Our primary and secondary schools are falling behind the rest of the world. Low-cost countries are turnning out large numbers of well-educated young poeople, fully qualified to work in an information-based economy. For the US the loss of technology leadership could be historic. If we only could get somehow our high-school math and science scores up to South Korean standards it, would be a gargantuan achievement. The No.1 policy prescription for solving the problem comes down to one word: education. The author concludes that in an economy where technology leadership determines the winners, education trumps everything. The greatest challenge will be changing a culture that neither values education, nor sacrifices the present for the future. This is what we too were saying all along this chapter.

Chapter Eight

The Arts in the Globalized Internet Culture: Commercial Aids and Shock Entertainment

"Art is the mirror of nature", said Shakespeare in his Hamlet, but the statement covers a very complex process. Art is the product of an artist. Nietzsche stated therefore that the artist creates his characters and does not imitate nature. He did not heed the basic thesis of Aristoteles in his Poetica, that even if one depicts people with more or with less virtue or mind as they have in real life, the point of departure is nature, and the artist is imitating it. Obviously, Aritoteles uses the concept of imitation in a very broad sense, referring to the actual existence of the depicted *elements*. One may remind the adage of Leonardo da Vinci, that nobody can imagine a dragon, the tail or the clews of which had not been seen in larger or smaller form in another animal. As such, art adds to our understanding of the world, art has a cognitive function, but it is different from science. Croce (1965) has stressed the intuitive character of artistic cognition relying on imagination, on the images of objects only. "Intuition, says Croce, is undifferentiated in the perception of real and possible things". At the same time science is an intellectual cognition relying on a logical process. Krau (1971) has demonstrated the personality-bound psychological mechanisms of cognitive activity working with concepts and alternatively with intuitive representations as elements of thought, and in the process of reasoning. The particular characteristic of the latter activity with images is, that they may evolve into *constructive images,* which, regarding their power of generalization, do not lag behind conceptual thinking, because they reflect the essential, permanent and necessary characteristics of the object. Art is rooted in images, but it also expresses them in an artistic genre, in painting, literature, music, and dance. Croce (1965) goes so far as to say, that all intuition is expression. He refers to Michelangelo, who has said that painting is done with the brain, not with the hands.

Good art works with constructive images. Thus good art reflects in a particular image the general characteristics of a cultural, social phenomenon. Fleming (1970) says, that in order to understand the inner life of people, the joys, values and drives that makes them find life tolerable and meaningful, one must examine their art, literature, philosophy, dances and music. At *one time* and in *one place* the arts, architecture, sculpture, music and painting share a common constellation of ideas in relation to the contemporary social order and its spiritual aspirations.

Society influences the arts through: 1.The existing natural and human landscape, shaped by society economically and in technology 2.The existing preferred technology of the artistic creation having the widest spread throughout society. 3. Society's preferential emphasis on certain aspects of content, dependent on widely accepted values. The artists become aware of these preferences by the public's feedback on their artistic production, also echoed by art critics. 4. The system of premial and punitive sanctions in force in each society, regarding the content and the style of artistic creations.

At the same time it is true that the work of art is most dependent on the artist's personality. Zola has defined art as "un coin de la nature vu à travers un temperament quelconque" (a corner of nature seen through a certain temper). Yet, Benton and DiYanni (1998) remark that the poetic language is revealing not only the writer's feelings, but also cultural attitudes meant to encourage or discourage particular types of behavior. In this appears the *normative aspect* of the arts. It may incite to revolutionary activity, but also to accepting the existing social order. In the latter sense the arts often serve to reinforce, demonstrate or celebrate the dominant values of society. We shall see that precisely this is the case with what is presented as art works in the Internet Society.

There are three main principles, which determine the artistic creation in this society. First, the aspect of *creation* is stressed in disregard of a true reflection of reality. The intent of the artist is sometimes to "correct" the reality, to give prominence to aspects, which the evolution of civilization has marked as ugly and unworthy. Thus the definition of aesthetics as the science of the beautiful becomes nonsensical. The ugly is forcefully put in the center of the artistic creation, which it is not, and should not be in accordance with reality.

The second principle of contemporary art is a positive one, and refers to the enhanced spread and acceptance of art works produced in all parts of the globe. The advancement in communication, and the ideology that accompanies economic globalization has produced an all-encompassing spread of inidigeneous art throughout the globe. "Primitive" African art and South-American art occupy a most distiguished place in all art collections. It is a welcome enlargement of the artisic taste, but with the twist characteristic to this society, it has immediately led to the very negative phenomenon of another principle, the third: It is the waiving of aesthetic criteria in the appraisal of an art work and of artistic activity. The artist is considered to provide services for the paying public, and the worth of the production is evaluated by the height of the price paid for it. The more shocking a production is, the more the groups with a low cultural level (and they are numerous) will be attracted to it, will pay for it, and an insipid horror movie or a urinal will be declared the summit of artistic activity. This practice overturnes the role of art in society, which is not a deepening cognition through reflection and aiding moral and aesthetical ascent, but imposes the lowest taste on the public. The art of the Internet Culture is a warped reflection of reality: of the now existing reality and of the older venerable masterpieces of art.

We have already shown in the last chapters, that today even published photographs are not true pictures of reality. Situations and characters are "arranged", and the digital photos are tampered with in the computer. In the literature this process of "correcting" reality according to the opinions of the contemporary public, and especially, of the writer himself/herself, has been known, but today every historic novel, movie or theater play is fictionalized history, or even worse, historized fiction. Hollywood has given such pictures a special name, *biopics* or biographical pictures, encompassing both the famous (and infamous) and the obscure. The British film professor D. Negra points out, that biopics is a genre that emerges in periods of uncertainty about the national experience and about national morality. Such films or TV shows allow voyeurist looks into the lives of people, create a sense that all lives should be free for public consumption (*Newsweek*, October 2, 2006). In order to enhace such consumption, real life stories or the stories of past literary masterpieces are transformed into "real" stories. Andersen's famous stories for children are remade to meet the sex expectations of modern youth (*Newsweek*, November 22, 2004), and Mozart is being "rethought" as a well-to-do XVIIIth century yuppie, who had an income of about $100,000 a year, and who spent money compulsively (*Newsaweek*, January, 30, 2006). It is however conceded that he has written more music than . . . the Beatles have recorded (for a writer-clerk of the Internet Society the Beatles are the embodiment of an absolute superlative in the arts). The truth on Mozart is told in the now obsolete genre of scientific treaties like the one of Wold, Martin, Miller and Cykler (1955/1991). Although they have surely heard of the Beatles, they write that Mozart was perhaps the most nearly perfect musical creator in the history of Western music. Contrary to the kitsch of modern biographical studies on Mozart, the authors add, that it is difficult to realize the personal tragedy that haunted most of the composer's life. Unlike Haydn, he was never successful in gaining the kind of position, court composer, that would have pleased him most, and he was left at the mercy of society. Today, it so seems, artists may be pretty well off with the mercy of society, but also get themselves shot, as John Lennon did.

The warping of reality, presented as its correction, takes several forms in the Internet Culture. Allen and Gonzalès (1999) present the subtle analysis Hitchcock makes of this phenomenon in his movies. The democratic press often fails to get its facts right. Newspapers' displaying a frontpage photo of a wrongly accused man is a recurring Hitchcock trope. There was a day, when we thought a free press was a sufficient guarantee of democracy. This day is gone. A free press is not enough, democracy needs intelligence, as well as freedom. Also, journalists often think more about how getting a story will benefit them and not the reader, whom it is their democratic mandate to alert and to inform. In his movie, *Saboteur,* Hitchcock describes the subversion of democratic freedom by journalists, through defamation of character, the falsification of the facts, by excitement or rumor. It is true, that in Hitchcock's view nature presents crudities, lack of design, monotony. In this imperfection he sees the great occasion of art. Art is our spirited protest and it corrects nature, he says. This last statement has to be qualified. The art work cannot and should surely not be a photograph of reality, the artists' creation contains an addition, a certain correction in acccordance with their analysis, emotions, i.e. with their personality. However, this addition must be the embodiment of *kalokagathia,* the antique Greek ideal of unifying the beautiful and the good. Art has an ethical dimension that raises people to a higher moral and aesthetic level.

The faithfulness to the essential aspects of nature must also extend to its already known reflection in clasical masterpieces of art, which embody the principle of kalokagathia. There is no inconvenient in recreating King-Kong, this time in a 3-hours long movie picture, as has been done in 2005. Those, who have the nerves and the patience, let them watch this new "creation". However, there are serious problems with Duchamp recreating the portrait of Mona Lisa with a moustache or Mel Gibson's bloodthirsty, blasphemous recreating of the Passion of Christ, in open contradiction with the teachings of the Church. The result is the distortion of reality and/or of an acknowledged monument of art, the destruction of all human achievements in aesthetics, as the realm of the beautiful, and their replacement with commercial utility and products adapted to the lowest taste existing in human mobs. Berman (1989) suggests that artistic avantgardism has contributed significantly to a profound reorganization of culture, integrating previously excluded domains (commodification, popular culture) into the realm of art. Nontheless, the abolition of opposition between high art and low art cannot be sustained and neither is sustainable the aboliltion of difference between culture and nature. The result of such "fertile" thoughts in the theory of art was Duchamp's "ready made art" (a work of art without an artist to make it). Duchamp's definition has found its creative expression in the image of a urinal under the name of *The Fountain.* Sassower and Cicatello (2000) point out that extracting the urinal from a public bathroom, and placing it in an art gallery or a museum (Sic!) distorts the uniform world view that separates the natural from the manufactured, the aesthetic from the commercial/industrial. Duchamp's "creation", the authors say, was the framing, the planning, the title and the perspective. They add that such artists push the limits of the art world, and force the public to find aesthetic value in the world of commerce. It is hard to agree even with this statement. Since when represents a urinal the world of commerce? It is true that some commercial commodities are artistically designed. The advertising posters of Toulouse-Lautrec were recognized pieces of art, but their content had been sufficiently decent. The urinal of a public toilette is a very necessary commodity, but even nicely painted, it is not a work of art. Its place is not between the exhibits of an art gallery, whether in its original form or as a painting. To place it there amounts to mere bad taste, which characterizes the Intenet Culture in its drive to shock the public. Some will perhaps say, that this judgement is exaggerated, as is the importance given to Duchamp's "fountain". Let us underline that not we are giving importance to it but the culture of our time. Duchamp painted it in 1917, towards the end of a war, which had produced a general abrutization of people. During a short time this exhibit has made sensation, then it has been forgotten, but it was rediscovered by the Internet Culture. As a matter of fact, sprouts of bad taste were to be found in appreciated artists too. Has not Baudelaire in 1857 written the poem *La Charogne* (the carcass), but who has ever given it prominence in public? The Internet Culture has canonized into art history the pissoir of Duchamp, and it happened in 1991, nearly 80 years after the original "fountain" has been "created", Sherrie Levine made a golden urinal, as an enshrined cultural symbol, and who knows, if not as a sign of worship.

If arrived at worship, let us take a look at a modern artist, who is flirting with the idea that he is Christ, and that it is his right to be worshipped. We are speaking of the Christos (Christo Javacheff and his wife). They are "environmental artists", whose work is consisting in covering 20 miles of valleys with colored umbrellas, or cutting a field by curtains, what has rightly or wrongly brought them renown. The effect on people is attributed to disrupting ordinary perception and astonishing the senses, by forcing the observer to grapple mentally with immensity and power (Nye, 1994). The immense force and labor required by the placement of the umbrellas and the giant curtains gives way to the modern sense of the sublime. It is an emotion experienced in a crowd and not in solitude as previous art has been. Nye exclaims, that these covered landscapes force onlookers to respect the power of corporations and the intelligence of their engineers (and of their God-like artists). This is the point, *hic iacet lepus*. The corporations fulfill the functions of God, and the avantgarde manufacturers of artistic pissoirs and landscape-covering umbrellas and sheets are his prophets.

The god-like feelings of contemporary artists breed the irreverential attitude towards the older artistic masterpieces. Indeed, a fashion of remaking any older masterpiece is raging. You cannot go to the theatre or to the movies and see a classic play set in its original environment and *couleur locale*. The opera *Carmen* is transposed from Sevilla into an American bootcamp with Sergeant Joe and Husty Miller instead of Don José and Escamillo, the toreador. Mozart's *Cosi fan tutte* is presented in Aix-la-Provence in 2005 as an Eurovision project conducted by Daniel Harding and directed by Chéreau, both renowned artists, with the title changed into "*tutti*", to fend off feminist critiques, transposed into a farmstead with a signboard "Vietato fumare" (Smoking Forbidden). The director explained later that the reason for his choice of Cosi fan tutte, was the significance of Mozart's play that marriage is boundage and adultery is a necessity of the heart. The original title and libretto of the opera show that not this was Mozart's intention. Yet, he may posthumously congratulate himself that people like Chéreau did not live at the imperial court of Vienna. It could have cost him his liberty. The art and the thought of this play in the Rococo era were jokingly playful, the art of today and the thought behind it is destruction: in this case it is the destruction of the family and of true love. *Cosi fan tutte* was a playful joke on women's flirtations, now it is turned into a feminist manifesto and supporting the pleasure-now seeking of the Internet culture. This last idea was also stressed at the Mozart Festival held in October 2006 in Baden-Baden, with the opera *Don Giovanni*. Don Juan was cast not as a tragic hero in full maturity of age, as it had been done everywhere during the last 200 years, but as an adolescent yuppie who performs churlish pranks, and out of irresponsibility defies every possible taboo, people and God. His sole motive is achieving immediate pleasure, like it is for any modern Internet Culture bird. In Shakespeare's theatre plays staged nowadays, characters wear modern street suits with James Bond cases, or to the contrary, they are dressed like bumps in Harlem or Soho. In some new musical shows, also "the king", Elvis Presley is presented like a stripper (*Corriere della Sera*, 10 April, 2005). There are numerous cases when the symphonic music of Beethoven or of other composers is jazzified. The directors of these spectacles justify the infringements of all aesthetic rules and of good taste with the need to bring art nearer to the people. We are told that the classics are reread and interpreted differently at various stages in life, fuelling the appetite for new takes. This is true, but a new or a deeper look or a new interpretation of an old artwork cannot justify making a mockery of the original. In some new version of Dumas' everlasting novel, the Count of Monte Cristo, Dantes, became a hero of proletar fight. We read in *Corriere della Sera* (26 October 2003) that the movies which are true to the original text cannot be sold, therefore, "*al cinema bisogno tradire*" the movie industry must betray the originals. This statement contains a disastrous idea, not only concerning the remaking of movie pictures, but about the art in the globalized Internet Culture. Mercantility supplants every aesthetical artistic standard. In earlier times we were accustomed to critics' rating of movies based on quality considerations of the story, the actors' play, of photo images, etc. Now it is the price tag, the box office performance. Here is a part of a classification, which appeared in *Newsweek* (July 17, 2006) together with a rating of the pictures' "coolness": Charlie and the Chocolate Factory - $206.4 million, Finding Neverland $53.7 million, both of equal "coolness". (Could somebody tell me what this coolness is, the number of sex copulations or the position of the partners?), Pirates of the Caribbean $305.4 millions, Sleepy Hollow $101 million, and so on. Wold, Martin et al.(1991) point out that the fields of literature, philosophy and the arts deal with a problem of values. One of the dangers to democratic society is the lowering of its values by mass communication, mass education and mass production, which all find their reflection in the arts. The authors add, that after World War II the buying power of youths increased very much, their relationship with their family and school, with its culture weakened in a proportion that widely caused concern. The result was a kind of pop culture and the spread of *kitsch*, worthless art productions. Spider-Man, graphic literature, which requires no effort to read and reflect, has broken out of hobby shops. Academics in the US and in Europe are teaching comics as literature in the classroom (*Newsweek*, August 22, 2005). As value-laden content is emptied from movies and literature, there is a dangerous increase in the taste for horror stories and horror movies. The corruption of innocents seems to have a wide appeal in modern public. This taste is forcefully sustained by the press, which underlines the artist's right to shock and provoke (*Newsweek,* February 20, 2006). A surprising, blasphemous name has been given to the representation of horror, *gothic art,* and the press speaks of "the lure of gothic", the macabre aesthetic (*ibid.*). The modern gothic has nothing to do with the medieval art known for its proud ogives, if reference is not made to a late medieval allegory, *La Dance Macabre,* which under the impact of the Black Death seems to hint at the universality of death, which unites all.

Like with pornography, recently this lure of the "macabre esthetic" has reached the stage, when children are being drawn in, to heighten the thrill of adults. The "creepy kid" has become the most abundant acting gig in town. There have been some successful forerunner movies like The Village of the Damned in 1960, The Exorcist or The Sixth Sense, but then the large number of such pictures has made them lame. Therefore the film makers have been in search for tricks to make the horror more potent. Says Tony Timpone, editor of the *Fangoria* magazine, "It's one of the last taboos of the genre, the possessed kid is sort of the ultimate problem child". Moore's casting director had a last-minute panic that they would not find parents ready to send their kid to be the spawn of Satan, but apparently several hundred parents thought their kid was perfect fort the part (*Newsweek,* June 12, 2006). As the film shooting succeeded, the crew exclaimed, "Man that kid's creepy. Mom and Dad must be so proud". With this, in the Internet Culture the perversion of the taste for the beautiful has reached its final stage.

As a matter of fact, the process has been going on for years, if having in mind the transformation of values we have spoken of. Already in 1946, French critics, seeing the American films they had missed during the war, noticed the new mood of cynism, pessimism and darkness that had crept into the American cinema. The lighting grew darker, characters grew corrupt, themes more fatalistic, the tone more hopeless. It was the *film noir,* which has no official definition, as hasn't the gothic art of horror, and it is evaluated by its "noir elements", color, tone disillusion and sordidness. The majority of scenes are fit for night, oblique and vertical lines are preferred to horizontal, there is much rain, dirty water. There is a convoluted time sequence, the characters are insecure, lack clear priorities (Belton, 1996). This film genre evolved ever since, embracing the greater part of Hollywood productions, but it is widely made in Europe too, in Germany, France, Spain and Russia. The differenee between them is that, while nearly the entire Spanish fim production is of this kind, in other countries only the thriller movies are so, in Russia also the movies on social problems. Only Italian film makers seem to resist this trend.

Some art historians (Mahon, 2005) contend that what we are seeing is the inheritance of surrealism, its combination of sex and subversiveness, born of Freud and the hideousness of the first World War, as artists, writers and thinkers are committed to the power of the unconscious. We have already pointed out that , while unconscious drives may influence human behavior, the latter is conscious, nevertheless. The painters or writers may "fly on phantasy's wings" but they are not somnambulant, and they know what they are doing. The proof is that they are in an elaborate way seeking the techniques, which would best express their phantasies. If some people play a dirty character, and speak not decently, they know what they are doing, and if they are attracted to such parts, it is clear that this is their inner nature. A film director said on Johnny Depp, the pirate-hero of the new block buster "*Pirates of the Caribbean*", "Johnny is a pirate in real life, he didn't have to be an outsider on the outside. He could be an outsider on the inside, it's the closest part he has ever played to his real self" (*Newsweek* July 17, 2006). The problem with the growing number of such movies, which reveal a true indecent self, is that they exhort more and more people to perform evil behavior in the real social environment. In the past, society's culture, the social institutions of award and punishment, forced people to restrain their "pirate" instincts. From Corneille's *Cid,* to Victor Hugo's *Les misérables,* Goethe's *Faust* and Lev Tolstoy's *War and Peace*, the sense of duty and benevolence have been rewarded, evil has been punished. The same appears in Michelangelo's paintings in the Sistine Chapel (*The Last Judgement, The Flood, The Creation of Man*), in Beethoven's IXth Symphony or in Berlioz' *Symphonie Phantastique*, in Rodin's sculpture *Les Bourgeois de Calais.* It is a sculpture figuring six leading citizens of the city, on their way to the enemy camp, having accepted to have their heads cut off on condition that the town be spared. Their faces are sad, but with the grim resolution that they are human has been born yet, who would love people as much as I do". This is also true of other doing the right thing. Which contemporary artist immortalizes such a heroic behavior?

The art of the old masters expresses a cosmic love for fellow humans. Said Michelangelo, "No classic painters. In the Prado Museum of Madrid there is a painting of Velasquez *La Rendición de Breda*, where the mayor of the town surrenders to the Spanish general Spinola and hands him over the keys of the town. In a serene landscape the Spanish general accepts the token of surrender with a gesture of respect and kindness. The men of the defeated army are sad, but express acceptance and not rage or vengeance. Contemporary art depicts a hopeless, unmitigated hatred as in Picasso's *Guernica,* or a moment's pleasure of the individual or for the individual, caused for instance by the pleasant impression of a colored canvas with or without objects or human figures. In tis latter art works, there is nothing to incite to deeper thoughts or to a betterment of attitudes. Take the canavas *Three Musicians* of Picasso. It produces a strong impression with its color composition and the sharp cut of the forms, but arouses a negative attitude in the spectator towards the depicted figures. This negative attitude characterizes Picasso as the forerunner of contemporary art. His biographer, Arianna Stassinopoulos Huffington (1988) names him a creator and destroyer, and points out that the struggle between the instinct to create and the instinct to destroy was at the heart of his life. He consecrated destruction in his art and he practiced it in his life. Convinced that the Universe was evil, he wielded his art as a weapon, and meted out his rage and his vengeance on people and canvases alike. In his private life he held a harem of women around himself, he lied, cheated and humiliated each of them, until they broke down. He immortalized his Afghan hound, painting his features superimposed on those of Dora, his mistress, who had helped him paint *Guernica*. As an explanation, he referred to the "animal nature of women". He often beat Dora and left her lying unconscious on the floor. No wonder that one after another the people close to him crushed. His second wife committed suicide, and so did Marie-Thérèse Walter, his mistress of many years, and also his grandson. Picasso has always obstinately refused to meet his grandchildren. His first wife had fallen into a psychic disintegration, and Dora Maar, a great artist herself, who had become his mistress and had helped him to create *Guernica*, fell into a severe nervous breakdown. No one of his close environment escaped unharmed.

We are so much concerned with Picassso, because, as Stassinopoulos (1988) writes, "he brought to fullest expression the shattered vision of a century, that perhaps could be understood in no other terms, and he brought the painting vision of disintegration, that Bartók brought to music, Kafka and Beckett to literature". The Internet Culture worships Piccasso and does not even see the horrific negative traits in his personality and in the substance of his art.

In June 2006 the Spanish government, in an attempt to express their veneration towards Picasso, who regarded himself as a socialistic Spaniard, organized a comparative exposition in the Prado Museum. They brought Picasso's works from the Reina Sofia museum and exposed them canvas per canvas in parallel with the classical Spanish painters El Greco, Velasquez, Goya. The decision was politically motivated and aimed at showing that the arts in the society of today are on the same level with the Golden Age. It should appear that the "son of the socialist revolution", Picasso is at the same level, if not on a higher one, with every genius of the past. Since Picasso constructed his own identity within the artistic tradition, themes represented in Velasquez' and Goya's paintings appear in the work of Picasso. The canvases of *Los Borrachos* and *Las Meninas* of Velasquez are the recognizable inspiration of Picassso's paintings *Three Musicians* and *The Maids of Honor*, while Goya's *Los Fusilamentos del 3 de Mayo* inspired Picasso's *Execution*. These facts should apparently favor the possibility of a public comparison in front of laymen. It is still a very risky enterprise, because of the differences in culture, personal styles and technical conditions. It is very significant that the Soviets did not even think of such a juxtaposition. Their treasure of the older foreign paintings was held at the L'Hermitage museum in Leningrad (today St. Petersburg), while the most renowned Russian paintings have been treasured at the Tretiakov Gallery in Moscow. Never did they mix up El Greco's *Apostles Peter and Paul,* or Rembrandt's *Return of the Prodigal Son,* treasured in the L'Hermitage with Ioganson's *Lenin speaking at the Komsomol Congress* or with similar socialistic paintings. The Soviets ventured all the time the slogan that the socialistic art is superior to the feudal and the bourgeois ones, because it underscores the essentials of the socialistic reality, but they never compared canvas to canvas the works of art, because they knew what would happen. Now the Spanish government did it, and Picasso lost in the comparison and lagged behind the Old Masters. Undoubtedly, Piccasso has the judgement and the technical touch of a very great painter. However, he lacks the vibrant humanity of the Old Masters, the love to his fellow humans, which appears in every stroke of their brush.

Let us make the comparisons by ourselves. We have spoken of the canvas of Picasso's *Three Musicians*. It arouses a cold negative attitude in the spectator. Compare it with the quiet joy and good will emanating from Velasquez' *Los Borrachos,* the drunkards' faces animated by wine, raising good will and friendly love between the members of the company. The same happens with *Las Meninas (*Velasquez) vs. The *Maids of Honor* (Picasso). The latter painting is in a repugnant gray-blue color, with women-like figures, who have no apparent common activity, dispersed in a room with a repugnant disorder. The king appearing in the doorstep has the attitude of a jailer. To the contrary, in Velasquez' *Meninas* we have a live athmosphere, where the center of interest is in the children, with the "infanta", the crown princess, in their midst, but she seems to mostly care about her dog. The children are surrounded and cared for by the maids of honor and the king-father, who is loking into the room from the doorstep, to see if all is all right. All figures are depicted with sympathy in what seems to be an every-day scene, at which the painter, present on the canvas, looks with an attitude of good will. Picasso is incapable of feeling sympathy towards any of his characters. Perhaps only the dog receives a slightly better treatment on the canvas. In the expression of positive human emotions, Picasso is handicapped by his wicked personality and his dogged self-aggrandizement. Precisely these are the traits so much appreciated in today's society.

What has been said does not mean that El Greco, Velasquez or Goya were servile "yes-sayers" without self-awareness and pride for their value. They have grasped the negative traits of their models of royalty, and reproduced them on their canvases, but always together with the positive aspects of their appearance. One may refer to the portrait of cardinal Nino de Guevara painted by El Greco with a stirn, merciless face, but with an impressive stateliness. Another example is the family of Carlos IV painted by Goya, where a somewhat cheap sensuality of the queen and a definitely not aristocratic *bonhomie* of the king stick out, but the whole group portrait purports to say, "Here is our royal family, they are ours, and we love them". Then there is Velasquez' portrait of the count Olivarez. The king's feared chief minster sits on horseback. At a first glane he appears as a courageous knight, but the painter makes him throw a look backwards, showing a sharp profile, like of a bird of prey, with an evil, wry look. The spectator does not see a valiant army commander, but an evil, greedy and rancorous courtier. Nevertheless, he sits on his horse, commanding genuine respect by his position. These paintings are the testimony of a sharp, vigilant critique, but one based on a basically sympathetic understanding of people and events.

Let us finally compare the two paintings of executions, Goya's depincting of the shooting of Spanish civil fighters by the soldiers of Napoleon Bonaparte on 3 May 1808, and Picasso's nameless "*Execution*". Goya shows the soldiers standing with their back to the spactator. They are brutal killers by order, lacking any chivalry and human compassion. The victims present the entire gamut of human attitudes in the face of a violent death, from fear, resignation till heroism. Goya depicts the murderous human cruelty and humans' frustrated and rebellious desire for liberty. He educates for patriotism through the admiration for the people who sacrificed their lives for the liberty of their country. Picasso in his *"Execution"* stays by the cruelty, emotionless, cold, mechanical. On his gray-blue canvas, the firing squad seems made of automata, programmed to do a job, looking even somewhat comical with their sophisticated weaponry. The painting arouses hatred and rejection, but not as a human emotion towards a definite historical event. It does not educate for patriotism and pride for the fatherland. It is a minor art work (as compared to Goya's), and reflects the nihilistic spirit of a society, wich Picasso sensed, would come. This society cannot produce a major art. Said Read (1938), "Art has long ago ceased to be monumental, as had been the art of Michelangelo and Rubens. In order to be monumental, the age should have a sense of glory, while the artist must have some faith in his fellow men and some confidence in the civilization to which he belongs".

Yet, Picasso did produce one monumental work, the *Guernica,* as a protest against the barbarian bombing of the town by the Nazis in April 1937, which left it destroyed and a thousand people dead. Picasso, living in Paris, was outraged, and during only one month produced a monumental canvas of 3.49x7.75 m. The painting is in black and white with shadows of gray. The central figure is a bull, in some opinions representing Spain, its heroism and tragedy, others say it represents the irrational forces of the human psyche, and still others see in it the symbol of the aggressor. There is a horse speared and dying in anguish, a woman with her baby, crying out in despair, dead and wounded people on the floor, while a man with a lamp apparently searches to understand what happened. Some see in him a soldier. The overall impression is one of terror and destruction, arousing a sense of indignation and a cry of protest. Then, perhaps, we have been exaggeratedly severe in our appreciation of Picasso, and he, nevertheless had a sense for other people's sorrow, and felt the duty to fight against the barbarian oppression of liberty and human dignity? Unfortunately, this is not the case. When in 1956 the Soviets used the same oppressive methods to quench and crush the aspirations for liberty in Hungary, their tanks wrecking havoc in the city of Budapest, as they left thousands of people dead, Picasso, member of the Communist party, remained silent. He did not paint a second *Guernica.* All what he did, was to send a downwatered letter to the Party Bureau. It earned him a reprimand, he swallowed it, and for Picasso the case was closed. *Guernica* had not been a cosmic protest for liberty and against oppression, but expressed the indignation of a party comrade at what had been done to his other loyal comrades. If the same happened to others, *tant pis pour eux*! (this is bad for them), but it was not his cup ot tea, since it did not concern him personally.

Guernica is a monumental work of art, but not for the liberty of mankind and against any oppression. In Read's (1938) words it is a monument to disillusion, despair, to destruction, and we shall add, it is one, which truly reflects the spirit of our time, plagued by terrorism and lack of understanding. By depicting the primacy of instincts, it mirrors, in a sense, the attitude towards the arts in our society. Today the role of the arts is simply not understood. How could one otherwise perceive and come to terms with the pillaging of irreplaceable works of art in Baghdad, at the time of the American invasion. Some 15,000 irreplaceable objects (Polk, Schuster and Abrams, 2005) have been plundered as US soldiers looked placidly at what was happening, and did not intervene, because "it was not their job". Now the new German Internet Culture has resolved to reinforce this process. In October Prime Minister Oertinger of the Land of Baden-Württemberg has proposed the selling at a public auction of the thousand-year-old hand written and painted manuscripts from the national library in Karlsruhe, unique for their value for German and universal history. What is needed today is entertainment and not art.

There is even more to come. In the culture of the present-day society a new phenomenon takes place: theft intending the destruction of the stolen works of art. In the past year the "gentleman thief", as he was called by the German press (his name is Breitwieser), stole 239 renowned works of art, like paintings from Bruegel and Cranach, and handed them over to his mother, who mostly destroyed them. Allegedly not one piece of them has ever been sold. The tribunal declared that "it was a colossal loss to to the heritage of humanity", but mother and son got only a three-years detention sentence each , because of the emotional plea of the defense lawyer about a tormented relationship between the son and the divorcerd mother (*Newsweek*, January 24, 2005). If there has still been any doubt as to the real attitude of this society towards the treasure of art works created by humanity, this case put it into a glaring light.

In many countries priceless art works are destroyed because of the criminal neglect to fund the necessary maintenance work. In Rome architectural monuments, which resisted for 2000 years, like buildings of the *Forum, The Bath of Caracalla,* or the *Domus Aurea* of Nero have begun to crumble, as the former government had proposed a 35 percent budget cut in the funds for architectural preservation. The problem is not only the decay and delapidation of architectural monuments. Italy's opera houses, like the Scala receive less government subsidies than the Paris Opera or the Vienna Staatsoper. However, generous subsidies are given to soccer teams and TV stations, the favorite entertainment of this society (*Newsweek*, December 26, 2005). Such things do not happen in Europe only. In the U.S.A. the National Park Service denied a grant for repairs to Boston's Old North Church, famous in the American War of Independence, using the "politically correct" justification that it was still an active parish. Even the church communities used to resist that their holdings be declared monuments and get state funding for repairs, because they want to be free to develop or demolish and sell historic properties in the real estate market (*Newsweek*, November 6, 2006). Such an attitude downgrades the arts.

In the Internet Culture art is stripped of all its cognitive and ethical functions. It remains a minor gender of entertainment, minor as compared to soccer, wrestling, pubs or a sex party. Judging by the numbers, today the biggest entertainment is browsing the Internet, staring at a little screen, and not giving a damn about what is going on around, the persons sitting next or a sunset in fantastic natural colors. Such entertainments tear out the person from her environment, often from her family and vocational life. The present-day miniaturization of computers into cellular phones enhances this process. Society does nothing to stop the resulting involution, the disappearance of unused human capacities, because entertainment is big business with giant investments. Craik (1994) points out that from a consumer's point of view, leisure is also a conduct of life, which must be regulated and managed. The growth of leisure style reflects the restructuring of the consumer society, and an increase in non-work existence. Such is society's purpose, and to it art is called to contribute, because art must be an arm of entertainment. In this conception art creates the dreams which money can buy, and coaxes people into buying them. The artist becomes a provider of services. Sassower and Ciccotello (2000) defend the view that artists are self-employed in today's society, but the dependence upon the commercial propaganda machine and the dominating utilitarian culture are too strong to allow an independent status of the artist.

The artists comply with the tasks required of them in several ways. First, through the already discussed break with classical art, the distortion of reality in what is presented as works of art. Then there is the introduction into the artistic domain of objects and activities, wich may serve natural purposes, like urination and urinals, but do not characterize the cultured, "sapiens" characteristics of humans. Defecation is proper also to animals and has nothing artistic in it. In the time of the successful (?) American painter Pollock, who with a paintbrush in his hand, ran around a canvas put on the floor throwing paint on it, they also presented an exhibition of a monkey's "paintings".

In the theatre the suppression of the taboos is achieved through an increasing politization in the style of Bertolt Brecht (1967). For him the stage was a sociopolitical laboratory, often aiming at alienation, a separation of the actor and role, role and audience. In the separation state one is free to think, to view the events objectively and consider alternative actions. To the sociopolitical laboratory one may also refer the dramas of minority discourse like *Ma' Rainey's Black Bottom, Bury My Heart at Wounded Knee*, as also *Love! Valour! Compassion!* or *Palermo, Palermo*, (for a more detailed analysis see Hartnoll, 1998). There is also an increasing number of gay and lesbian dramas, starting with Sherman's uneasy equation of homosexual persecution with the Holocaust and Nazi death-camps in his *Bent*.

By the way, the theatre has preserved a most influential status in controlling the crowd. Crary (2001) relies on Le Bon, stating that nothing has a greater effect on the imagination of crowds of every category than theatrical representations. There the most personal conscience is vanquished by the levelling magic of the great numbers. Stupidity has the effect of lasciviousness and contagion (the TV multiplies this effect). In the theatre the neighbor reigns, one becomes a mere neighbor. Less and less are the plays presenting an intelligible action. An existentialist sense of the absurd dominates the many plays substituting a storyless action for well-contrived plays, and a disconnected dialogue for witty responses and speeches. Benton and DiYanni (1998) point out that absurdist dramatists reject the idea that characters can be understood, just as they are rejecting the order and coherence of characters and action in everyday life. People are incoherent and inconsistent, and life is confused. In such conditions art cannot fulfill the healing function Landy (1996) ascribes to every creative process, to the frames of mind that produce dance, music poetry or literature. Through such expressions we should create ourselves anew.

The art of today preaches senselessness and violence. In contemporary movies violence appears as acts of senseless brutality, pathology and indifference to human suffering. Says Giroux (2001), "I am not arguing that Hollywood films such as *Fight Club* are a cause of these problems, but they are symptomatic of a wider symbolic and institutional culture of cynism and senseless violence that exerts a powerful pedagogical imfluence on shaping the public imagination. .. In the films of Quentin Tarantino *Reservoir Dogs* (1992) and *Pulp Fiction* (1994) excessive and brutal violence is estheticized, contributing to a cynical and nihilistic cinema".

At the beginning of the XXth century a program of self-censorship was installed in the U.S.A., and in the '1930s a Production Code was instituted, asking to avoid the presentation of vulgarity and "repellant" subjects, crimes against sex, religion, etc. However, often film makers ignored this code, especially since in 1952 the Supreme Court ruled that movies were an expression of free speech. Consequently, gangsters were portrayed as tragic heroes. It amounted to making a mockery of the code principle that "the sympathy of the audience shall never be thrown to the side of the crime, wrong doing, evil or sin". In the style of expression as also in the content, there is today an erosion of the older distinction between high culture and the so-called mass culture. The latter breeds an environment of philistinism, schlock and kitsch, of *Reader's Digest* culture and pastiche, a parody that has lost its sense of humor (Cf. Belton, 1996).

The same happened in music too. If in the Pythagorean tradition music had healing powers and was an instrument for social cohesion, it now seems to be an element of social anomie (Crary, 2001), the lack of values which also induces changes of taste. It has been repeatedly spoken of the declining of symphony repertoires in the US orchestras, especially regarding Berlioz, Mendelssohn, Schubert, Liszt and Rubinstein. Even Beethoven's formerly very popular *Wellington's Victory* is currently nearly neglected, and there is a decrease in the popularity of the *Ninth Symphony* (Lieberson, 2000). Musical tastes are responding more and more to the demands of a popular audience. The Boston Pop Orchestra became a national institution. Unfortunately, the mass media have led to an abundance of aesthetically popular art and kitsch that appeals to the uneducated public created by sensationalists, and by those who try to give the public what they think it wants and will buy. Globalization intervenes in this process. Coca-Cola and jazz, which had been symbols of American culture, are now global "property". Pop art emphasizes mass-produced objects and symbols of the mass-media. It is opposed to the so-called fine arts. Andy Warhol, one of the pioneers of modern art, used multiple images of mass-produced items (e.g. green

Coca-Cola bottles and the obligatory toilet) as symbols to characterize our culture. More recently pop cuture has turned to MTV (music television), a continuous presentation of rock music and surrealistic television imagery. The universal availability of technical media that receive and reproduce music, has made its dissemination one of the biggest industries in the world. The peculiar situation of popular music is in that every original performance is unique, because spontaneous improvisation is a must of this style (Wold, Martin et al., 1991). Aleatoric or *indetermined music* is also a kind of improvisation. Modern composers use a number of new devices of notation, which are in effect indicators for directed or even free improvisations. For instance, Penderecki in his Threnody in Memory of the Victims of Hiroshima, does often not even indicate a definite pitch, and there is no traditional indication of a rhythmic pulse or meter. The problem with all this is that the improvisation treatment is nowadays applied to classical music too, which should be performed under rigorous rules and with the greatest respect for the original.

In its entire history, till the XXth century, music has meant melody and harmony within rhythm, now all had to be reassessed in order to stress the revolutionary tendencies of the *Zeitgeist*. It is true that also the Romantic composers piled dissonance upon dissonance, to the end that musical tension or expressive quality might be heightened. In the XXth century dissonance has been appreciated for its own sake, but presently, the melody has vanished completely, and the musical phrase is drowned in what seems to be plain unpleasant noise. Be it an operatic perfomance or a talking movie, the orchestra is set to play an accompaniment with such intensity, that the opera aria or the spoken text becomes undistiguishable. The public ask themselves, what is the intention of the film, or of the spectacle director, to convey the music arias, the story of the plot, through the text spoken by the actors, or the noise of factory machines and cars on the street? Critics and musicians of renown are abhorred with the present-day music, especially with rock'n roll. "It fosters almost totally negative and destructive reactions in young people", said Frank Sinatra, who also called it "a rancid aphrodisiac". "Music today is money", points out E.Y.Harburg, "it's rhythm, it's hypnosis, it's a good deal of hysteria". The words spell out the terror of the age in which the young are growing up. He added, "Good music and good lyrics should belong to all times". Let us also present another quotation from Gary Allen, "Music is now the primary weapon used to make the perverse seem glamorous, exciting and appealing. Music is used to ridicule religion, morality, patriotism and productivity, while glorifying drugs, destruction, revolutions and sexual promiscuity (Schapiro, 1978). All this means that in the Internet Culture, art loses the functions it had hitherto, and vanishes *qua* art. It becomes an arm of commercial or political propaganda, and its main functions are the *Blickfang*, the captivation of attention (inclusively shocking the audience), and to make the public accept the propaganda message. Such have always been the classical functions of publicity and advertisement. I wrote about them back in 1967 as public relations of the enterprises (Krau, 1967), but today the whole of society see themselves as a free market enterprise, harnessing all social acticvities, including the arts, to this purpose. Andy Warhol's exhibit of a water closet is not an advertisement for a factory or a shop selling such items, it is a statement on the new role of the arts, integrated into a utilitaristic culture. In it there is nothing apart from money making and the basic lowest human activities, like using a toilet. One should, perhaps, appreciate the compromise Warhol made. He could have very well answered the call of nature going into the backyard of his house, and then paint what has been going on, (there are today movies with such scenes) but then there would have been no occasion to make commercial propaganda for commodities.

If contemporary artists do not make commercial propaganda, they are presenting political propaganda with the slogans of the moment, renouncing the truth and even a steadfast engagement to their own ideological positions. Alessandro Piperno, author of the most discussed Italian novel of 2005, *Con le peggiori intenzioni* (With the worst intentions) declares, "I do not believe in literature, because this would impose assuming responsibility, and a writer must have the right to be irresponsible. When it comes to it, literature is a useless thing treated with religious seriousness. A writer should not take up social responsibility. His sole divinity is the style" (*Corriere della Sera*, 5 October 2005). The writers do not even sense the contradiction between the tendency to make political propaganda and their "irresponsibility". As a matter of fact, the Internet Culture is irresponsible, and what you say now, in no way will oblige you tomorrow. Claude Simon, the famous French writer, said in acceptance of the Nobel Prize of 1985 for literature, "I write only to write. I have nothing to say", adding then with politeness, "in a Sartresian sense of expression". However, the critics point out, that this affirmation of Claude Simon only refers to the last decades of his activity, when his stories seemed enshrined in a thick veil of annoyance. It is the annoyance produced by our culture, which led the writer think that he is just writing without influencing the world in any way. Yet, it was precisely then that he was awarded the Nobel Prize! The same happened to the Oscar Award for movies. Today it is given for political reasons, and does not reflect the top talent of performers or the highest quality of the product (*Time*, February, 25, 2008) In one of Simon's known novels, *Le chemin de Flandre,* a soldier receives from his father a letter telling him of the destruction of the great library in Leipzig, when in a few minutes humanity has lost an inherence of centuries. The soldier answers, that if the contents of those books had not been capable of saving the library, they had no utility, and he adds a list of much more valuable things he needs, like soap, underwear, sweaters, socks, etc. The mistake is here twofold. Humanity needs both, underwear and books, i.e.spirituality and aesthetics, and the one cannot supplant the other. Books cannot be used in lieu of underwear and neither vice-versa. The second mistake is ascribing books the capacity to prevent destruction, if the existing culture pushes in this directioin, *and* there are writers like Claude Simon, who declare that they have nothing to say, and that they are writing "just to write".

This means that the people who today call themselves artists, actively participate in the destruction of the arts. The most sordid book as content, imagery and style, which I have ever read was *Una vita violente* (A violent life) by Pier

Paolo Pasolini. The writer feared the Italian public, who comprises of many people with an outstanding taste and culture, and therefore wrote it in dialect, not in Italian, and then used this fact to reject the existence of a unified Italian language. He contended, that the literary Italian is bourgeois and therefore he tried to write in a proletar language, as spoken by the lowest level laborers and vagrants. He did not know, or did not want to know, that a similar attempt by E. Marr failed precisely in the Soviet Union, being brandmarked by no other than comrade Stalin in person, in an essay on Marxism in linguistics published in 1950. Stalin understood well that the common language is a key instrument to unify the nation, and that dismantling it is contrary to sound civic thinking. This attitude towards the nation's language, and perhaps the squalid content of Pasolini's writings caused, that after being murdered in 1975 by a male prostitute, Pasolini fell in oblivion for some 15 years, until the ascent of the Internet Culture. The latter readily discovered him, since filth is a key element of its "art". From then on it was a march of triumph. Only in 1990 *Vita Violente* reached three printings in Milano, and was immediately translated into several languages, including Hebrew. With this the degradation of literature has reached its peak. Let us examine this process in another artistic genre, the comedy. While tragedy, which presents the fatal destiny of people animated by ideals, is less present in the landscape of the arts in our time (there are hardly any ideals and there is no destiny recognized as such), the comedy can speak of a strong comeback. Were we to speak malicy, we would refer to Aristoteles, who in his *Poetica* stated that comedy imitates people with inferior moral traits. One should bear in mind that for Aristoteles art is the imitation of reality. While tragedy shows people better than they really are, the ridiculous behavior shown by comedy is indicating bad habits, but causes no pain and does no harm. The comical masks worn by antique Greek actors were ugly, but had no expression of suffering. This thesis of Aristoteles, readily accepted by all authors ever since, does not stand in modern culture. Consider the joke reproduced by the *APA Monitor on Psychology* (37, 6, 2006, p.55 after humor researcher Vaid). A woman walks into a bar with a duck on a leash. The bartender says, "Where'd get the pig?" The woman answers, "This is not a pig, it's a duck". Then the bartender says, "I was talking to the duck". The article continues with sophisticated theories on frames of reference and the results of experiments with students, to which this "joke" has been presented. There is not a single word that this alleged joke has been a plain offense, and that it is inadmissible to make such "jokes". I wonder why there had been no feminist protests.

Humor is a most researched issue in contemporary psychology. Martin (2006) mentions over 4000 journal articles, and they contend that the heart of humor is incongruity, when an idea or an object is out of place. Humor is working only in a playful atmosphere, when the incongruity represents no real threat. Was the atmosphere in the bar, in Vaid's experiment with a mean bar tender and drunkards a playtful one, that would allow to consider the rude offense of the woman as a joke? Ritchie discovers (Cf. APA *Monitor, ibid.* P.56) that enjoying humor is also linked to a mental gymnastics to get the true meaning of a joke, tapping into some uncomfortable or unspoken truth. Ritchie writes, "Humor points to the truths that everyone knows, but nobody admits". He gives the following example of such a joke-statement. "By the time Mary had her 14th child, she would finally run out of names to call her husband". There certainly is a hidden incongruity here, but where is the unspoken truth? Are you inferior and do you deserve to be laughed at if you have many children? Here the Internet Culture adds a political edge to comedy. Innocent incongruity is not enough. It must also have a political edge. Then, naming a woman a sow is politically correct?

It is true that a funny person seems to us inferior mentally or culturally, but the heart of the phenomenon is not this inferiority, but a behavior (also a statement) incongruent with what we would have expected. Many years ago, (Krau, 1962, 1964) I hasve spoken on the orientation towards action (set) in my doctoral thesis. I have analyzed the inadequate orientations to perform an action (Krau, 1962,1964,1977). Such inadequacy comprises of the faulty evaluation of the situational components, where secondary details are given a decisive weight, and the important ones are neglected. Freud (1922) has presented numerous examples of *lapsus*, e.g. the man with a belly ache who reads "Klosethaus" instead of "Korsethaus", the speaker of the Austrian parliament, who declares the opening session which he feared, would be stormy, as "closed" instead of "open.", etc. In his widely known book on the "brave soldier Svejk" (pronounce Shwake), Hasek puts his hero, who is enchained and led by a police man to jail, to stop before an army mobilization poster, take a military upright position and shout, " Long live Emperor Franz Josef"! It is the result of an inadequate orientation (set), and it provokes laughter. The phenomenon has psychophysiological causes, charging with nervous energy perceptional components, which in the objective constellation have a secondary character, and should not receive the acknowledgement of the situation by the cortical control center. The inadequate orientation happens on the basis of habit, a repeated performing, a momentary acute physiological or psychological event, open or hidden wishes, etc. All of them charge the wrong nervous centers with energy. Of course, not every inadequate orientation is funny, only those, which are harmless, and represent no real threat.

Funny situations provoke laughter, and they are at the heart of comedy, as an artistic genre. Contrary to the affirmation of modern searchers (*APA Monitor on Psychology 27, 6, 2006, p.59 sqq,), that until the late 1980s the* field was unexplored territory, it has proccupied thinkers along centuries, starting with Aristoteles and continuing with Hobbes, Kant, Bergson, etc. The concept of comic incongruence was introduced by Schopenhauer some 150 years ago, but the quoted researchers do no know it. This is funny by itself, were it not tragic in shedding light on the ignorance of the Internet Culture. Be this as it may, modern research has stressed the importance of the social presence for ejoying fun. This is of course, true, and since time immemorial there has been much talk on the contagious character of laughter. Yet, the modern emphasis on the human collective in enjoying comical sites or expressions, raises two weighty problems.

The first is in the content of the funny remarks and of the comedies presented to the public. In the moment the Internet Culture introduces political edges into comedies, the comedy becomes a tool for propaganda. Sometimes this edge appears in dashing on mass stereotypes, like the presentation of all aristocrats as idiots. Some, of course, were, as are some of the Internet birds of today, but generalization is not only a deformation of the truth, it is harmful to honest and capable people and impedes their activity. Where would the modern world stand without the duke of Wellington, the marquis de Lafayette, the earl Bacon of Verulam, count Tolstoy, Alexander von Humboldt, count Cavour, etc.? The cheap mockery made of traditional institutions in modern comdies is harmful, and degrades the comedy as a genre.

The second problem resulting from the recent research on the social link of fun and laughter is the ethically doubtful conclusioin that we *are using* laughter as a tool for social bonding. In conversations and lectures, speakers are 46 per cent more likely to laugh than their audiences are, punctuating their own talk with laughter (Provine, 2000). Laughter, especially a loud laughter, is contended to elicit positive reactions from other people and communicates to them that we mean no harm. According to this conception, people are laughing in the presence of a sympathetic group, and they have something to gain from the *captatio benevolentiae*, i.e. from catching their good will. A true son of the Internet Culture gives nothing away without some form of retribution, payment. This means further, that people in this society have lost the sense of authentic humor, and they are laughing not as a spontaneous manifestation, but artificially, in order to get something from the others.

It used not to be so. When I was still a child, I very much liked the then very popular movie pictures with Stan Laurel and Oliver Hardy. Watching them I used to burst into laughter, it had no importance whether there were other people in the movie hall. I laugh even now, when there is something funny on the TV screen, even if I am alone in the room. I do it essentially for myself, as a kind of aesthetical enjoyment. It appears therefore, that the Internet Culture lacks the pure aesthetical enjoyment of a comedy, aand there only remain gestures to get certain things from the surrounding group, the spectators. This means that the comedy is not aiming at presenting witty conversations and funny behaviors to produce hilarity and good humor in the public. It becomes a conscious attempt to sell the writer (or the speaker), his ideas, the actors to the public for financial and political benefits.

Apart from what has been said, in this society comedies have another big problem. Orthodox playwrights see in them merely the fun, which is only a part of the psychological and aesthetical base of the phenomenon. The authentic comedy effect is produced by the *combination of the witty and the funny*. The two may be related, but are not identical. The witty results from the association of incongruent representations, as does the comic, but the association is unexpected, paradoxical, and the link is suddenly discovered by the public. Says, for instance, G.B.Shaw, "Youth who is forgiven all, do not forgive anything, old age who forgives all, is not forgiven anything". The listeners' mind is contemplative in the comical event they are presented with, but in the case of a witty speech, they have to discover the "point" by themselves. The joy of this discovery produces the aesthetical pleasure, which has pronounced intellectual components. In the comic situation we are laughing *at* the funny person, upon a witty remark we are laughing *together* with the people who understood it.

In a good comedy the witty and the funny go together. In the Internet Culture the witty side of comedies is missing, and they are only based on situational fun, frequently addressing the lowest tastes. One may refer to dozens of Hollywood TV serials, soap operas, which constitute our everyday portion of entertainment. The aim is not any more to put into evidence and laugh at social inadequacies, in order to improve general behavior, but to approve existent misbehaviors with a forgiving smile. The laughter itself is no more a social chastisement, the way it had been seen by Bergson. It is an instrument to get social approval for speakers who want to be "popular" or for deeds that are not crimes, but are neither a part of what is accepted by social conviviality. .

The degradation of the arts is a general characteristic of all artistic genres in the Internet Culture. This becomes evident when comparing the modern and the older art works. The famous film *Love Story* of the '1970s is a tragedy of modern times. So is Kushner's *Angels in America*, dating from the '1990s, but the difference between them is enormous. After viewing *Love Story*, a human tragedy with an only hinted, nearly hidden political allusion, the audience used to leave the spectacle in an emotional storm expressing catharsis. The identification with the actors and the story has always been total. No eye remained without tears. The modern *Angels in America* is also a tragic story, but a play in which "the gay theatre asumed its full political maturity, framing a homosexual love story within the historical context of political corruption and religious ecstasy" (Hartnoll, 1998). The spectators leave the spectacle with mixt feelings, because of the dirty scenes and the dark despondent setting. Many spectators felt repulsion.

If we compare the "fairy-tale" genre represented by the older works like *The Wizard of Oz* or *Snowwhite* with the superproduction after Tolkien's *The Lord of the Ring*, the result is again in favor of the older productions, which elicited unmitigated positive, joyous feelings. *The Lord of the Ring*, despite the computerized technological feats.leaves a depressing impression, because the ugliness and filthiness of numerous characters is repulsive, the setting of the scene is again "*noir*", making impossible an identification with the story or its protagonists. We shall discuss one more praised modern art production, *The Da Vinci Code* of Dan Brown. Howard recently made of it a movie picture. The press called it a "joyless blockbuster". The plot embroils Robet Langdon, a Harvard symbology professor in a murder mystery of biblical proportions, a combination of a thriller, religious manifesto and art-history lecture (*Newsweek*, January 23, 2006). This spreading through genres is constructed with ability. The undoing is that all is based on half-truths, and is finally false. It may be said in Brown's defense that, historic inexactitude would be a problem with a scientific work, but not with an artistic production, if the artist (the author) would declare or let understand that the work is fiction. *Quo Vadis* of Sienkiewicz was also fiction based on half-trruths, and had been in its time the most widely printed and read book. Brown, on the contrary, starts the book with a declaration that certain secret organizations, its members and the described rituals are facts, without indicating the fictious character of the persons and events he describes. He intentionally lets the reader presume that the events presented in the book are also facts. This is a dishonest procedure.

The plot of the book hinges upon an inflammatory conspiracy theory, that Christ was married to Mary Magdalena and fathered a daughter, whose bloodline gave birth to the Merovingian French royal dynasty, and then went over to England. It allegedly exists until this very day. It is stated that all the time the Catholic Church has been covering up the truth (*Newsweek*, January 2, 2006). Leonardo da Vinci enters the story as a person who knows the plot of the Church, and spread about it hints in his art works. According to Dan Brown, Leonardo painted Maria Magdalena sitting next to Jesus in the *Last Supper*, and in order to bear testimony to him (Leonardo) as being gay, he painted Mona Lisa as a bisexual being. He then emphasized the higher power of women, like a true feminist would have done today. All this appears in the theory, which the chief protagonist, Robert Langdon exposed before a gathering of art-loving convicts in a state penitentiary, the most trustworthy and expert public the author could think of for listening to such an exposé. Langdon later on developed the feminist fundaments of his theory on the Christian doctrine and the saint reliques, arguing that the Holy Grail is not a cup, but a woman, Mary Magdalena, who received the semen of Jesus. This holy quality she has passed to all her descendants, until it arrived at Sophie Neveu, who holds in Brown's book the role of Jesus' descendant and that of the great detective. Together with the other characters she cracks the Da Vinci code.

The communication of Brown-Langdon's new theory on the Christian faith in front of conmen seems very symbolic. As a matter of fact, the code-cracking squad did all the things conmen do. They took down from the walls of the Louvre the most valuable paintings, scribbled messages on their back, they threatened to destroy the irreplaceable values of humanity, if they would not be given their way, like true children of the Internet Culture do. For them their own messages scribbled on the master pieces of art were more valuable than were the paintings made by the giants of mankind. An arrogant disobedience is shown vis-à-vis all representatives of the law, the guards of the Louvre museum, the French and the English police. It seems to the group that their own agenda is above all law and authority. Towards the end of the book, Brown tries to amend this situation, but the conception instilled along hundreds of pages remains, and is reinforced by a last concession to the Internet Culture. The chief criminal (an English scientist), the organizer of the whole complot, who was caught by the police, would not be judged, according to the French police chief, he will plead insanity.

We have insisted so much on the Da Vinci Code, because the degradation of the arts in the Internet Society is not only a matter of theory, it happens before our eyes. It is the same irreverential disregard graffiti scribblers have for the walls of city houses or art monuments. It roots in the realization that contemporary art is not the embodiment of the beautiful. Perhaps the street graffiti are even executed with greater art than are the urinals of Duchamp or other contemporary "environmental statues" of tin or rusty iron, or their image on a canvas.

At this point, I do not want to leave the reader with the impression that the arts are doomed. As there are encouraging signs that this society is about to change (see the next chapter), we are witnessing the courageous call of men and women of culture for the saving of the arts, which are expressing the beautiful and spiritually sublime. Martha Nussbaum (2006) points out, that although the domination of the profit motive would suggest that only education in science and technology was crucially important to the success of nations, we should worry that other abilities, equally crucial, are at risk of getting lost in the competition flurry. The abilities associated with the humanities and the arts are also vital to the creation of of a decent world culture. We should cultivate sympathy towards the other, and the best way to do it is through instruction in literature, music, theatre, fine art and dance. The arts educate students in both freedom and community. They can also be a great source of joy, they make the world worth living in (Nussbaum, 2006).

The conditions for this to happen are first, the creating and fostering of true art, and second, the creation of real possibilities to teach true art. Lip-service solutions in some European universities (e.g. in Oslo) with a single pot-pourri art course, taught at the same time to more than hundred students in an auditorium, are worthless, and give the mere illusion to have received some philosophical and aesthetical education. Today the classical genres, including painting and poetry, operas and symphonies are "endangered species", driven out by pulp fiction, TV (endangered itself by the cellular phone), rap and hip-hop music. It is heartening that recently a generation of young artists arises, who are revitalizing the old genre of "core" classical music and other already forgotten artistic activities. In the domain of music, until now, producers assumed that the only way to expand the classical market was by introducing pop beats, flashy lights and scantily clad singers. The production costs of classical recordings were steep. Now successful artists, like the soprano Anne Netrebko from Russia or De Niese from Britain, understand that it is not only the music making that sets you apart. It is also the personality of the artist and their ability to communicate with the public, the "dramatic arc that you create onstage". Thanks to the new DVD technology, singers with theatrical talent are increasingly prized. The audience remembers the singer's energy and personality brought to the performance. Forgotten arias of Salieri were restaged in 2003 and Cecilia Bartoli recently relaunched "Opera Proibita", a collection of little-known works written during the early XVIIIth century (*Newsweek*, August 28, 2006). This means that gradually top talent returns to the traditional treasure of art, and finds a broad public having the same concern. In Milan the season 2005/2006 of the Scala was opened with Mozart's half-forgotten opera Idomeneo, and conductor Harding received an ovation of 12 minutes, what in this summit theatre happens rarely, indeed.

The new fact in poetry, had written the *Corriere della Sera* in January 28, 2004, is that the higher the quality of the poem, the larger will be the public who read it and try to understand. The public has again the wish to receive nourishment for their mind and soul. They want a new approach towards the problems of life, help to control their passions, their anger and violence, to use their reason without being conditioned by political opinions. This aspiration can be only fulfilled by good poetry, in the lecture of the classics. In the U.S.A, this new tendency is echoed in Hollywood, e.g. in the film made by Giovanni Fago on the Renaissance painter Pontorno. We are witnessing the same restauration phenomenon in architecture, picture, and hopefully, with literature. Says the proverb, "*Ars longa, vita brevis*", real art is enduring, only life is short.

Chapter Nine

Toward Globalization with a Human Face

Arrived at this point, the reader has a right to put a very uneasy "Quo vadis?" question, and ask where this culture will lead society. If it should change, then in which direction, and which would be the moving forces and the mechanism of such change? It is a very difficult question, because the prediction of economic and social developments stands on shaky grounds, In Leser's (1969) words, the motto of economic forecasts is "Father peccavi", and there can be little comfort in the fact that sometimes it is not the model, but the economy, the culture and the social factors which are at fault. More and more we are hearing today, that the world is totally random, humans are unable to figure it out, and the proof is that experts were no better than nonexperts at predicting the future. Although they were much more confident in their predictions, they could not explain more than 20% of the variability in outcomes, and the more famous the experts were, the worse they performed (*Fortune*, February 6, 2006, p.24). A good example was the assumption of power by managers, as a consequence of the dispersion of ownership into a large group of shareholders which did not participate in management, and did not even always try to exercize control through their voting rights. Burnheim (1941) has called it a managerial revolution. Koontz (Cf. Maynard, 1967) has seen in the separation of management from ownership a fundamental process characterizing the modern enterprise. Towards the end of the '1990s the revolution has clung down, the legendary CEOs like Iacocca, Nasser, Welch have all been sacked by shareholders, and Iacocca has been sued for insider information trading. CEOs are still fabulously paid, but only as "humble and obedient servants" to the shareholder owners. Those who abused the trust of the owners sit in jail, like Martha Stewart, the managers of Enron, Parmalat, etc.

The "managerial revolution" is over, and with it the trend which spoke of power being achieved and exercized by professionals for professionally conceived economic goals. Only the professional rhetoric has remained.

The "brave new world" will not be entirely new. The problem is to ascribe the correct weight to the various variables, having in mind not only the impact they have in the present, but the power they will have in the future. This is a "mission impossible", but we must try to accomplish it if we intend to cast a daring look towards the future. Twice I myself have tried to predict the economic process, in 1993 and in 1998, using as point of departure the existing economic and social trends, but the success has only been partial, to say the least. I did not succeed in predicting the Internet Society. Nobody did. In 1993 I tried to foresee the management style of future organizations (Globerson and Krau, 1993). The point of departure was an international study of the group "Managers of Tomorrow"headed by Claude Lévy-Leboyer from the University René Descartes in Paris, in which I participated representing Israel. Other participants were France, Germany, the U.K., Australia, China and Japan. The aim of the study was to construct the cognitive map of the middle manager in the different countries and industrial branches. The map comprised important, frequent and disliked activities and their characteristics: challenging, creative, freely chosen, done for others or alone, self-developing, etc. In the book I published together with A. Globerson in 1993, I added to these items characteristics of the manager's personality, his/her values and salient life domains. The working hypothesis of the book, concerning the future organization and mangement, was that, since "the organization is the people working in it" (Perrow, 1970), it could be assumed that the chief managers of tomorrow would be the middle managers of today. Therefore their aspirations and pesonalities would shape the organizational style of tomorrow. At the same time, organizations and managers would be under the influence of the larger social system, which at that point tended towards a further development of the post-industrialist values of the '1970s. In the macro-economy it was assumed that the main trend would be the merger of high technology with telecommunications, resulting in a reduction of the number of people employed in production, and a parallel increase of jobs in the service industry. However, I qualified such statements by cautioning that the process of organizational development depended upon the trends of political decision making in the existing social systems, determined by socio-cultural characteristics. I developed this idea in a later book (Krau, 1998).

It appears that the forecasts regarding the direction of technological development, the external and internal constraints of organizations, the power policy of managers were outborn, but not the main socioeconomic direction of development. The hypothesis had been that the cultural and psychological trends existing between 1950-1990 would essentially continue and further develop, but they did not. This trend had coincided with the flourishing of the welfare state, as the working (and consuming) human person was put at the center of the economic process. It was assumed that every technological development would strengthen this tendency, making the process of work and the products themselves more human friendly, more accessible for the large masses of people, and contributing to the betterment of their material situation, their physical health and life satisfaction.

It was not to happen that way. Instead, the development of automated technology, advances in the creation of more developed computers and in the technology of communication, the internet, have led to the idea that humans, especially human workers and performers of economic and production tasks are expendable. The aim of economic and public social activity is no more the benefit of all, but of the strata who have the power and the money to impose on the economic process a direction yielding a maximal profit for them. Lowering production costs through retrenchments has become a fashion, in many cases not justified by objective indicators. Actually, only about a third of the companies which performed major lay-offs, reported increases in productivity and profit, while a plummetting morale surfaced in 80% of the cases. More and more such organizations were getting, as it were, "lean and lame" (Henkoff, 1994). One of the causes of this situation has been the fact that the companies were not just laying off, they were flattening their structure. Middle managers were a preferred target for having their jobs terminated. Even if some of them have been maintained, they were disempowered by top management, in order to appear as modern, but in fact to enhance their own power aspirations (Krau, 1995). As a consequence, participative management was simply no more feasible, nor were the workers interested in it any more. Presently, top management does not want to share their power prerogatives, middle management has ceased to be a factor of importance in the enterprise, and the workers exposed to continual lay-offs have no feeling of loyalty towards the enterprise and its management. More often than not vacancies in the organizational hierarchy are filled with outside candidates. While the theoretical positions and conclusions of the "Managers of Tomorrow" research project remain valid as a sociological and psychological document, precisely its economic benefit has been annihilated.

Professional managers are aware of this situation, but they too are powerless. The days of the "managerial revolution", heralded by Burnheim (1941) are definitely gone, and so are the days of employee participation and the "new mandate of busines" and its social responsibility. The exclusive aim for organizations today is the bottom line of the cash register to be handed over to the shareholders. However, here the latter have a problem, because this policy damages the organization's image, whence also the cash register. Some brisk lawyers and economists immediately came up with a method to make money also of the image problem and devised the London think tank AccountAbility which rates the world's largest companies according to their "sins", the infringement of their social responsibilities (*Fortune*, October, 3, 2005). The problem is, however, to define the social responsibiltiy, and here we are again witnessing the characteristic twist of the Internet Cultue. The image rating is about green energy, deep water drilling, candid reporting. No word on massive lock-outs of employees, on the reduction of their salaries, as working hours increase, nothing on corruption, on the lack of moral values. The rating does not seek to lable the good or the bad, but rather to identify the smart. It is a business rating, not a moral one. Even in the narrow environmental problems it is not a self-sacrificing attempt to save the planet, but in the words of GE CEO Immelt, "we plan to make money doing it" (*Fortune*, October 3, 2005). The newly baked corporate social responsibility is not referring to the own employees, or to the citizens of the country, but through the media it is addressing the world. Organizational leaders are widely publicized when they are sending checks to Africa, or getting photographed with some sick children in Asia or Africa. It is of course a good idea to help the population of other continents, but not when at the same time you crush the livelihood of your own employees, neighbors, citizens.

We are presented with a fools' psychology, but it is so deeply entrenched in the culture of this society, that it appears in every theoretical work of scientists and in every speech of a political leader. At every meeting in which the French president Chirac participated in the last years, he spoke of the need to help the population of Africa, until in November 2005 a savage violence broke out in his own capital, involving looting, arsoning, torching cars and houses. The rioters were mainly young immigrants, who felt deprived of any possibility to lead a normal life at a decent level.

This phenomenon of extended rioting at a worsening economic situation was foreseen by me (Krau, 1998). I pointed out that our society was not facing temporary market difficulties, but a much deeper and wider crisis with only one root in the worldwide economic developments, while other roots were social and psychological. The occurrences labelled as economic are by no means only in the domain of the economy. They involve the total behavior of people with their social and psychological background. Therefore the economic situation is not only a cause, but also an effect of organizational management behaviors on the macro- and micro-levels and guided by society's values. The latter create *models of strategic socioeconomic management,* characteristic of the various types of society. My book (Krau, 1998) analyzed the management model of collectivist-authoritarian societies (China, Russia), liberal-individualistic societies (e.g the U.S.A.), collectivist societies with participation in decision making (the Japanese model), and the model of cultural pluralism within an individualist society (the European model). The analysis retained as the most positive trait for the economy of the future the collectivist participative element linked to a free market economy.

At this point, however, we should like to see which forecasts were today outborne and which were not. The culture-bound models of socioeconomic management are facts, which had been predicted and they exist, each one with the mentioned characteristics. Outborne was also the predicted bubble in the American economy and its burst causing a recession. It spread all over the world, because of the globalization of the economy. However, the resilience in the tradition of societies, as bearers of the various models, did not realize. The forecast had assumed that a government conception that came into being in a country by the will of the nation, represented this society in national and international matters. This basic premisse has partly proven false. Let us take the example of Japan, as a society with very strongly entrenched traditions. The inner strength of Japanese tradition could not withstand the combined external and internal onslaught brought by American pressure to make structural reforms. The latter aimed at abolishing the tenure system of the work force, deregulate the economy, abolish the tradition of saving and spend more (on American goods), strengthen the curency, so that the Japanese commodities should be less attractive on the international market, strengthen American intellectual property protection and lower trade barriers. Japan caved in, hailed the reformist prime-minister Koyzumi, and can today be pleased to announce the world that its for-merly not existing unemployment is already climbing towards the 5 percent. Ast the same time, the recent privatization moves for the post system is dealing a deadly blow to the saving tendencies of the public. What did this economy, still flourishing in the nineties, get in return? They received a scary recession, which even today is not entirely over. Rightfully, does Jeffrey Garden (2005) believe that Japan's meltdown towards the end of the '1990s was due in part to Ameri-can pressure for a stimulating monetary policy at just the wrong time, and to pressing the entire region in to overzealous deregulations.

The second inadvertence I committed in my forecasts in 1998 refers to the underestimation of the tremendous influence psychology has today on the econ-omy and on governance. Surprisingly, and due perhaps to the dominance of communication media, in the modern world economic and polling behavior be-come a psychological problem. The facts, even the own economic situation are disregarded. In the middle of the recession in the US, the big surprise was the robustness of consumer spending, which helped ensuring that the downturn was mild. However, instilling an optimist atmosphere is a virtual remedy, like the entire Internet Culture. Disinflation is the large triumph of Alan Greenspan, the big economic wizard. Although it has delivered huge benefits, as people felt wealthier and spent more, it has also left big potential problems. They are: heav-ily endebted consumers, a housing bubble, massive trade deficits, a zero saving rate, the rising exchange rate of the dollar, which has made US exports less competitive (*Newsweek*, February 13, 2006), followed by its downfall. At any rate, it is easier to control inflation and stabilize the economy, if people don't believe that inflation is inevitable and they try all the time to raise wages and prices. The crown of the matter comes now: Prices are being raised, while wages are not, and the public accepts this behavior of the system. The public does not react, neither economically, nor politically at the polls or through strikes, be-cause the corporations' propaganda machine hammers the slogans of general accessibility and satisfaction into people's minds, through TV and the other me-dia channels. The new economic analysis always arrives at the conclusions the analysts want to reach (*Fortune*, 143,5). When it became aleady obvious that actually the bull market was a bear, they kept saying that there would be no bear, and that the public should continue buying and spending. And the public listened to them.

This effect does not appear in the economy only, but also in the behavior of the electorate. The objective material economic and political situation does influence it in a slight manner only. It is the same German elections in 2005, which are furnishing the proof for the decisive impact of psychological factors, together with the elections in Spain, India, Britain and even in the US. In Spain the Popular Party, like the Bharata Party in India, had brought to the country a never seen economic boom, but they were ousted. Spain is now entering a period of intestine struggle between the autonomous regions and the central authority, between believers and anti-religious citizens. These fights may easily lead to the dissolution of the unitary country. Nobody of the hotheads gives any thought to how a small Catalunya, Euskadi or a tiny Galicia wuld cope with the great economic and social problems. In Britain and in the US the governments have been reproached to have started a war on the basis of a wrong (some say a possibly intentionally misleading) information. In Spain precisely such was the reproach that ousted the government (the reference was to the terrorist attack in Madrid in March 2004), in England and in the US the leaders were re-elected despite such allegations. In Germany there are 5 milion unemployed, but dogged voters clinged to the social-democrats, and the election results of Novemvber 2005 gave the conservatives a far to small majority for a smooth governance. Such events can only be explained by psychological factors not linked to a logical assessment of the general and the own material situation. It is a question of parochial identities and the values of those "parochies". The weighty conclusion is that in all social and economic forecasts this trend has to be taken into consideration.

In the events which have been discussed, the globalized "Internet Culture" has an easier standing. It offers its followers affilliation and vocal protection, no matter what they would have done, it emphasizes individual success, revelling and amusement, it declares morality as inexistent and legitimates vice, liberating the individual form the pinch of morality feelings and from guilt, except the guilt of loosing. The winner is consacrated, whatever means he might have used. In order to win and be supported and protected by his/her party fellow members, the individual must hate political opponents, not because they have done something to him, but because they are a danger to the party. Therefore, if the party is elected, hatred is the word of order, consumed in public denunciations and harassment by the police and the magistrates (in most countries they identify with the left). All happens like in the well known aria of calumny in Rossini's Barber of Sevilla, where Don Basilio sings,"Il meschino calunniato, avvilito, calpestato, sotto il pubblico flagello per gran sorte va a crepar" (The poor fellow slandered, vilified, crushed will perish under the public scourge). There usually are bursts of laughter in the audience, but in real life there is nothing to laugh at, the picture Don Basilio presents is accurate. Is it the Ship of Fools? It is not only the politicians who are playing fool. They are supported by a choir of numerous scientists and professional analysts. Some acknowledge an intentional "foolish behavior" in order to present a more acceptable image. The editors of the *Scientific American* (292, 4, 2005,p.4) published a declaration pleading that henceforth the journal would present all the facts objectively, without a political censorship and interpretation, but then, surprisingly, they drew the public's attention to the scientifically irrelevant fact that the declaration was published on April 1, the Fools' Day. A number of readers welcomingly echoed this aspect (*Scientific American*, August 2005), and unfortunately, they were right. It had been a simple abuse of the public's confidence.

Curiously, today the common attempt of scientists is to presage a global catastrophe. They see it, but do nothing to fend it off. Our triumphant species may be partying towards a collapse of global civilization, say Paul and Anna Ehrlich (2004). They point out that we are on a collision course with nature, brought about by accelerating the depletion of our natural capital by the trends of population growth and the worsening in economic and political inequality. (Nota bene, they are speaking of inequality among nations, not of the socioeconomic inequality within the countries). Therefore the matter is complicated by social and psychological problems, because we cannot tackle the environment if we are at one another's throat.

Once again we get civil rights and the environment, both so dear to the Internet Culture, and now joined together. The problem is, neither of them can be cooked and eaten, perhaps parts of the environment may, but then there would be vocal protests from civil and animal rights activists. The fixation of thought in the single direction of the mantras of the Internet Culture is the real predicament and the root of all evils that befall our planet. Of course, earth quakes, hurricanes and tsunamis are events of nature, but their prevention and relief from them are linked to human actions, which for reasons of corporate profitability and economic liberalism are not implemented. It is well known that the US has withdrawn from the Kyoto Protocol of environmental protection. Scientists know that we are heading for disaster, but as true voyagers on the Ship of Fools do, they don't budge, and are only searching for theories justifying this attitude. In 2004 a Nobel Prize was awarded to the psychologist Dr. Kahneman, who found out that in economy people behave illogically. One has to ask, whether the prize was given for the novelty and the intrinsic worth of the theory or for finding a learned label justifying the attitude of passivity and refusal to search for the real causes of what happens.

There is little use in writing about the future as it seems to be or should be in the understanding of a writer, an analyst. We have seen that the sole logic in really occurred development is *the logic of aspirations and sustainable power* by the class of people who exercizes political dominance. The characteristic feature of a 250-years long history of power, rights and power sharing shows that the rights conquered by the lower middle class were preserved by the following generations. This pattern abruptly changed in the '1990s, when all progress towards power sharing was halted and acquired rights were cancelled de facto. During the previous 250 years there was a steady gain of rights for working people, and an assimilation of moral principles in enterprise management. It reflected the necessity of agreed collaboration among the factors of industry. This was not only an economic necessity, but also a sociopolitical one, given the threatening presence of the Soviet Union with a cold war fought by both sides. It happened despite the fact that the USSR was ruled in the name of the working class by a merciless clique oppressing civil liberties and perpetrating heinous crimes. The Soviet Union constituted a threat for the ruling classes in the West, and therefore they felt they had to care for the needs of their fellow citizens in order to ensure their support, even if this reduced their possible additional profits. The implosion of the Soviet Union changed this situation.

In the meantime there had been tremendous advances in the domain of communications, computer technology and automation. Originally, these advances were linked to military needs, in order to fight the cold war and to prepare for a "hot" one, but now all inventions and discoveries were put at the disposal of the civil market.Here two elements appear, which will have a growing influence on society and its culture. They must be taken into consideration in every forecast. Both are backlashings of the economic and political globalization, forcing on peoples and countries a culture which contradicts their tradition. The first element is massive illegal imigration overflooding Western countries. People from underdeveloped countries and material products from there are legally and illegally introduced into Western countries on such a scale, and with such intensive pressure, that all defenses of the US and the EU are crumbling. Recently a British sting operation busted a pan-European ring, that according to Scotland Yard, has smuggled as many as 200,000 people into the United Kingdom during the last few years. In the US the number of illegal entries has stayed about half a million each year, notwithstanding the severe security measures taken after 9/11. Naim (2005), who presents these data, adds that concomitantly there is also a dark trade with arms, drugs and smuggled consumer products going on. This is the second element of influence on today's economy and society. It is driven by the same global forces, which now threaten the smooth functioning of the legitimate world. Changes in technology and politics have reduced the obstacles that distance, borders and governments had imposed on the movements of goods, money and people. Money laundering has grown tenfold in the last years. Governments everywhere are lowering tariffs, eliminating currency controls and opening their economies to foreign traders and investors. Analysts present a scenario according to wich Asian counterfeiters contact African people-smugglers to have illegal immigrants sell fake Guci gags in Paris or New York. Meanwhile law enforcement budgets have dwindled as a rsult of attempts to downsize government, and because of a shift towards anti-terrorist defences. So, smugglers have less to fear from being caught. Technically, modern society is incapable of dealing with these problems created by itself. Only when we realize that that illicit trade is damaging high profits, we will start to beat back the scourge" (*Newsweek,* October 24, 2005, p.62). This means we should investigate and prosecute only actions and behaviors that harm the high profits of corporations. So, is the torching of thousands of cars and the arsoning of houses, perpetrated by young immigrants in France in November 2005, a minor offense (not to be prosecuted) or a serious harm to profit? French interior minister Sarkozi (the President of today) declared it a serious infringement of the law, but he was promptly criticized by human rights activists. They contended that the matter should be dealt with by improving the material situation and the integration of immigrants. However, in doing so, great sums of money would have to be taken from the privileged and used for measures developing the material and cultural situation of immigrants. Such measures reduce profits, and are therefore not accepted, and neither would they be accepted in the future. We have found a focus of unrest that will persist and and must forcibly be discussed in all possible future scenarios.

At their arrival in the host society, immigrants are led by a sincere wish of integration. However, the economic and social situation in the new country and the attitudes of the host population are far from fitting the initial positive images cheered by the immigrants. The result is what has been termed a *culture shock,* whereby the immigrants take refuge in their own culture, in order to preserve their self-image and collectively cope with anxiety. This is the point where presently, especially in Europe, militant Islam takes over. We are asking the immigrants to cope with the situation, but coping should include solving the external problem, and this solution is resisted and blocked by the host society. The moves are not only or specifically directed against immigrants, although anti-immigrant rhetoric is high in Western countries. The Greek tragedy-like development causes that in behaving this way (and they cannot otherwise, because such behavior defines the Internet Culture) society unleashes a sometimes murderous, merciless Islamic fundamentalism, not in accordance with the teachings of the Holy Quran. The latter preaches peace and tolerance

> To you be your religion,
> And my religion mine! (Sura 109, 6)

Even today important Muuslim countries, like Malaysia or Turkey try to defuse the unholy alliance between poverty and fundamentalism. This moderate Islam is the only chance the West has, if it plays its cards wisely. For the moment the West is rewarding Turkey's moderation with an attrition game having the undeclared aim of preventing her entry into the European Union. They don't seem to grasp , or do not care, that this is the surest way to to send the country into the welcoming embrace of fundamentalist turmoil, like it happened in Algeria. Europe cannot "play the fortress" as it tried 40 years ago, and refuse to let people with an alien culture in, because the immigrants are already there, 5 million in France, millions in Britain and in Germany. They must be recognized as a sociopolitical force having an uncanny attraction to the masses. In Spain analysts speak of a "reconquista in reverse", as the Spanish society discovers its Muslim past and its Muslims. The number of small mosques in Spain is on the rise, and so is the number of Christians converting to Islam (*Newsweek,* March 14, 2005), and all this one year after the bloody bomb attack on the Madrid railway. Again, to one's mind come the verses of the Quran (Sura 110, 1-3):

> When comes the Help of God and Victory,
> And you see men embracing God's religion
>
> In many a legion,

Then praise your Lord, and seek his Mercy,
Since He's most Prone to Pardon

The West has been caught unprepared for this phenomenon for two reasons. As we have seen, the Internet Culture depises tradition, and considers that today all people are living in the same historic time and culture. This is not so. The modern unification of historical time is an illusion. The conflicts raging today are faught in the name of values, which are not linked to the evolution of Western thought in the XIXth aand XXth centuries, but in the name of much more profound and old values like those at the cradle of Islam or Hinduism. Globalization dramatically reveals to us that peoples and civilizations live in different historical times (Lepre, 2005). Therefore modernism appears as the enemy of the own culture and tradition. By propaganda, education and administrative pressure modernist values are forced upon the Islamic masses, but these values only penetrate a limited cultivated upper structure, like it happened in Iran during the days of the Shah. The values of globalization and of the Internet Culture do not reach the lower strata hurt by society's economic and immoral attitudes. This is the second reason for the Establishment's perplexity at the eruption of popular sentiments. The surprise rejection of the European Constitution in France and in The Netherlands is a good illustration of this phenomenon. The problem of the West is not only Islam as such, but the religious fanatism of certain Islamic groups, and the abnegation and self-sacrifice with which they wage the war.

Despite a snoring rhetoric of not bowing to terrorists, the establishment of the Internet Society (except perhaps G.W.Bush) readily caves in, however maintaining an uncompromising stance in financial and in value matters, as it rejects all moral restraints and furthers antireligious blasphemy and sexual débaucherie. This is to say, that the establishment incites fundamentalism with its own hands, while continually preaching against it, and then bowing to its outcomes. It so seems that like in a theatre tragedy the characters are irresistibly driven to their destruction, as they are continuing their hitherto known behavior. The Internet Culture tries to subvert Muslim fundamenatalism from the inward, applying the American jingle of "bringing democracy" to Arab countries. This "democracy" means the way of life of American corporations. It allures the upper strata of society, but not the masses, from which the fundamentalists draw their support. A further problem is that the project of bringing democracy is different from bringing liberty. In the Middle East the whole endeavor reflects the confrontation between the Shah, supported by the West, and Chomeini. The former lost, and could not even rely on his American allies. They dropped him when the situation got precarioius. They did such things all the time, except in Korea. This lesson of history means, Islamic fundamentalism will not change, it is us who must make some changes for the sake of a peaceful coexistence. Islam has proved it can live in peace with Christianity, with Judaism, with classical capitalism, but not with an all-encompassing mercantilism, atheism, sexual depravity and the abolition of family structures. The reader will ask why it should be so important with what the Islam can or cannot live. The answer is simple. The

Internet Society's globalization policy of profits brought the Muslims here and among us. Now they are here, and if displeased, they go after us, as the attacks of 9/11 in New York, of 11/3 in Madrid or of 7/7 in London have proved. The West has successfully fought in Afghanistan, unsuccessfully in Iraq, and then recoiled before Iran and Syria, and this means defeat. They, the fundamentalists do not fear to fight and to die for their faith (we do!), and this makes them stronger in the confrontation. The slogan of bringing a Western lifestyle and democrcy to them is an easy and convenient illusion. The two lifestyles are different, neither is genuinely accepting the other, and Muslims will not waive an inch of their faith and its symbols, the way scores of Christians and Jews are doing. In September 2005 the Italian judge Luigi Tosti refused to administer justice in a courtroom with a crucific on the wall. (*Corriere della Sera*, 26 October, 2005). He stands trial amidst the usual circus of the "freedom-loving" leftist press accusing Ratzinger (?!). They even do not give the Pope his title. You will never find a Muslim judge doing the same, or a Muslim journal to attack the own religious symbols. The worldwide riots because of the Danish cartoons figuring the Prophet Mohammed are more than eloquent in this respect.

Today you may find a Western philosopher, like Onfray (2005), with a book largely marketed in France and Italy, whose main problem is to save mankind from God. He sees the problem in the fact that even modern atheism is "Christian". No one stating that some Christian values are acceptable or that the gospel has something good is a true ateist, he says. There is a need to build a post-Christian atheism, deconstructing the mythology of Jesus. No Muslim will say, or only think such words, by the way, he would not live to see the next morning. And what has the West to present in the spiritual confrontation: the craving after additional profits and good sex? History teaches that in past final confrontations it was the civilizations believing in hedonistic pleasures which crushed. An illustration is the fall of the Roman Empire with its licentious Hellenistic culture, the fall of the Ancien Régime at the onslaught of the French Revolution, the take-over of the Bolcheviks in Russia, in Cuba, etc. All tell modern society, *De te fabula narratur,* the story is about you. The educated public will read these lines with a smile. In modern confrontations the victor is always the nation with the more advanced technology, and there is no doubt that the Western developed countries belong to this club. American military power smashed the Talibans in Afghanistan and occupied Iraq. Then, perhaps the ever-advancing technology could save the Internet Society with its culture?

There are several considerations that put the technological superiority in a more doubtful light. Although important journals like the *Scientific American* (July, 2002) have proclaimed the United States the most scientifically and technologically advanced nation, as they leaned on Luca's concept of the "American Century" (Cassidy, 2004), the enthusiasm with technology should be dampened. It is true, hitherto unheard of progress has been made with the miniaturizing nanotechnology, robotics is advancing. Robots with sensors are developed, even television becomes obsolete, despite its 600 channels on tap. The growth of digital communication is changing the way TV is produced, distributed and consumed. It can be delivered not only by traditional broadcasters, cable or satellite operators, but also by telecoms and portals over the Internet (Internet Protocol Television, IPTV). All this, however, means big losses for industry and media companies (*Newsweek*, July 13, 2005). A time comes when the technological boom stops paying off (*Fortune*, May 17, 2004).The newly discovered devices, pharmaca and other products become obsolete before they have paid off the lengthy and very costly labor of research and development.

The new technology also becomes too complicated to be handled by the human operator, especially with the lack of willingness to work, which characterizes modern culture. Good examples are NASA's repeated lack of ability to put into orbit thoroughly checked spaceships, so as to avoid lethal accidents. After the Challenger explosion in 1986, the next launched Discovery (1988) was a success, it delivered the Hubble telescope and revived NASA. However, after the Columbia disaster in 2003, at the next launching, the space ship presented the same sloven work, that, a report said, "was hampered by a lack of rigor, both in developmant and testing". Chunks of insulated foam broke off, and pieces fell off the ship. Some people in the space industry are wondering if NASA read its own findings carefully (*Newsweek*, August 8, 2005). One year earlier, Genesis, NASA's first automated extraterrestral sample return mission ended with a crash in the Utah desert, having on board 20 micrograms of solar-wind particles painfully collected over three years in space from original material of the primitive nebula that coalesced into the Sun and planets. It would have been an epoch making scientific realization, but it went off in smoke.

In the midle of the XXth century scientists considered the discovery of the man-machine system a major scientific achievement for the improvement of work (McCormick, 1964; Bednii, 1975). It is one of the systems decribed by von Bertalanffy more than 50 years ago, whereby the inclusion of the human person increases its complexity, because the human person is a system in itself, a probabilistic and not a deterministic one. The factors influencing the probabilities of the system's states and behaviors are so numerous, that the interaction of the two components cannot be precisely determined beforehand. In the man-machine system it is important that there should exist a physical arrangement of the equipment components that will facilitate their use by the human operator. The functions of the system are information receiving, storage, processing, then decision and action functions. The Internet Culture wants to convince us that the increasing role of computers and automatic devices makes the human person redundant, and the automatic machine components are sufficient for executing most if not any work activity. This is a costly and ominous illusion, because the behavior of the system is always led by the human component. Even if the current command and control is transferred to a computer, the supreme lead is performed by humans, the system becomes a man-computer-machine system, but its overall characteristics must be compatible with the human agent. Long ago Chapanis, Lucas and Jacobson (1960) have stressed that one should not confound distant command with complete automation. In airplanes without a pilot, the human operator is not sitting in the cockpit, he is on the ground, but performs from there all necessary command functions. It is always the human operators who exercize the ultimate command and control, they repair the machine component or take over the concrete control, if parts of the system are failing. The technological progress may reduce the number of humans working with the system, it may change their location, but it even increases their responsibility. The computer and the machine components of the system perform with greater speed, sometimes even with greater precision, they do not feel tired or depressed, and neither do they go on strike (if there is no problem with maintenance), but these advantages are poised against a greater reliability of humans in situations of uncertainty, in which the system must behave with flexibility in gathering information and reacting, and in situations in which social responsibility is required.. The computer remains a human auxiliary The system must not require activities which surpass the biological limits of the human operator, or which are incompatible with his/her values. The system must give the human operator real responsibilities.

Technology has a future only in combination with and in adaptation to the human factor. Driving technology ahead, while despising the human component of the system, presages system failure at the micro- and the macro-level. It is therefore an historic necesity to renounce and change such a cultural conception. The whole question has an additional aspect, which makes it appear in a new and very dangerous light. We are referring to the energetic and environmental conditioning of the technology-human system in its macro-aspect. J. Diamond (2005) gives the Rwandan 1994 genocide an explanation relying on the ecological factor. A vast population explosion has left Rwandan farmers unable to feed their families, desperate and primed for violence. Farms had shrunk to a size, which did not allow for rational farming. As the world looked on impassible, genocide was the only logical outcome. In other cases, societies have brought ecological suicide on them by abusing their natural resources. Most Easter Islanders starved to death after a competitive frenzy between chiefs to erect the famous giant stone statues, as they cut down all the tries of the islands. Similarly, the Vikings, who in the Middle Ages had settled Greenland, died out after they had squandered valuable fields for houses and fodder for cattle which was impractical in this climate. The fish-eating Inuits have survived.

The great natural disasters in the last years are seen less linked to human failure. We are speaking of the devastating hurricanes, like Katrina which destroyed New Orleans, the South-East Asian tsunami, the Kashmir earthquake or the draught and fires which swept along the Mediterranean countries from Portugal and Spain to Greece, except the fires in Portugal which were arsons. Many experts see here the initial symptoms of an enduring climate change produced and exacerbated by overpopulation and technological overdevelopment of a fragile ecological lanscape and agricultural overexploitation of the soil. Actually, a 300,000 square kilometer coast of Europe's Mediterranean territories is threatened by desertification. In Spain this process has extended already to the inland and destroyed a third of the soil. The land dies and becomes agriculturally improductive, even if people still build there cities and roads. Summer temperatures in France and Italy are expected to rise by 7-8 degrees Celsius, and the number of scorching days to multiply.

Of course, one cannot ascribe all these changes to human actions, especially since the worst thing of all is their abrupt character, which neither scientists, nor governments could foresee, in order to enact efficient defense strategies. It appears, however, that humans, eager for technological development, are pushing certain aspects of climate closer to the thresholds that could unleash fatal changes. The first such dangerous behavior is deforestation, which despite all warnings is unabashingly going on in Brazil, Ucraina, Romania, etc., then there is the emission of greenhouse gases. They deplete the ozon layer of the atmosphere, and constitute a main trigger of global warming. The problem is that stopping the emission of greenhouse gases would be getting in the way of industry. An international protocol on curbing greenhouse gas emissions has been signed in Kyoto, but the USA, the country with the most powerful gas emissions, has simply withdrawn from it. In December 2005 a conference on this issue was held in Montreal, and the reach of an understanding was trumpeted very loudly, but without any concrete actions and targets.

Part of the problem is that a number of scientists had been telling everyone exact the opposite on climate change. We have already seen how some scientists are on industry's payroll, and are telling what the industry wants to hear. In this case they were telling that an ice age is coming. However, most investigators have found that greenhouse gas concentrations were rising rapidly and that the Earth's climate was clearly warming up. It is obvious that cultural and political motivations prevent the world to enact efficient defense strategies against the menacing natural disaters. In the issue we are discussing, it is true that precisely the warming which is causing the melting of the ice cap in the Arctic Sea, is bound to disrupt the ocean currents which are keeping Northern Europe warm. They have already slowed by 30 percent in the last 12 years. However, the possibility of a catastrophic freeze looks remote.

Hand in hand with the dangers to the planet's soil are the dangers to its population by the already discussed natural catastrophes, infectious diseases like AIDS and overpopulation. Today putting a hold on the spread of infectious diseases is a problemn of education and of reducing the price of pharmaca, allowing the production of indigenous generic medication. These possibilities of remedy are halted and twisted by the Internet Culture. The spread of AIDS can be stopped by the use of condoms, but also by abstinence till marriage, which goes counter to the pleasure seeking modern culture. Cheaper pharmaca contradict the profit seeking policy of the pharmaceutical firms, so all measures are taken half-heartedly only, and HIV merrily expands further. The same has to be said on TBC, malaria, etc.

The danger of overpopulation eating away all increases in food production, has already been spotted by Malthus in the XIXth century. The Marxists have criticized this theory on the ground, that the overexpanding industry can absorb the population growth, while providing the additionally needed food. However, such develoment again goes counter the cherished values of today, such as reducing the payroll in order to increase profits. Jöchle, a key figure in the Millenium Village Project, proposes a voluntary reduction of fertility, a "demographic transition" including improved child survival, women's empowerment for abortion and availability of contraception (*New York Academy of Sciences Update*, November/December 2005). All is mixt up here in one pot, and a fairy tale candy is addded. It says that each household will voluntarily have only two children, because their survival till adulthood would have been ensured. Jöchle forgets that child survival till adulthood is mainly a social problem of availability of material means and education, and only secondarily a medical one. So, in the cost-reducing Internet Society we are back to square one. The "knowing" Chinese have not much trust in volunteerdom and reduce fertility by simply killing redundant children at birth. For the moment, the West kills old people only, and this not legally, but under cultural pressure, using also illegal, brutal methods. Ogden (*Scientific American*, June 2005) studied 34 euthanasia cases and found that half of them were botched, which resulted in increased suffering.. Even Ogden sees problems in the "raging culture of death": there is no medical or counseling personnel to assess mental competence, no informed consent, and no exploration of treatment alternatives. The solution of the problem is a change in the dominant culture, allowing for cuts in profits, not in costs, which allegedly are making the killings necessary.

The solution of the heavy problems raised in this book, and especially in this chapter, does not entail the renouncement of the achievements in technology and in the global economy this society undoubtedly has, but a shift in its value emphases and priorities. It should and will hopefully turn into a *globalization with a hnuman face*, sustained not by the greediness for ever bigger profits for a few, but by the solid foundation of morality leading to the wellbeing of large masses of people, the respect for their national and spiritual traditions. Unfortunately, distinguished members of the inteligentsia, who should spearhead such a movement, are against it. The German Catholic theologian Schockenhoff (2003), wrote a lengthy book on the possibility of founding morality and law on superior principles, like the natural law. He concludes at the end of 300 pages, that it is impossible to deduce the sphere of positive law from some higher level of validity, which would also have legal binding. In his conception the sphere of law is an historical manifestation of the practical reason, similar to that found in the moral convictions and values adopted by the individuals (pag. 303). Does this mean maximal profits, good sex and the killing of the elderly? With such "guides" the leadership of the betterment movement is deposited in the hands of radical, violent populist leaders. Against them the intelligentsia reiterates her belief in scientific prediction based on computer models. Popper, Lampert and Bankes (2005) recommend not to look for optimal strategies, but for robust ones that will work well enough and that are adaptive. Because of the uncertainty of predictions of the future, the basic idea is to liberate ourselves from the need for precise predictions by using the computer to find strategies that work well over a wide range of possible futures. This reasonng is false, because values are also intoduced into the scenarios, whether obtained by computers or not. As the human operator feeds the data into the computer, he makes a value based selection. The authors sense this problem, when they say, we should not seek to predict the future, but ask what actions today will best shape the future *to our liking*. The computer will search for possible scenarios and design robust strategies that perform well across a sufficiently diverse set of them. These are plausible futures and a sustainable development. Finally, the authors strongly criticize the 1970 report *The Limits to Growth,* issued by the Club of Rome group of scientists. It said that the world would soon exhaust its natural resources, unless immediate action is taken. Impending resources will melt away, but new technologies will make production more efficient and provide alternatives to dwindling resources. Were Popper, Lampert et al. (2005) right, there would be no outcry to save the planet, no desperate tentatives to save its enegy resources. However, the problem exists, measures are being proposed, but immediately declared unnecessary by corporate-paid scientists, publicists and executives, who perhaps sincerely believe in what the publicists are saying. This way the problems cannot be solved and result in disaster.

Many scientists and economic analysts see in the continually rising oil prices a negative and dangerous economic and social phenomenon, but others (Sharma, 2005) vocally disagree. Of course, in this technologically advanced society attempts are being made to discover alternative sources of energy, like eolic and solar energy. Hybrid cars have been invented, which partly use electricity, but the capturing and the use of these new energies is very costly, and is less comfortable. A more promising avenue is Ethanol produced from sugar cane or corn, but it would mean easing import tariffs from Brazil, which can produce it cheaper than the US is capable of, and convincing big companies like Shell to commit to cellulosic ethanol on a commercial scale. Instead, the shortsighted analysts declare that what happens is in accordance with the economic aims of society. Stocks and bonds are sold, the higher energy prices have been or should be passed on the public, all is well as it is, no cause for worry. In the meantime deforrestation and the emission of greenhouse gases merrily continue, but there are enough analysts paid by corporations to loudly proclaim that no new measures are necessary. Nonetheless, the dangers in both cases are real, and they cannot be averted as long as what we have called by the name "Internet Culture" will dominate society. Is it, however, reasonable to assume that this well entrenched, ferocious culture will change? We are using the term "ferocious", because this culture is officially based on deceit, it advocates the destruction of the family, the liquidation of the old and sick, it throws out of work millions of people, robbing them of their human dignity, of all amenities of life and of spiritual religious comfort, and it does nothing to prevent the depravity of children, their use for pornography. Such a society can only be characterizedas ferocious. Fortunately, there are some encouraging signs attesting to the fact that the masses of people are fed up with this state of affairs. There are occurrences clearly indicating that the peoples do not want society to go ahead with the same world conception and behaviors that spell destruction.

Let us first speak about what is happening in the USA. The last key event was the election of Barack Obama as the first Afro-American president, and he has led his campaign under the motto "change for America". The intended details and the depth of this change are not yet clear, but the elections have shown how deeply the desire for change is pervading all the strata of the American public.

In the last years the political debate was joined by the growing power of American Evangelicals. If in 1970 only 3 percent of the US population was evangelical, today more than 20 percent are, and they broaden the movements's focus from the traditional warring about sex to include issues of social and economic justice. They turn from "the garden of Christ's Church" to fight the battles of the wildernesss of the world. At the same time, the American press (Washington Post, New York Times) speaks of a rebirth of American neopuritanism at the place of work. The New York Times has recently fired Susan Sachs, one of its best reporters, because she had exposed the adultery of some other reporters. The Boeing company has sacked his president, Harry Stonecipher, because he maintained an extramarital relationship with one of his female managers. Similar cases have occurred also in Europe. Britain's m.p. and director of the Spectator, Boris Johnson, was constrained to resign last autumn, because of a secret relationship with a female colleague, P.W., who remained pregnant. I have no intention to either approve or disapprove such occurrences, but to underline the novelty of the trend. In a culture obsessed by sex and which is depreciating the family, we should have expected shareholders, management and the public opinion to look the other way at such galant happenings, and feign that nothing has happened. Instead, more and more support is expressed for the family. *The APA Monitor on Psychology* (December, 2005) has dedicated an entire issue to the American family, writing on strategies for family success, psychologists' need to support poor minority families, on the ingredients of step-family success, parenting plans, the renaissance dad, etc. There were no more elucubrations on sex gratifications and self-realization through divorce. New books speak of virtue and psychology, the need for psychological practitioners to integrate their life with their work in a way that is rewarding personally, for those around them and for society at large (Fowers, 2005). Something in this society is beginning to move in the right direction.

In Europe the political surprise was the rejection of the European Constitution by France and The Netherlands, after all references to Europe's spiritual roots had been cut from the draft, and its content had not really been publicly discussed. In this atmosphere struck the car torching in France, the assassination of the playwright Theo Van Gogh in Netherland, who criticized the inequality of women in Muslim families, and the violent riots everywhere, because blasphemous cartoons on the Prophet Muhammad had been published in a tabloid of Denmark. These violent breakings of the law have made it clear that the Muslim minorities did not consider themselves as an integral part of the European host nations. After years of wavering and appeasing, the European nations are now hitting back, to defend themselves, their spiritual and national being. The port city of Rotterdam published a code requiring Dutch spoken in public, the Dutch Parliament banned the burqa wearing in public. A high-court judge in The Hague said,"We demand a new social contract. We no longer accept that people don't learn our language, we require that they send their daughters to school and stop bringing in young brides from the desert and locking them up in third-floor apartments". Denmark's minister of cultural affairs said,"We have gone to war against the multicultural ideology that says that every thing is equally valid". Danes and Dutch agree to create a multiethnic, but not a multicultural society, where different cultures live by different norms (*Newsweek*, March 8, 2006, p.44-45). These are new voices and new tendencies in Europe.

If the tendency for change we have discussed so far was related to the resolve to preserve and strengthen the nation's spiritual tradition and character, there is a second powerful trend of change fighting the economic and social injustice inflicted by globalization in its present form. The social actors of this trend are different, and usually come from the extreme left. Let us illustrate the case. Recently in Italy the government wanted to build a high-velocity train, in order to facilitate the access to the Winter Olympics, held in Northern Italy in 2006. The problem was, the Italian government was center-righht, and so the left-wing opposition initiated a violent wave of protest in Val di Susa. Buildings were set on fire and scores of people were badly injured. The protesters have been not only local citizens, who were afraid the track of the future train might bring damage to their farmland. They were "No Globals" from all of Italy and from other countries, who saw in this project another submission to globalizing interventions. They are known as "Disobbedienti" (the mavericks) and anarchists, whose only desire is to fight authority. The point of interst is, however, that as a matter of fact, those people are fighting the present-day Internet Society and its culture: globalization, the modernist high-speed trains in this case. Although they do it all wrong, they are agents of change, and their violent protests can no more be discarded with equanimity. Those people are fighting against what they perceive as lack of social justice. Their world conception stays in sharp difference to the outlook of the new culture's representatives, who see society in terms of economic processes only, especially in terms of increases and decreases in the values of the stock exchange. The only role economists ascribe to the masses of people is to support by their spending the upward movement of the stocks.

Recently, Glain (2005) published dithyrambic praises on China's leadership for being on the same side with Western economists, who believe that the benefits of a mobile labor force far outweigh the risks. The author points out that China has created a dynamic labor market, which is closer to Americas's flexible work force than to the static societies of Europe and Japan. Economists are advocating the mobility of capital and labor. Capital trades internationally, but labor does not, which is why domestic migration is so important. In the last years there was an estimated annual movement of 200 million rural Chinese, comparable only to the movement of 40 million Americans during the same period. Migrants with their low pay are the key components of the low "China prices". It is a horrific price to pay for this economic bonus in the US, as well as in China. The migrants live in shanty towns or in overcrowded rooms, they receive a miserable pay, much less than stable locals, and between 14-18 percent of them, in the US and in China, spend annually less than six months in their areas of primary residence. The backlash of the attempts of a crazy global worker uprooting policy is that parts of the occupationally redundant do not seek the miserble jobs available in remote locations, but become migrant professional protesters, turning up in every place where protests or global economic conferences are being held. They are mobilized, and allegedly paid by local organizations, planning to stage violent protest actions. They do it not only for the money, but for the ideological significance of the protest against a society which disregards people.

We are touching here a crucial point. In opposition to the ruling conception that it is only the economy that counts, we are relearning that there are other worthy things in life. Says Alvaro (2005), The West is not only economy, and neither is the Eeast. Europe is explained by chivalry and politeness, where the respect for women and the search for truth are embedded. Also in China the Great Sage, Confucius (VIth century B.C.) is again in vogue with his endeared values of unity, morality, respect for authority and the importance of hierarchical relationships. Today the official Chinese slogan is harmony, which could help stave off economic stagnation and social upheaval. Chinese leaders say that in a world where there are no moral standards to regulate how people treat each other, their business partners, friends and family, there is a need for a spiritual ideology, and Confucian values are the answers to China's new go-go culture (*Newsweek*, March 29, 2006,p.30). All this is the opposite of modern culture conceiving an economy without individuals, and the individuals without a soul. Every day the propaganda machine of the Internet Culture hammers into our heads that we are living in a post-idealist world. This is not what people want. They want something to believe in, to fight for, the are just not yet sure what that is. Many return to faith. At any rate, in the former Soviet Bloc the revival of the Church has been remarkable.

In the U.S.A. there is a renewed flair up of the controversy whether to teach evolutionism or creationism in schools. Data show that 80 percent of the population believe God has created the Universe, and less that half believe in evolution, despite the very vocal propaganda in favor of Darwinism. Darwin has suggested a different creative force, an undirected, morally neutral process he called natural selection, which ensures the survival of the fittest in the struggle for life (Underwood and Adams, 2005). Against this conception, the newly posited Intelligent Design theory presumes an intelligent force behind the emergence of life and of the complex biological systems. They argue that the empirical basis of Darwin's theory is weak inasmuch macroevolution is concerned. There is no factual evidence for the appearance of life from anorganic matter, and neither for the gradual transformation of an existing species into a new one with new organs. Fossils of intermediate organisms have not been found, and the new organs in the new species are of an irreducible complexity. The circulatory lungs of birds could not have appeared through the accumulation of small differences in the "bellow" lungs of reptiles. Even the flagelli of monocellular animals could not have appeared by small modifications. These apparatuses can only function when all their parts are fully developed (Denton, 1986). Darwinism also encounters most serious objections regarding its theory of the chemical evolution of life from anorganic matter, the so-called abiogenesis, from a pristine soup of chemical elements, inducing the formation of coacervates (Thaxton, Bradley and Olsen, 1984). Besides, this theory had already been put forward in the late '1940s by the Soviet academician Oparin, but because of the impossibility to prove it, it has been utterly discarded.

The only theory that gives an answer to these problems is the assumption of an Intelligent Design. It is a theist theory, though its proponents would not take stance to name the designer. At any rate, in the whole of the evolutionary process an ascendant pattern clearly emeges. The more developed organisms are indisputably standing on a higher level, and not only biologically – and this is the point. To compose symphonies and to drive cars goes beyond survival, and beyond sexual pleasure. Is this not evidence for an Intelligent Design? It does not mean that every move of every individual (human or animal) is pre-established. All have their relative independence, their "free agency", but if they relinquish the way of the Design, their fate turns to the worse (Krau, 2003). In his travels and research Darwin never found God, as Underwood and Adams (2005) say, nor did the Soviet cosmonaut Iuri Gagarin, who vaunted himself of the same thing. Both of them simply did not want to find Him. Believers say, God has been in all what they saw. Besides, there is an obstinate rumor, that Darwin converted on his death bed and expressed repentance for his theories.

For much that the scientific arguments in favor and against Darwin's theories of evolutionism are important, the problems with this theory and the reason we are dealing with it, lie in the cultural-political coercion construed on it. Darwinism has become a metaphysical naturalism (Woodward, 2003) which identified itself with science, delegitimizing any other opinion. This theory impacts not only on the truth in science, but on the possibility of a free expression of opinions, the freedom of speech. "We should ignore Intelligent Design proponents, and offer them no credibility by giving them a platform in the magazine (Natural History Magazine) or at the museum", urges the new thought police (Cf, Woodward, 2003, p.30). Not only that those who claimed the existence of an Intelligent Design were not allowed to make their point, but the Academy also ruled against a negative argument, which would discover the flaws in the evolutionist theory.

The scary aspect of today's version of Darwinism is its anachronicity. You have the impression to find yourself in the Soviet Union of the years 1955-1975, when dissenters could not even present their case, and if they tried, they would be ostracized and lose their jobs. During long years, in the U.S.A the proponents of the Intelligent Design were not arguing and enlarging their theory, they were simply fighting for their survival as scientific workers. Woodward's book is not an argumentation for ID, but a praise song on how skillfully the ID proponents

circumvent the censorship of the scientific Establishment, and how they succeeded in coaxing some evolutionists to speak with them or return a smile. I
read this book, and I suddenly felt thrown back in time and space for some 40
years, assisting at an inept debate of two groups, each attempting to show that
they are the better Communists. Also here the Intelligent Design group take an
utmost care not to hint at the identity of the "Designer". If need be, they could
always say that it was the local Party secretary. Yet, nowadays finally it seems
that the Intelligent Design group are daring to proclaim their opinions, and there
are indications that they are also getting the public's ear.

We are today witnessing a revival of traditional values, even if not accompanied by a strict observance of religious canons. In Italy the recent years witnessed a trend for youth to enter classical high schools with curricula in Latin
and Greek. In 2005, 50,000 new students inscribed and found Virgil and Par-
menides enough attractive and efficient for educating the qualities of a logic
mind (*Corriere della Sera,* 8 December, 2005). Elsewhere in Europe the spiritual revival regards more the skepticism and dissatisfaction of an entire generation with what the Internet Culture has to offer. The German film director Wein-
garten captures this dissatisfaction in his film "The Edukators". Warningly (?)
he says,"You hardly notice, then one day, at your surprise, at the polls you vote
consevative" (*Newsweek*, May 16, 2005). As a matter of fact, in the recent elections the German electorate voted conservative. Nonetheless, the world trend of
renewal is much more complex, and also imcludes the votings in Latin America,
where indigenous and populist movements are surging and gaining elections in
tandem with the widespread rejection of neoliberal economic policies. They
constitute an increasingly assertive underclass, which negates the values of
modern capitalism. The indigenous communities have led the region against
globalization. It is not just a cultural revival, but a vibrant, sometimes explosive
outpouring of civic and political activism. Since 2000 indigenous uprisings have
been instrumental in toppling four presidents in Ecuador and Bolivia, while qui-
eter upheavals have taken place in Colombia, Venezuela, Guatemala and Nica-
ragua (*Newsweek*, December 12, 2005). So, what has the Bolivian Evo Morales
in common with Angela Merkel and G.W. Bush? They all fight for the link with
tradition, with the despized and forgotten spiritual values of the common people.
They stand for a "culture of life", as G.W.Bush has called it, and are leading
towards globalization with a human face. In the same trend Pope Benedict XVI
fights for the re-Christianization of modern Europe. Before he has become pope,
he said in his visit to Subiaco, "Europe has developed a culture, that in a manner
unknown to humanity, excludes God from the public conscience, and this has
led to "the edge of abyss". Muslims, he pointed out, do not feel threatened by
the Christian moral foundations, but by the cynism of a secularized culture that
denies its own foundations" (*Newsweek*, August 15, 2005). The recent political
changes in the world center on bringing back these "own foundations". One
might think of Napoleon's adage that only a nation with a past has also a future.

The "own foundations" find their expression in some apparently unrelated
trends of the recent years. First, the already discussesd "parochial identities"

have to been mentioned. Apparently linked to a narrower basis than a national ethos and tradition, most of these movements flow into the broader unity of national heritage. In places where this does not happen, like in Spain, the leftist disintegrative proecss has gone too far, and narrower identities tend to gain supremacy (Euskadi, Catalunya, Andalucia). All of them uphold their past condition, in order to justify their separate identity on their way to (a separate?) future. In normal conditions the clinging to provincial tradition does not lead to the dismemberment of the state. The best examples are the Federal Republic of Germany with her Bundesländer, and the United Kingdom, where a degree of autonomy given to Scotland and Wales has brought no threat to the unitary state.

The "own foundations" draw their substance not only from public life. The family is one of the strongest pillars of society. We have already discusssed how the modern culture subverts, rejects and renegates it. It is therefore surprising that the new trend all over the world contributes to the strengthening of the family. Up to now we had been accustomed to the praise of singleness and divorce, to the idea that it is better to separate than to put sufferance and grief on the children, who live the permanent shameful spectacle of fights in the family. Now an entirely new message is sent out. There is no "good divorce" for the children, it is better to live in a low-conflict family, than the separation of the parents. Marquardt (2005) points out that when a marriage breaks down, the children's life is very adversely affected. Often the outcome of the breakdown appears in drug consumption, adolescent pregnancies and delinquency. The children feel raised in two families, parallel worlds with different values, and this causes inner psychological conflicts. Therefore it is better to learn to repair the edgy differences between the parents and to keep the family together. Similar opinions are expressed in Italy by S.V.Finzi and A.O. Ferraris (*Corriere della Sera*, 26 October 2005), as they also are in other European countries. Still, in some very conflictual families divorce is necessary, but its terms must take into consideration the need to care for the children's happiness, and not only for the ego-satisfaction of the parents. The slogan used to be that divorce is restoring the woman's self-esteem. The new idea is that self-esteem has to come from being ethical, not from pleasure-given satisfaction. Therefore American opinion polls deplore that ethics are not taught in American schools (*Scientific American*, May 2005).

These changes in the public's conception of social life phenomena are parallelled by changes in the mentality regarding banal everyday occurrences, for instance, attitudes linked to repair vs throw-away-and-buy-a-new. The Internet Culture promotes the latter in order to keep big business going. However, the buying hysteria was accompanied by payroll cuts and salary reduction. It has caused a class of "new poor" to emerge.They cannot afford to throw away the things they already have, and besides, in Europe, 48 percent of the families do not save, again a result of the vocal publicity to buy. This situation has revived cohorts of tinker-plumbers, repair cobblers, tailors and seamstresses, who suddenly have more customers than they can handle. In Italy it has bacome a new mass behavior (*Corriere della Sera*, 7 November, 2004).

What happens has surely an economic aspect in its causes and effects, but there is also an undeniable cultural face. The big corporations begin to lose their grip on the masses, who take refuge in a past lifestyle, which better tends to their needs. If this is so, then the forcefully imposed jingle on the ineluctability of continuing the present direction in the economy and culture has been broken. Like in the tales of Andersen the king appears naked. This does not mean that globalization must be completely discarded, but its rhythm, style and dimensions must change, in order to put a human face on it to the benefit of the people and not only of the corporation shareholders. The modification of the economic habitus will go in parallel with a modification of the ideological sphere, reviving the humanistic values of the past. It is a process that has happened many times in history after periods of social and ideological aberrations. It happened in England after Cromwell, in France after La Terreur of the French Revolution, in Germany after the Nazi regime, and in Russia after the Communist rule, precisely as it is happening now in China after Mao. It is not true that the values of the past never return. However, their comeback is always on the basis of the newly achieved technological infrastructure, which surely has also some ideological consequences, but the latter are capable to live in harmony with the old-new values. So, the Internet will surely stay, but its use and effects will adjust to society's newly found values and lifestyle.

The process is developing before our eyes and presently its spearhead is Europe, as I had foreseen it in my 1998 book (Krau, 1998). The violent and continual criticism from the American and the americanized press speaking in each article on an "European decay", because she is not willing to give up its social and national traditions, only reinforces what we are saying. Europe clearly discards the American model, which today has no satisfactory welfare system, no safety net for the out-of-work, and whose economy is a prey to speculative bubbles from high-tech to real estate. It has a massive debt and a currency propped up by Asian governments (*Newsweek*, September, 5, 2005). Europe criticizes this situation. They are talking of new models, which would embrace both globalization and welfare. They speak of the Anglo-Social model of Pearce, the Social Market model of the German CDU, and of the Swedish model of social citizenship, which some say, has been copied by the other two. Sweden has a life-long health care, a good educational system with renowned universities (Lund, Uppsala), but also big industrial brands, such as Volvo, Scania, Erikson, the world highest per capita ownership of second homes and pleasure boats.

Contrary to the position, that all what happens with globalization is a tide which will never turn back, we are contending that the tide will have to be turned back, and the remaining incertitude is only the timing and whether the process will happen peacefully. The tide has gone beyond its reasonable scope, and its continuation in the same direction spells catastrophe in the environment, in the economy and in the social domain. Says Prestowitz (2005), president of the Economic Strategy Institute, "For most of the last 50 years, globalization has been a win-win proposition making America richer, while lifting hundreds of millions in the developing world out of poverty. Recently, however, it has begun to operate differently, undermining US welfare, while creating imbalances likely to end in a global economic crisis". The US trade deficit is now around $800 billion (from $24 billion in 2004), and is steadily growing, as America consumes more than it produces. Even the US high-tech trade surplus made in 1998 ($30 billion) has today collapsed into a deficit of about $40 billion. Also agricultural trade is in deficit for the first time. Then there are "dollar crashes", sell-offs, which hurt housing with increased mortgage rates (they have reached 6.3 percent from 5.6 percent in June 2005), and depress consumer spending (*Newsweek*, January 9, 2006).

In September 2008 the global economic mismanagement finally imploded, paying the "price for greed", as the press calls it. Driven by greed, investors and financial institutions took risks that proved too large. To keep profits growing, Lehman borrowed huge sums relative to its size, its debts became about 35 times its capital. After such a feat the pressure to reduce the debts leads to dumping assets, which policy drives prices down, the financial crisis enters the economy. In a globalized economy the *deleveraging* becomes global. It is not only the Amrican stock that crumbles, but also the European and the Asian exchanges. If one cause of the economic implosion was the lack of fear in maneuvering risky stocks, now fear is spreading, banks are afraid to lend money to each other, to institutions and to citizens. Enterprises must lay off workers in order to be able floating, but people out of work cannot spend money, and the economy is slowing down further.

In the desperately looking situation the states all over the world intervened with generous bailout programs. The US Treasury poured $700 billion into the bankrupt businesses, but nevertheless imposed some financial regulations. Two problems still remained unanswered: 1) What happens to the masses of people who lost or will shortly lose their jobs and their homes, will the Treasury salvage them too, or only the bankrupt managers and shareholders? 2) Are the bailout measures sufficient to turn around the economy and prevent further crises? The answer to the first question had only been nice speeches with vague promises. As to the second quesation, each day the press says the crisis will shortly be over, but they all are living in denial, as they have done hitherto. Already in the XVIth century Francis Bacon stated *Manente causa permanet effectus* (If the cause still exists, also stays the consequence). The downfall of the economy will happen again, because it was not an accidental occurrence, but a logical consequence of the systemic failure in the globalized socioeconomic order. The roots of the crisis are deeper than envisaged, they are in the culture, which sets the values driving the disastrous behavior of greed and unjustified self-reliancee at an unimpeded striving for self-satisfaction. To beware of crises and depression, there must be changes in the faulty Internet Culture of the present globalized society, in its values and life conception. The leading groups are not yet ready for change, and they are convinced that the crisis has passed and all would continue the usual way, with perhaps only a slight fiinancial tinkering. This is a disastrous mistake. Bailout has a temporary impact only. How many times can the US Treasury pour 700 billion dollars into bankrupt businesses?

For the US globalization has meant building its economy into the largest service economy of the world, a giant consumption machine. Easy consumer credits, loans with tax-deductible interest payments, an accomodative monetary policy and other incentives have led Americans to forfeit savings, while borrowing at record rates. For the others globalization has meant export-led growth by managing to keep the dollar over-valued vis-à-vis their own currency, and their export prices low. These countries can save, invest and export their production to the US, which is living above its means. At the World Economic Forum held in Davos (2006) panelists, from Chancellor Angela Merkel to the former Clinton adviser Laura Tyson, raised questions about the benefits of globalization for the rich countries. They considered that in its present form globalization has had negative consequences for the industrialized world. Job creation and wages have lagged behind historical norms. Economic recoveries have either been jobless or wageless, or both. While productivity growth soares, gains in worker compensation have lagged, defying the hitherto admitted principle that labor is alwayas paid in accord with its productivity. *Newsweek* (February 20, 2006, p.43) concludes that more and more the overall stability of the economy as a whole is based on an increased instability of individual industries, which causes instability of individual careers.

Acknowledging some of the facts, Schwab (2005) has seen a rosy outcome, as he declared the year 2005 as a tipping point of globalization. The world of tomorrow, he said, is not based on a suprastructure of nation states. It is a world where business is a major shaper, not only of economic developments, but also of social developments. The legitimacy of its platforms will depend less on a traditional "representative" process, and much more on ongoing public acceptance and measurable gains (Sic!). Here is the finally outspoken logical consequence of socioeconomic processes driven by the globalized Internet Society: an economic and political dictatorship of corporations, i.e. of their leaders. Would it be some kind of Business-Mao or Business-Hitler? They too shunned the "traditional representative" process. Fareed Zakaria from the editorial staff of *Newsweek* enthusiastically praises China, because her present government has achieved growth at a pace no other country has achieved, in disregard of all local protests of the population. "Every time you see a dam, Zakaria writes, remember that it displaced whole villages and towns, every time you see a gleaming new highway in China, remember that there were homes, shops and farms, where it now runs (*Newsweek*, December 26, 2005, p.21). What a truly modern leadership, isn't it?

In the already quoted series of articles, Robert Reich (2005) professor of social and economic policy and former US secretay of labor makes an analysis of the future stratification of society. He starts from the analysis he made 15 years ago, when he described a three-tiered work force. At the bottom were workers who offered personal services in retail outlets, restaurants, hotels and hospitals, the second tier comprised of production workers in factories or offices, performing simple, repetitive tasks. Personally, I don't see the social and economic differencs between these two tiers, the division makes some sense only from the point of view of the Internet Society, which is destroying the second tier, the group of production workers, and makes of them a kind of modern *"Lumpenproletariat"*.

Corporations, we are told, need to decide what to do with their newly found riches. Ideally, they will increase capital spending and prolong the global expansion of their companies. But that means assuming that they can find profitable investments, what today is hard and uncertain. Expansion just for the sake of getting bigger, without having ensured viable economic advantages leads to falling profits, and an early end to spending (*Newsweek*, November 14, 2005, p.35). So, this part of the future equation is leading to an economic and social crisis, as does resisting the necessary actions for energy saving and for preserving the environment.

Like in a logical dilemma-exercise, the other side of the equation, the social situation, is also leading to a crisis. We have already discussed this matter. New data may be added any time. In China, ten years ago, there were some 10,000 local protests a year, now figures speak of 74,000, about 200 a day. France, this autumn, saw torching riots in Paris, Toulouse and in other cities, where thousands of cars, shops, buildings were destroyed. It is not the entire nation on food, not yet, but the masses are in a state of negativistic despondency, yearning for change, as they also are in Germany, Italy, The Netherlands, Russia. With these masses of followers the leadership, be it national or international, want to ensure the "great leap" forward? Or do they wait for the Business-Hitler to do the job? All hitlers used to have a miserable end. Mao died in his bed, but his wife and security chief were sentenced to death, although the sentence was not carried out.

It is of common knowledge that motivating people to great deeds asks for a great vision, which would benefit every individual, make possible the realization of their cherished dreams. Such a vision incites people to accept even great hardships, but for a limited time, set beforehand. In his famous speech in 1940, Winston Churchill told Britons that for the moment he can promise only tears and sweat, but the engagement will ensure victory over a cruel dictatorship, restore freedom and national well-being. The same did Roosevelt and even Stalin, who spoke to his "brethren and sisters", telling them that there would be celebration also on their street. The global Internet Society's leadership has no such vision to spread for people. Their vision centers on the superrich. The picture-journals of large circulation, like Newsweek or Fortune have introduced entire new sections of "Good Life", where the marvels obtainable for astronomic sums are enticingly pictured and described. There has been vocal criticism from the readers, but to no avail. One reader writes to Newsweek, "Good Life left me feeling very poor indeed. So does the Tip Sheet, which has no item I can afford". In other letters the critique is much more severe, "For me, seeing this free publicity section of the good material life seems so cruel and frustrating, after reading articles that are about war, terrorist attacks, hunger and poverty". Finally, somebody directs his arrows at the superrich themselves, "Completely missing from your coverage is the slightest element of these people's sense of duty and responsibility to a wider community" (*Newsweeek*, November 21, 2005, p.18). There is some talking in the media on the advancement of science and technology, better TV screens, but nobody can be willing to endure misery for such marvels, many of them will only benefit the richest. The main question is, why should people be disposed to suffering in the first place, lose their jobs, be constrained to relinquish their home and move to other places, why should there be continuous cuts in the payroll, in wages and in the services given to the public? Is there a war going on, a siege, a national catastrophe, which would justify the massive suffering and renouncements? We only hear of the need for corporations to expand, for the must of national economies to grow, for democracy to be brought to Iraq (who does not want it), but the man or woman on the street asks,"What is there in for me?"And the answer is only à la Hitler and Stalin,"Otherwise you wil lose even what you have". If in Sweedeen the ratio between the salary of a waiter and a CEO is in the average 1:4 , why should it be 1:30 in Israel and even larger in the USA? The people in every country are asking: Why should every theatre, hospital or other public facility, like even the mail, play the eternal jingle of reducing their service offers to the public because of budget insufficiency, when before the start of globalization there was no such a situation? Must we continue to endure this economic and social style which cripples us, only because in Tony Blair's words, it is a tide?

The Japanese minister in charge of reforms, Heizo Takenaka, was asked in an interview (*Newsweek*, December 19, 2005,p.42), whether he is not worried because of the slight growth of the Japanese economy. He answered that the level of 2 percent is quite comfortable, Japan is not moving too slowly. "There is no need to make a permanent comparison with China and India. Japan has her policy targets, and they have theirs. What is important for Japan is to sustain the growth of per capita income, to sustain the standard of living". This is a very clear statement of priorities, and if they are actually adopted in Japan, they express a feasible policy, accepted by the nation.

There was a time when in brainstormings, enterprises and politicians rewarded the unorthodox maverick questions of the type "What would happen should we not accept this or that stongly proposed action, but which has unwelcome side effects?" This way the best solutions used to be obtained. In regard to our subject, one should ask,"What would happen if we reduced the economic corporational growth, which cripples our people?". Europe is doing precisely this, the growth in France, Germany and Italy is reduced to 1.2 – 3 percent. The leftist critique in the press is terrible, so is the American pressure and the pressure from the own corporations. However, if a country has the courage to look in the face of both, then it is able to save important parts of its welfare system and save the common people from starvation and suffering. The Internet brought an enhanced global communication and made global competition easier. Competition does not threaten the people, it is a threat only for corporations, if the governments are not willing to defend their economy and their citizens. The American government, for instance, very well defends the country from being flooded with cheap Chinese imports. If there is a will, there is a way to keep globalization in check.

We have been repeatedly told, that today what counts is to have ideas and to valorify them. An unprecedented war for top talent is raging in the economy. Today after 500 years or so, the scarcest, most valuable resource in business is no longer capital. Shareholder wealth is the real scorecard in capitalism (is here anything said about the masses of people?). Companies like Microsoft and Google are great examples of how today's information-based economy lets business create vast shareholder wealth using very little financial capital (*Fortune,* February 6, 2006, p.52). The article continues telling us that money isn't what today's firms need most. The best companies desperately need talent. The greatest shortage is in skilled, effective managers (*ibid.*).

Two things are sticking out in this new manifesto. First, all the slogans putting a permanently developing advanced technology at the core of this society, are mere propaganda, as is the need of capital accumulation. The economy is saturated with them, and it does not support them any more. It is an obvious sign of the decay of this society. It had completed its task, if it ever had one, and it is ripe for change. The second point is, that the social mechanism of the Internet Society blocks the developing and the recognition of talents in the broad masses of the population. It is self-evident that the biologically conditioned aptitudes are distributed within the entire population, and are not traits only attributable to the megarich for whom the "Good Life" section of journals is edited. If they have no privilege of talented offspring, they *have* the privilege of the best possible education and career furthering for their children, talented or not. By the same token, they put a halt on the attempts of the economically less fortunate people to compete for positions. Then there is the spiritual censorship of the leftist press on all opinions contrary to the values of the Internet Culture, and it restrains even more the expression of talents, who often are nonconformist. One should remember that blocking people's ideas and their active participation in society has brought down the Communist empire. Now the Internet

It is not clear today, how far the ominous policy of the Internet Culture will be allowed to go. Both its economic and social policy is spelling crisis, and the broad masses of people want change in the economy, in values and in lifestyle. They want a link with their spiritual and national tradition. The problem is not only to get jobs, but an unacceptable lifestyle is forced on people by the Internet Culture, and the loss of the job is only a part of it. This does not mean to bring back the '1950s-1970s. People want a *sustainable welfare state.* A 35-hour working week had been an exaggeration, which is not sustainable economically. However, there are more vital issues such as a pension system for retirees, family assistance, some form of job security and medical insurance which *must be* sustained by the economy, even if the result is a decrease in business profits. The sustainable welfare state should be based on a sound ideological basis, tolerant for freedom of thought, and it should enhance the preservation of humanity's cherished spiritual values, national and cultural traditions. It should forbid their desacralization and the corruption of youth. Things that in the past have always been forbidden will also hitherto stay off limits. No hypocritical jingle can justify the murder of elderly sick people. No scientific fairy tale can justify fraud in scientific experiments, no psychological acrobatic feat can justify an eduction system in which the teacher has only the role of an observer, and therefore the level of knowledge and moral education is hardly above the zero point. No chatter on civil rights can justify the lack of punishment for murder and other heinous crimes, no chat on modernization can justify the degradation of the arts and the corruption of artistic master pieces. In all these domains the social institution of a severely enforced taboo will be reinstated, subjected to the decisions of the representative system of the nation.

Analysts are saying (e.g. Moravcsik, director of the European Program at Princeton, see *Newsweek*, December 26, 2005) that the uneasiness and rioting in Europe are merely an economic problem, and that Europe is destroyed by the bankruptcy of its own socialist ideals. The ideals of Europe are not exclusively socialist. The socialistic ideals further the welfare state, and true, also its exaggerations, while the conservative ideology, which time and again is the ruling one, helps keeping the right balance. The democratic countries of Europe need the bi-partisan political structure in which both social-democrats and conservatives (the names of both vary from country to country) are vital for a balanced, sustainable economic system to emerge. Both Clement Attlee and Margaret Thatcher were necessary, so the England of today could emerge. It took Kohl, Schröder and Angela Merkel to create a unified, free Germany, with chances to thrive economically. The violent Internet Culture cancels this healthy democratic governance mechanism. Today, when the left gains power in democratic ways, it deligitimizes the former conservative rulers, if possible, puts them on trial, and immediately introduces measures of no return. Every individual or group holding other opinions is stigmatized as belonging to the "extreme right". This latter ought to be marginalized and deprived of the slightest influence. Spain and Israel are good examples in this sense. Some of these tunes were heard even in Germany from the Schröder government, ironically also precisely as they lost the elections of 2005. The return to true democracy and true freedom is a must for a peaceful development. We have seen this process in its positive action after World War II, after the implosion of the Soviet empire,after the toppling of Haile Mengistu's terror regime in Ethiopia and of Apartheid in South Africa. There is always a return to a lifestyle of freedom, and the logic of history indicates that it will happen also in the present society.

We are arguing that corporation gains should be compatibilized with the welfare of the people. If Europe of the '1950s and '1960s could maintain full occupation and a good pension system, in a much narrower market, there is no logically compelling reason why this should be impossible today, with the tremendous advancements in the creation of new products and the opening up of new markets.

Remains, however, the question of power, and if corporations are exercizing it exclusively, the chances for shredding a policy which cripples the less privileged classes are slim. Since Montesquieu from the XVIIIth century, and except the Soviet regime, the theory of the state upholds the principle of the separation of powers. The trend of the Internet Culture, to put business in command of society, infringes this principle. The state embodies the will of the people. Therefore the economy of a country has to be regulated by the state. The recent economic crisis has proven that the market is unable to provide an automatic regulation of the economy. For long years there had been an experiment with self-regulation by business, but the state had to be brought in, when all went wrong. The bailout catastrophically drew on national resources and many businesses and jobs still could not be saved. A pre-emptive state regulation would have avoided this fallacy.

Corporations are a part of the people, but if their loyalty is given to globalization and not to their own nation, they do not any more belong to the people. Economy is a vital function of society, but the other functions have also to be properly taken care. The economy does not only comprise corporations. The national labor market and the masses' standard of living also belong to the country's economy. Business used to fire people, who then are of no more concern. The state cannot offshore its activities and cease to care for the citizens out of their jobs. If this is what it does, it risks a political upheaval, which may even put at risk the physical life of government and corporate leaders. It has happened in history.

A dangerous momentum arises when a company decides to outsource its activities. It is a move contradicting the interests of the people, of the nation, seen in its entirety. On the other hand, in a free market society business will claim the right to implement its intentions to offshore jobs. Of course, from an ethical point of view solidarity has to be with the own nation, they should not decide to go against their own people (do they have something like that in globalization?), but today "greed is cool". Here is the fulcrum point. The state has to make offshoring a very costly enterprise, not paying off. It should use bureaucracy and taxation methods to halt the move. Such measures are on the agenda in France, although they are not yet fully implemented. The last twenty years have shown that if both sides behave reasonably, the necessary radical changes can be accomplished through Velvet Revolutions, as in the former Soviet Bloc, or through the Orange Revolutions in Ucraine and Bolivia. Fanatic obstination of the ruling regime has only led to bloodshed in Romania, in former Yugoslavia , Ethiopia, etc.

Modern economists and managers are directing fierce attacks against the economic role of the state. They are asking for the removal of any limitations on bussiness. The idea seems attractive, but its consequences are a nightmnare. Consider the jubilating prospects announced by Google, Microsoft, etc. regarding the tracking of bypassers on the street in order to learn their consumer preferences, purchases, to track their movements and correspondence, know their private lives. All this happens unbeknownst to them and without their permission. The purpose is to target them with personalized advertisements. It is only a small step to register beliefs, love life, political opinions. It means the end to privacy, and we might be afraid to engage in any activity others could find controversial (*Newsweek*, April 3, 2006, p.38). Even free trade has its limits of usefulness and it is not a magic bullet. It has not much helped the 47 least developed countries. Their share of world trade has sharply declined since 1950, and the number of people living in poverty has risen and is expected to further rise to 471 million by 2015, up from 334 million in 2000 (*Newsweek*, January 2, 2006). China's great economic success is due to her stepwise entering the free market economy and maintaining a tight government control on the process. The European Union is trying to do the same with her welfare systems, as her cultural, ideological and lifestyle problems are involved. Perhaps the concept of "sequencing" coined for entering globalization should also be the leading paradigm for *dismantling* the noxious characteristics of the Internet Culture. Indeed, there are timid signs for this process. One of them is the newly proposed idea of "thinking smaller". Said Bill Ford in an attempt to save the Ford company, "For too long we have used the advantage of size to avoid change". He encouraged his employees to think like a small company (*Newsweek*, February 6, 2006). Another sign of change is the admission that the unipolar world has come to an end (*Time*, February 25, 2008).

At this stage the social groups who want to dismantle globalization are not in majority, but a majority wants to impose restrictions on it. They want *globalization with a human face*, global business which is not allowed to harm economically and ideologically the masses of people and their conceptions on life. Society must proclaim that greed is not cool, and that the supreme value is people's wellbeing and not shareholder wealth. We do not want to be the "low cost gheneration", are shouting the young demonstrators in France and in Italy. The struggle is for rights that had been already conquered since 1968, but taken away by this society: jobs, work agreements, consumption for the large masses. The young generation is considering the attitudes towards people in the globalized world as lacking human dignity and a human face. One must add that the people's welfare has also its limts and does not mean lilving in a Luna Park. It cannot be a working week of 30-35 hours, but neither is it the "24/7 working week" of 80 hours, "softly" imposed in the US, under the threat of losing one's job. This is an inhuman and murderous practice. How long can people resist to such a lifestyle? *Fortune* (December 5, 2005) which brings this story to the attention of the public, has on its cover page a dog in a business suit with the title "Get a Life". Corporations which have positively reacted to this problem, have emended the working schedules of the big executives only. This is inadmissible. The rank and file worker or clerk has also the right to be treated like a human person and not as a dog. It is the change of values, which must be imposed.

In order to do so, an important requirement is the existence of a genuinely free press, not intimidated by governments or party comrades, and not corrupted by corporations. It would put before the public all the relevant facts, and either let the public themselves make the judgement, or present the commentaries of *all the shades* of public opinion. Presently the interpretation of the Internet Culture is dominant, and when reading the journals or watching TV you have the impression of a giant indoctrination going on. It is not only the written press to which this definition applies, but also the electronic one. It has been a key demand of the Soviet Union during the cold war.

In every copy of Newsweek, Fortune, or any other important international journal, Europe, Japan or Latin American nations are blamed for not renouncing their welfare policy and their national traditions. There are censured for not hastening what is called "reforms". This is not a free press, it is an "engaged" press, functioning as an instrument of cheap indoctrination. In the eyes of these "engaged" people Europe is in the process of decay, because its economic growth measured in stock value increase is small, as she puts up a ditch fight to ensure a decent living for all of her citizens. She also upholds its national lifestyles based on tradition and family, and refuses to become a multinational conglomerate dominated by immigrants from Asia or from the Sahara. We are thinking, that to the contrary, this same behavior constitutes a resurrectional process heralding in a new era of globalization with a human face, which will go on with or without the engaged journalists of the Internet Culture.

Be this as it may, the return to a healthy social life and to common sense, will not obstruct the technological development, because technology is socially neutral. It would, however, put limits on what big corporations are allowed to do, and would enhance action taken against destructive shareholder greed. To give greed a limitless go has always spelt catastrophe in private and in public life as well. What will happen to the Internet? As a communication technology it is neutral, and will continue to develop, but it will have to be made sure, that it does not serve terrorism and crime, and it does not corrupt youth, nor set out to control people's private life, phone calls or entertainment.To ensure such conditions is a technological and partly a legal issue. Surely, the "stormy advance of technology" will be able to find the right solutions. Unfortunately, the power struggle among the big corporations like Microsoft and Google has already begun in this domain, and the danger is that the Internet could be drawn into the war. It should be understood that all technology is only an auxiliary to humankind and so must be the Internet. To make of it a tool for profit raising, for indoctrination or an object of a cult, to create around it an entire culture, which swallows up all the values of society, does not serve society's progress. By the same token, progress has not been served by the worshipping of stones or stars in the old days. These adorations disappeared, and so will the Internet *Culture*, together with all the values and behaviors which deprecate and degrade human solidarity and dignity. The technological advancement will remain to serve people's needs on their way to a happier life.

No advice is more loyal than the one given from ships that are in danger. (Nessún consiglio è piú leale que quello che si dà dalle nave che sono in pericolo). *Leonardo da Vinci, Aforismi.*

References

Albin, F., M. (1989). *Consumer economics and money management*, 2nd ed. Englewood Cliffs, NJ: Prentice Hall

Allen R. and Ishii-Gonzalès, S. (Eds.) (1999). *Alfred Hitchcock centenary essays,* London: BFI Publishing.

Alvo, G. (2005). *L'anima e l'economia.* Milano: Mondadori.

Anaud, M. (1995). *The art of sexual magic.* New York: G.P.Putnam's Sons.

Anderson, W.T. (1997). *The future of the self.* New York: Tarcher/Putnam.

Asch, P. (1988). *Consumer safety regulation.* New York, Oxford: Oxford University Press.

Bacharach, S, B. and Lawler, E. J. (1961). Power and politics in organizations. San Francisco: Jossey Bass.

Bailey, D. S. (2003). Alternatives to incarceration. *APA Monitor on Psychology, 34*, 7, 54-56.

Barasch, I. M. (2000). *Healing dreams.* New York: Riverhead Books.

Barber, R., J. (1966). Government and the consumer. *Michigan Law Review, 64,* 1203-1238.

Baudrillard, J. (1983). *Simulations.* New York: Semiotext.

Bauman, Z. (2001). *The individualized society.* London: Polity.

Bazin, A. (1968). La politique des auteurs. In: P. Graham (ed.): *The new wave.* New York: Doubleday

Beccaria, C. (1764/1939). *On crimes and punishment* (Russian translation). Moscow: Juridical literature.

Beckler, S., J. (2004). The practical need for basic science. *APA Monitor on Psychology, 35*, 6, 37.

Bednii, G., Z. (1975). *Engineering psychology.* (Orig. in Russian). Kiev: Visha Shkola.

Bell, D. (1953). Crime as an American way of life. *The Antioch Review,* June 13, p. 131-154.

Bell, D. (1980). Beyond modernism, beyond self. In: *Sociological Journeys.* London: Heinemann.

Belton, J. (ed.) *Movies and mass culture.* New Brunswick, NJ: Rutgers University Press.

Bem, S.L. (1987). Probing the promise of androgyny. In: M.Roth Walsh, *The psychology of women.* New Haven and London: Yale Univ. Press.

Bennis, W.,G. (1966). *Changing organizations: Essays on the development and evolution of human organizations.* New York: McGraw Hills.

Benson, E. (2003). The science of sexual arousal. *APA Monitor on Psychology*, 34, 4, 50-52.

Benton, J.,R. and DiYanni, R. (1998) *Arts and Culture* (Vol.2.)Upper Saddle River, NJ: Prentice Hall.

Berman, R., A. (1989). *Modern culture and critical theory*. Madison: Univ. of Wisconsin Press.

Bernasek, A. (2002). Is this where the economy is headed? *Fortune*, 146, 3, 53-56.

Bierstedt, R. (1950). An analysis of social power. *American Sociological Review, 15*, 730-738.

Blair, T. (2005). Europe is falling behind. *Newsweek*, Special edition, December,18-20.

Booth, A., Crouter, A. C. and Shanahan, M. (Eds.) (1999). *Transitions to adulthood in a changing economy.* Westport, Connecticut, London: Praeger.

Bourdieu, P. (1998). *Acts of resistance*. New York: Free Press.

Brecht, B. (1967). *Gesammelte Werke*. Frankfurt am Main: Suhrkamp Verlag.

Brinkley, A. (1998). *Liberalism and its discontents*. Cambridge, Mass., London: Harvard Univ. Press.

Brown, E. (2000). So rich, so young – but are they really happy? *Fortune, 142*, 6, 37-42.

Brown, W. (1998). Freedom's silences. In: R. C. Post (Ed.) *Censorship and silencing*. Los Angeles: The Getty Research Institute.

Bruner, J. S. (1967). *Toward a theory of instruction*. Cambridge, Mass.: Harvard University Press.

Campbell, J.P., Converse, Ph.E., and Rogers, W.L. (1976). *The quality of American life*. New York: Russell Sage

Campbell, J.P. Dunnette, M.D., Lawler, E.E.III and Weick, K.E. (1974). Theories of motivation. In: R. Dubin (Ed.) *Human relations in administration*, 4th ed. Englewood Cliffs, NJ: Prentice Hall.

Carr, A. (1968). Is business bluffing ethical? *Harvard Business Review*, January-February.

Cassidy, D.C. (2004). *Robert Oppenheimer and the American Century.* New York: Pi Press.

Castells, M. (2002). The network becomes the social structure of everything. *Fortune, 142*, 8, 106.

Catani, M. (1982) Changing one's country means changing one's flag. In: *Living in two cultures*. Gower: The UNESCO Press.

Cauer, P. (1911) *Das Altertum im Leben der Gegenwart*. Leipzig: Teubner.

Chapanis, A., Lucas, A., Jacobson, E.H. et al. (1960) *L'automation. Aspects psychologiques et sociaux*. Paris: Beatrice – Nauwelaerts.

Charan , R. and Useem, J. (2002). Why companies fail. *Fortune, 145*, 11, 26-44.

Chomsky, N. (1999). *Profit over people*. New York Seven Stories Press.

Churchman, C.W. and Emery, F.E. (!966). On various approaches to the study of organizations. In: L.R. Lawrence (Ed.). *Operational research and social issues*. London: Tavistock.

Cibelli, J.B., Lanza, , R.P., West, M.D. and Ezzell, C. (2002). The first human clone embryo. *Scientific American, 286*, 1, 42-49.

Cole, L/ (1970). *Psychology of adolescence*. New York, London: Holt, Rinehart.

Colvin, G. (2001) Value driven. *Fortune*, 143, 2, 22-23.

Cooke, P. (1988). Modernity, postmodernity and the city. *Theory, Culture and Society*, 5, 475-492.

Craik, J. (1994) *The face of fashion*. London and New York: Routledge.

Crane, M.W. (2003). Criminal justice policy and its discontents. *NYAS Update*, January/February, p. 6-7

Crary, J. (2001). *Suspensions of perceptions. Attention, spectacle and modern culture.* Cambridge, Mass., and London : The MIT Press.

Creswell, J. (2000) Raiders reborn. *Fortune, 142*, 2, 10-12.

Creswell, J. and Prius R. (2002). The emperor of greed. *Fortune*, 145, 13, 55-58.

Croce, B. (1965). *Estetica come scienza dell'espressione e linguistica generale* (XIth ed.). Bari: G. Laterza e Figli.

Curzer, H.J. (Ed.) (1999) *Ethical theory and moral problems.* Belmont, CA, London, Tokyo: Wadsworth Publishing Company.

Daly, K. (1994) *Gender, crime and punishment.* New Haven and London: Yale University Press.

D'Andrade, R.G. (1965). Trait psychology and componential analysis. *American Anthropologist, 67*, 258-265.

De George, R. (1982). *Business ethics.* New York: Mc Millan. London: Collier McMillan.

Denton, M. (1986). Evolutioon: *A theory in crisis.* Bethesda, MD: Adler and Adler.

Diakonov, I.M. (Ed.) (1952) The laws of Hammurabi, the king of Babylon (Orig, in Russian). *Vestnik Drevnei Istorii*, 3, 225-261.

Diamond, J. (2005). *Collapse: How societies choose to fail or to succeed.* Sierra.

Dottrens, R. in collab with Mialaret, G., Rast, E. and Ray M. (1966). *Eduquer et instruire.* Paris: Nathan UNESCO.

Dunwich, G. (1998). *Magick potions.* Secaucus, NJ: Citadel Press.

The Educational System in Germany (1999). Washington, DC :National Institute on Student Achievement.

The Educational System in the United States (1999). Washington, DC: National Institute on Student Achievement, US Department of Education.

Ehrlich, P. and Ehrlich, A. (2004). *One with Ninive.* New York.

Elkind, P. (2001). Where Mary Meeker went wrong. *Fortune, 143*, 19, 93-100.

Ellis, R.D. and Ellis, C.S. (1989). *Theories of criminal justice: A crritical appraisal.* Wolfeboro, N.H.:Longwood Academic.

Emery, F. E. and Trist, E.L.(1965).The causal texture of organizational environments. *Human Relations,* 18, 21-32.

Epstein, A. C. (1993) Should cancer patients be dialized ? *Seminars in Nephrology, 13*,3, 315-323.

Ewen, E. (1980). City lights: immigrant women and the rise of the movies. *Signs, 5*, 3, Supplement S45-65

Eysenck, H.J. (1995). *Genius. The natural history of creativity.* Cambridge University Press.

Feinberg, J. (1973). *Social philosophy.* Englewood Cliffs, NJ: Prentice Hall.

Felman, Sh. (1987). *Jacques Lacan and the adventure of insight: Psychoanalysis in contemporary culture.* Cambridge, Mass.: Harvard University Press.

Fields, R. D. (2004). The other half of the brain. *Scientific American, 290*, 4, 24-33.

Fisher, H. (2004). *Why we love.* New York: Henry Holt.

Fitzgerald, L.F. (1986). On the essential relations between education and work. *Journal of Vocational Behavior*, 28, 254-284.

Fleming, W. (1970). *Art, music and ideas.* New York, Chicago, London: Holt, Rinehart and Winston.

Fogarty, R. (1995). *Best practices for the learner – centered classrom.* Palatine, Ill.: IRI/Skylight Publishing.

Fowers, B.J. (2005). *Virtue and psychology.* Washington, D.C.: APA Books.

French, J.P.R., Rogers, W. and Cobb, S. (1974). A model of person-environment fit. In: G.V. Coelho, D.H. Hamburgh and J.E. Adams, *Coping and adaptation.* New York: Basic Books.

Freud, S. (1922). *Zur Psychopathologie des Alltagslebens,* 8th ed. Leipzig, Zürich: Internationaler Psychoanalitischer Verlag.

Freud. S. (1954). *The interpretation of dreams.* London: Allen and Unwin.

Fuegi, J., Bahr, G. and Willett (Eds.) (1983). *Brecht; Women and politics.* Detroit: Wayne State University Press.

Fukuyama, F. (2002). *Our post-human future: Consequences of the biotechnology revolution.* New York: Farrar, Straus and Giroux.

Galli della Loggia, E. (2005). Le pagine bianche del romanzo Italia. *Corriere della Sera,* 23 may, 1.

Galton, F. (1978). *Hereditary genius.* New York: Julian Friedmann.

Garbarino, J. (1999). *Lost boys.* New York: Free Press.

Garten, J.E. (2005). Déjà vu all over again. *Newsweek,* October 24, 63.

Gavison, R. (1998). Incitement and the limits of law. In: R.C. Post (Ed.) *Censorship and silencing.* Los Angeles: The Getty Research Institute.

Gibson, J.J. (1941), A critical review of the concept of set in contemporary experimental psychology. *Psychological Bulletin, 38,* 781-817.

Gibbs, W.W. and Fox, D. (1999). The false crisis in science and education. *Scientific American,* 281, 4, 65-70.

Gielen, U. (1990). The United Nations and the emergent world order. *International Psychologist,* XXXI, 4, 9-11

Gimein, M. (2002). You bought, they sold. *Fortune,* 146, 3, 38-44.

Giroux, H. A. (2001). *Public spaces, private lives.* Lanham, New York: Rowman and Littlefield.

Glain, St. (2005). China is on the move. *Newsweek,* December 12, 46-49.

Goodall, J. (2005). *100 Perceptions on science and religion.* Templeton Foundation Press.

Goodstein, D. (1996). Conduct and misconduct in science. In: R.P. Gross, N., Levitt, M.W. Lewis (Eds.)*The flight from science and reason.* New York: The New York Academy of Sciences.

Gowers, E. (1956). *A life for a life? The problem of capital punishment.* London.

Greene, R. (1998). *Power.* New York: Joost Elfers, Penguin.

Gross, P.R., Levitt, N. and Lewis, M.W. (Eds.) *The flight from science and reason.* New York, NY: The New York Academy of Sciences.

Hall, S. S. (2003). The quest for a smart pill. *Scientific American, 289,* 3, 36-45.

Haney, C., Banks, C. and Zimbardo, P.G. (1973) Interpersonal dynamics in a simulated prison. *International Journal of Crime and Penology,* 1, 69-97.

Harris, Th. (1998). *Value-added public relations.* Chicago: NTC Business Books.

Harnard, S. (2001) No easy way out. *The Sciences, 41,* 2, 36-42.

Hartmann, H.J., Kraut, R.E. and Tilly, L.A. (Eds.) (1986). *Computer chips and paper clips – technology and women's employment.* Washington, DC: National Academy Press.

Hartnoll, Ph. (1998). *The theatre, a concise history,* 3d ed. Thames and Huddson.

Harvey,, Th. (2001). *Driving Mr. Albert: A trip across America with Einstein's brain.* Delta.

Hechter, M. (1993). Values research in the social and behavioral sciences. In: M. Hechter, L. Nadel and E.R. Michel (Eds.) *The origin of values.* New York.

Henry, W.A.III (1994). *In defense of élitism.* New York: Doubleday.

Herman, E.S. (1999). *The myth of the liberal media.* New York, Bern: Peter Lang.

Herman, E. S. and Chomsky, N. (1988) *Manufacturing consent.* New York: Pantheon.

Holstein, W.J. (2002). Canon takes aim at Xerox. *Fortune, 146,* 5, 70-76.

Honderich, T. (Ed,) (1995). *The Oxford companion to phiosophy.* Oxford, New York: Oxford Univ. Press.

Jameson, F. (1996). Postmodernism and consumer society. In J. Belton (Ed.) *Movies and mass culture.* New Brunswick, NJ: Rutgers University Press.

Joas, H. (2000). *The genesis of values.* The University of Chicago Press.

Kanter, R.M. (1989). *When grants learn to dance: Mastering the challenges of strategy, management and careers in the '1990s.* London: Unwin.

Kellner, D. (1988). Postmodernism as social theory: Some challenges and problems. *Theory, culture and society,* 5, 239-269.

Kellner, D. (1989). *Jean Baudrillard – from Marxism to postmodernism and beyond.* Cambridge : Polity Press.

Keynes, J. (1936). *General theory of employment, interest and money.* New York: Harcourt Brace.

Kissinger, H.A. (2004). America's assignment. *Newsweek,* 19 November 8, 38-43.

Kitson, H. D. (1927). *The mind of the buyer.* New York: McMillan.

Kluckhohn, C. (1962). (Ed. R. Kluckhohn). *Culture and behavior.* New York: The Free Press.

Kohn, M. L. (1969). *Class and conformity: A study in values.* New York: Dorsey.

Krau, E. (1962). The problem of illusions (Orig. in Romanian). *Romanian-Soviet Annals, 3d Series Pedagogy-Psychology,* 2, 89-103

Krau, E. (1964). Contributions to the problem of orientration in action. (Orig. in Romanian). *Studia Universitatis Babes-Bolyai, Series Psychologia-Paedagogia,* 21-41.

Krau, E. (1965). Acquirement of knowledge in history through programmed instruction. *Revue Roumaine des Sciences Sociales, Psychologie,* 9, 1, 29-37.

Krau, E. (1971). Thinking in rpresentations – an alternative way of reasoning. *Studia Psychologica,* XIII, 3, 199-202.

Krau, E. (1977). Subjective dimension assignment through set to objective situations. In: N. Endler and D. Magnusson (Eds.) *Personality at the cross-roads: Current issues in interactional psychology.* Hillsdale, NJ: Lawrence Erlbaum.

Krau, E. (1987). The crystallization of work values in adolescence: A socio-cultural approach. *Journal of Vocational Behavior, 30,* 103-123.

Krau, E. (1989). The transition in life-domain salience and the modification of work values between high school and adult employment. *Journal of Vocational Behavior, 34,* 100-116

Krau, E. (1989).(Ed.) *Self-realization, success and adjustment.* New York, Westport, London: Praeger.

Krau, E. (1991). *The contradictory immigrant problem. A sociopsychological analysis.* New York, Bern, Paris: Peter Lang.

Krau, E. (1995). The Israeli WIS project. In E. Super and B. Sverko (Eds.) *Life roles, values and careers.International findings of the Work Importance Study.* San Francisco: Jossey-Bass.

Krau, E. (1997) *The realization of life aspirations through vocational careers.* Westport, Connecticut, London: Praeger.

Krau, E. (1998). *Social and economic management in the competitive society.* Boston, Dordrecht, London: Kluwer.

Krau, E. (2003) *A meta-psychological perspective on the individual course of life*. Dallas, Lanham, New York, Oxford: University Press of America.

Krau, E. and Yona-Kimelman, D. (1991). The connection between organizational characteristics and the use of short-term employment. *Man and Work*, 3, 43-61.

Labich, K. (1996) Fire people and still sleep at night. *Fortune, 133*, 43-47.

Lainez, S. and Callao, J.A.(1999). *Contabilidad creativa*. Madrid: Civitas.

Landy, R.J. (1996). *Essays in drama therapy*. London, Bristol (Pennsylvania): Jessica.

Langan, Th. (2000). Surviving the age of virtual reality. Columbia: University of Missouri Press.

Lapham, L. (2000). School bells. *Harper's Magazine*, August, 8.

Lawrence, P. and Lorsch, J. (1967). *Organizations and environment*. Cambridge, Mass.: Harvard Univ. Press.

Leaf, C. (2004). Why are we losing the war on cancer? *Fortune, 149*, 5, 42-59.

Lederer, L. (1980) (Ed.) *Take back the night*. New York: William Morrow & Co.

Lefkowwitz, M. (1996). Whatever happened to historical evidence? In: P.R. Gross, N. Levitt and M.W. Lewis (Eds.) *The flight from science and reason*. New York, NY: The New York Academy of Sciences.

Lepre, A. (2005). Dell'era delle ideologie riemersero le tradizioni. *Corriere della Sera*, 10 January, 18

Lévi-Strauss, C. (1956). The family. In: H.L. Schapiro (Ed.) *Man, culture and society*. Oxford: Oxford University Press.

Levant, R.F. (1997). *New psychotherapies for men*. New York: Wiley.

Levinson, S. (1998). The tutelary state: "censorship7", "silencing" and "the practice of cultural regulation" In: R.C. Post (Ed.) *Censorship and silencing*. Los Angeles: The Getty Research Institute.

Lewis, Ch. and O'Brien, M.(Eds.) (1987). *Reassessing fatherhood*. London, Beverly Hills: Sage.

Lieberson, S. (2000). *A matter of taste. How names, fashion and culture change*. New Haven, London: Yale University Press.

Lineweaver, Ch. H. and Davis, T.M. (2005). Misconceptions about the Big Bang. *Scientific American,292*, 3, 24-33.

Linton, R. (1945). *The cultural background of personality*. New York: Appleton-Century-Crofts.

Lombroso, C. (1876). *Trattato antropologico-sperimentale del uomo delinquente*. Milano.

Longman, Ph. (2004). Which nations will go forth and multiply? *Fortune, 149*, 7, 27-28.

Longman, Ph. (2004). *The empty cradle*. Perseus.

Luca, N. (2001). *Il sopravissuto*. Bucarest: Sempre.

Lumsdaine, A.A. (1960). Teaching machines – an introductory overview. In: A.A. Lumsdaine and R. Glaser: *Teaching machines and programmed learning*. N.E.A

MacKinnon, C.A.(1993). *Only words*. Harvard University Press.

Maddox, J. sir (1999). The unexpected science to come. *Scientific American, 281*, 6, 30-43.

Magnet, M. (1993). Why job growth is stalled. *Fortune, 127*. 5.

Mahon, A. (2005). *Surrealism and the politics of Eros*. Thames and Hudson.

Marconi, J. (1996). *Image marketing*. Lincolnwood, Ill.: NTC Business books.

Marquardt, E. (2005). *Between two worlds*. Crown Publishers.

Martini, R. (2006). *The psychology of humor*. Academic Press.

Marx, K. (1953). *The critique of the poitical economy.* Preface. (Russian translation). Moscow: Publishing House for Political Literature.

Masters, R. and Houston, J. (2000). *The varieties of psychedelic experiences.* Rochester, Vermont: Park Street Press.

Mayer, A. and Herwig,B.(1961). *Betriebspsychologie.* Göttingen: Hogrefe.

McChesney, W.M. (1999). *Rich media, poor democracy: Communication politics in dubious times.* Urbana: Univ. of Illinois Press.

McCormick, E,J. (1964). *Human factors engineering,* 2d ed. New York, London: McGrow Hill.

McLean, B. (2001). Why Enron went bust. *Fortune, 144,* 533-58.

McLuhan, M. (1962). *The Gutenberg galaxy.* Toronto: Toronto University Press

McNamara, D.E.J. (1969). Convicting the innocent. *Crime and delinquency, V., 15,* 1, 57-61.

Mendelsohn, B. (1956). La victimologie. *Etudes internationales de psychologie criminelle,*1

Merton, R.K. (1938). Social structure and anomie. *American Sociological Rreview,* October, 672-682.

Miles, R. (1980). *Macro-organizational behavior:* Scott.

Milgram, S, (1965). Some conditions of obedience and disobedience to authority. *Human Relations, 18,* 57-76.

Mill, J.S. (1944). Utilitarianism. In: *Utilitarianism, liberty and representative government.* New York: E.P.Dutton.

Moles, A.A. (1967). *Sociodynamique de la culture.* Paris, La Haye: Mouton.

Montefiore, A. (1967). *A modern introduction to moral philosophy.* London: Routledge and Kegan Paul.

Müller-Freienfels, R. (1916). *Das Denken und die Phantasie.* Leipzig: Johann Ambrosius Barth.

Naim, M. (2005). Broken borders. *Newsweek,* October 10, 21.

Nestler, E.J.and Malenka, R. (2004). The addicted brain. *Scientific American,* March, 51-57.

Nietzsche, F. (1917). *Der Wille zur Macht.* Leipzig: Alfred Kröner.

Norton, R. (1998). Why Asia's collapse won't kill the economy. *Fortune,* 137, 2, 8-10.

Norton, R. (2002). Dumbed-down economics. *Fortune, 145,* 1, 16.

Nussbaum, M, (2006). Teaching humanity. *Newsweek,* August 28, 74-75.

Nye, D.E. (1994). *American technological sublime.* Cambridge: MIT Press.

Onfray, M. (2005). *Trattato di ateologia.* Fazi editore.

Osgood, Ch.E. (1964). Semantic differential technique in the comparative study of cultures. *American Anthropologist,* 66, 3, 171-200.

Overbye, D. (1993). Who's afraid of the Big Bang? *Time,* May 24, 72.

Parkinson, N.C. (1959). *Parkinson's law and other studies in administration.* London: Tarcher/Putnam

Parsons, T. and Bales, R.F. (1955). *Family, socialization and interaction process.* New york: Free Press.

Pavlov, I.P. (1924/1951). *Course on the functioning of the great hemispheres of the brain* (Orig. in Russian). Moscow: Academy of Medical Sciences.

Persson, G. (2005). Why Sweden is so tough. *Newsweek, Special edition,* December, 44-46.

Peters, T.J. and Waterman, R.H. (1982). *In search of excellence.* New York: Harper and Row.

Pizzato, M. (1998). *Edges of loss.* Ann Arbor: The University of Michigan Press.

Polk, M., Schuster, A.H. and Abrams, H.N. (Eds.) (2005). *The looting of the Iraq museum*. New York.

Popper, St.W., Lampert, R.J. and Bankes, S.C. (2005). Shaping the future. *Scientific American, 292*, 4, 49-53.

Post, R.C. (Ed.) (1998). *Censorship and silencing*. Los Angeles: The Getty Research Institute.

Powell, B. (2001). The new world order. *Fortune, 143*, 19, 48-50.

Powell, B. (2002). We're not turning Japanese. *Fortune, 146*, 5, 67-59.

Prause, G. (1966). *Niemand hat Kolumbus ausgelacht*. Düsseldorf, Wien: Econ-Verlag.

Prestowitz, C. (2005). The world is tilted. *Newsweek, Special edition*, December, 18-20.

Provine, R.R. (2000). *Laughter: A scientific investigation*. New York: Viking.

Read,H. (1938). Picasso's Guernica. *London Bulletin*, 6, October.

Reich, R.B. (2005). The new-rich gap. *Newsweek, Special edition*, December. 44-46.

Remuzzi, G. (2004). Scompare la ricerca indipendente. *Corriere della Sera*, 3 October, 16.

Resnik, H. (Ed.) (1990). *Youth and drugs: Society's mixt messages*. Rockville, Maryland: US Department of Health and Human Services.

Rohmer, J. (1998). Asia's meltdown. *Fortune*, 137, 3, 24-29.

Ronald, M.E. (1991). *The ideas of Ayn Rand*. La Salle, Ill.: Open Court.

Sageman, M. (2004). *Understanding terror networks*. University of Pennsylvania Press.

Sassower, R. and Cicotello, L. (2000). *The golden avant-garde*. Charlottesville, London: Univ. Press of Virginia

Sayers, D. (1923). *Whose body?* New York: Harper.

Schapiro, N. (1978) *An encyclopedia of quotations about music*. Garden City, New York: Doubleday.

Schneiderman, L.J., Jecker, N. and Jonsen, A.R. (1999). Medical futility: Its meaning and ethical implications. In: H.J. Curzer, *Ethical theory and moral problems*. Belmont, CA, London, Tokyo: Wadsworth Publ.

Schockenhoff, E. (2003). Natural law and human dignity. Washington, DC: The Catholic Unversity of Amrerica Press.

Schwab, K. (2005). The tipping point. *Newsweek, Special edition*, Deceember, 16.

Selden, L. and Colvin, G. (2002). Will this customer sink your stock? *Fortune, 146*, 5, 78-81.

Sennott, S. (2004). Ideas from thin air. *Newsweek*, August 23, 44-45.

Severino, E. (2004). La tecnica sconfiggerà economia e poitica. *Corriere della Sera*, 14 March, 23.

Shaevitz, M.H. (1984). *The superwoman syndrome*. New York: Warner Books.

Sharma, R. (2005). The oil shock with no pain. *Newsweek*, October 31, 59.

Shaw, W.H. and Barry, V. (1989). *Moral issues in business*. 4th ed. Belmont, Calif.: Wadsworth Publ.

Sigmund, K., Fehr, E. and Novak, M.A. (2002). The economics of fair play. *Scientific American*, 286, 1,81-85

Simpson, A.Y. (1998). *The tie that binds*. New York, London: New York University Press.

Singer, P.W. (2005). *Children at war*. Pantheon.

Sperber, D. (1996). *Explaining culture: A naturalistic approach*. Oxford: Blackwell.

——*SS im Einsatz – eine Dokumentation über die Verbrechen der SS* (1958). Berlin: Kongress Verlag.

Stan, A.M. (1995) (Ed.). *Debating sexual correctness*. New York: Delta.

Stassinopoulos Huffington, A. (1988). *Picasso creator and destroyer*. New York, London: Simon and Schuster.

Stefflre, B. (1966). Vocational development: Ten propositions in search for a theory. *Personnel and Guidance Journal*, 4, 611-616.

Sternberg, R.J. (2003) To be civil. *APA Monitor on Psychology, 34*, 7, 5.

Stewart, Th. (1993). Welcome to the revolution. *Fortune, 128*, 15, 32-39.

Stokes, D. (1997). *Pasteur's quadrant*. Brookings Institution Press.

Super, D. E. (1980). A life span, life-space approach to career development. *Journal of Vocational Behavior, 16*, 282-298.

Super, D.E. and Sverko, B. (Eds.) (1995) *Life roles, values and careers – International findings of the Work Importance Study*. San Franciso: Jossey Bass.

Tappan, P.W. (1947). Who is the criminal? *American Sociological Review*, 12, February, 96-102.

Tedlow, R.S. (2005). The education of Andy Grove. *Fortune, 152*, 11, 33-41.

Thaxton, Ch., Bradley, W. and Olsen, R. (1984). *Doubts about Darwin*. Grand Rapids, MI: Baker Books.

Thomson, J.J. (1971). A defense of abortion. *Philosophy and Public Affairs, 1*, 1, 47-66.

Tiger, L. (1999) *The decline of males*. New York: Golden Books.

Tomlinson, R. (2002). L'Oréal's global makeover. *Fortune*, 146, 3, 30-36.

Tupes, E.C. and Christal, R.E. (1961). *Recurrent personality factors based on trait ratings* USA FASD Technical Report, 61-97.

Uexküll, Th. von (1964). *Grundfragen der psychosomatischen Medizin*, 4th ed. Hamburg: Rowohlt.

Underwood, A. and Adams, W.L. (2005). Charles Darwin, evolution of a scientist. *Newsweek*, December 12, 56-58.

Vencat, E.F. (2006). Student cheating is reaching new levels forcing an overhaul of tests. *Newsweek,* March 27, 45-47.

Viorst, J. (1998) *Imperfect control*. New York: Simon and Schuster.

Want, R. (2004). RFID a key to automating everything. *Scientific American, 290*, 1, 48-55.

Ward, B. (1995). *In the mind of a monster*. Boca Raton, Fl. Cool Hand Communication.

Weber, M. (1947). *The theory of social and economic organizations*. New York: Mc Millan, London: Collier McMillan.

—— Welcome to cyberspace (1995). *Time*, Special issue, Spring.

Wheeler, Th. C. (1971). *The immigrant experience*. Baltimore, Maryland: Penguin.

Whitford, D. (1998). The party keeps cooking. *Fortune, 137*, 5, 8-10.

Wold, M., Martin, G., Miller, J. and Cykler, E. (1991). *An introduction to music and art in the Western World*. Dubuque, IA: W.C. Brown.

Wolfenstein, M. and Leites, N. (1950). *Movies: A psychological study*, New York: Free Press.

Wolfgang, M.E., Savitz, L. and Johnston, N. (1962). *The sociology of crime and delinquency*. New York, London.

Woodward, Th. (2003). *Doubts about Darwin*. Grand Rapids, MI: Baker Books.

Wouk, V. (2001). Power train. *The Sciences*, 41, 1, 38-42.

Zakarias, F. (2005). The Germans: A lot like us. *Newsweek*, October 19, 21.

Zytowski, D.G. (1970), The concept of work values. *Vocational Guidance Quaterly, 18*, 176-186

About the Author

Edgar Krau earned his Ph.D. in 1964 at the University of Cluj (Romania). He taught there until 1977, and from 1968 he was in parallel head of the section for psychological research of the Cluj Branch of the Romanian Academy. In 1977 he emigrated to Israel, where he was appointed professor at the University of Haifa, and in 1981 professor at the Tel-Aviv University. He stayed there until his retirement. He has published over 70 papers in scientific journals from 10 countries. Among his books are: The Contradictory Immigrant Problem (1991), The Realization of Life Aspirations through Vocational Careers (1997), Social and Economic Management in the Competitive Society (1998), A Metapsychological Perspective on the Individual Course of Life (2003). His scientific activity has earned him the membership of the New York Academy of Sciences and of several civil orders, like the American Order of Excellence, American Order of Ambassadors, Order Education, Science, Culture (Belgium). He has been awarded the Vasile Conta Prize of the Romanian Academy (1972), and received an honorary award from the Superior Centre of Logic and Comparative Sciences in Bologna (Italy), he received homagial articles from the Revue Européenne de Psychologie Appliquée (1993) and from the Journal of Vocational Behavior (1986). Recently he has been appointed honorary director general of the International Biographical Centre in Cambridge (England).